Cre

Creativity is experiencing a global revolution. Since the 1990s, in many countries, it has assumed increasing importance in the school curriculum, contrasting strongly with previous approaches to creativity in education. But whilst the tide of opportunities rises, there are questions to ask. What is 'creative learning'? How does it relate to 'creative teaching'? How do we organise the curriculum to nurture creativity? What pedagogical strategies support it? How is creative learning different to effective learning? And, more fundamentally, what dilemmas and tensions are raised for the curriculum by these models of creativity? What responsibilities do teachers and schools have for stimulating creativity with reference to the social and ethical framework, and the wider environment?

This book looks hard at these and other questions. Part One uses a number of lenses associated with the school to discuss creativity and learning, the development of a creativity language, curriculum and pedagogy. Part Two takes a broader view, which encompasses *principles*. It explores creativity with reference to cultural specificity, environmental degradation and the destructive potential of creativity. Finally, in Part Three, the implications of tensions and dilemmas in terms of pedagogy and principle are explored.

For teachers and schools who work with pupils who are pre-school age, through to those in post-compulsory education, this book synthesises practice, policy and research in order to critique some current assumptions, to lay out an agenda for further development, and suggests practical ways of taking forward pupils' creative development, celebrating their unique generativity in a more thoughtful way.

Anna Craft is Senior Lecturer in Education at The Open University, Director of The Open Creativity Centre.

'Anna Craft combines a thorough mastery of the literature on creativity with a far-reaching reconceptualization of standard aspects of teaching as seen through the lens of creativity. She does not spurn controversy. Whether or not one agrees with particular points, everyone will learn from this book.'
Professor Howard Gardner, Hobbs Professor of Education and Cognition, Harvard Graduate School of Education, USA.

'Creativity is being widely recognized as "good thing" in education. But good practice needs clear thinking and here, as always, Anna Craft provides plenty of it for teachers and policy makers alike.'
Sir Ken Robinson, The Getty Foundation, Los Angeles, USA.

'Finally, a book for teachers that recognises that creativity is complicated. Anna Craft dares to question some of the soft platitudes in which the wheels of liberal education have become stuck.'
Professor Guy Claxton, University of Bristol Graduate School of Education, England.

'In 'Creativity in Schools' Anna Craft has produced a coherent, deep, wise, scholarly and yet fully practical book that will, without doubt, be of immense value to the field of creativity studies as well as to those in education who hope to make schools and classrooms more creative places.'
David Feldman, Professor of Developmental Psychology, Tufts University, USA.

'The reflective reader will find much food for thought in this refreshing, provocative and stimulating book.'
Ng Aik Kwang, Nanyang Technological University, Singapore.

'Anna Craft herself has taken a creative risk – exposing and questioning the contradictions found throughout the creativity debate. It is a risk which succeeds. Whatever your perspective on creativity and Learning, this book will inform, challenge and inspire.'
Joe Hallgarten, Learning Director, Creative Partnerships, The Arts Council, England.

Creativity in Schools
Tensions and Dilemmas

Anna Craft

Routledge
Taylor & Francis Group

LONDON AND NEW YORK

First published 2005 by Routledge
2 Park Square, Milton Park, Abingdon, Oxon, OX14 4RN

Simultaneously published in the USA and Canada
by Routledge
270 Madison Ave, New York NY 10016

Routledge is an imprint of the Taylor & Francis Group

Transferred to Digital Printing 2010

Typeset in Goudy by Keyword Typesetting Services Ltd

British Library Cataloguing in Publication Data
A catalogue record for this book is available from the British Library

Library of Congress Cataloging in Publication Data
A catalog record for this book has been requested

ISBN 0-415-32414-9 (hbk)
ISBN 0-415-32415-7 (pbk)

For

Hugo and Ella

in hope that creativity and wisdom will guide you,
your peers
and those that come after you;

and

for Simon

with love, thanks and appreciation
for co-creating the story.

Contents

Preface

Creativity is an important element of the zeitgeist in the early twenty-first century, world wide. It is described as a significant part of the education process by politicians and other policy makers, educators and researchers. This perhaps ineffably human characteristic is one that has long fascinated many commentators, and it has had my attention for the past 10 years. It has, almost universally, a positive press. Many have explored how it can best be promoted in education.

Is it, though, as simple as that? What does the positive perspective mask? What kinds of tensions and dilemmas face us as educators as we promote the creativity of pupils?

This book aims to unpick some significant tensions and dilemmas that accompany the adoption of creativity as a prominent part of learning in schools. It takes a hard look at how possible it is to foster learner creativity and asks some fundamentally challenging questions, including how appropriate it may be to do so. Although the book ultimately has an optimistic outlook, proposing that to foster creativity is an important element of an education that encourages critical scrutiny, different perspectives and new ways of thinking, it treads some difficult terrain on the way, attempting to make visible some of the bars on our worldview 'cage', as Tim Smit describes it in his Foreword.

The evolution of this book has benefited enormously from conversations with fellow academics, as well as teachers, pupils and policy makers, mainly in England where my work at The Open University and as a freelance consultant brings with it regular and fascinating opportunities to explore creativity in education. The book has also benefited from conversations with researchers and teachers in the United States, where I have been fortunate to be a (mainly remote) visiting scholar at Harvard University for a two-year period. It has also benefited from the inspiration and support of my partner Simon and our two children, Hugo and Ella, aged six and four respectively. During several spells abroad with the children in the last 2 years, I have been particularly struck by the ways in which these two particular children have made sense of and engaged with the generative thinking that we might describe as facilitating creativity in many domains of knowledge in the worlds around them. Their experience of entering a new culture for a few days or weeks at a time has been a reminder of the ways in which we perhaps take for granted the cultural mores and values that provide a context to any learning, in or beyond the classroom. For, as Tim Smit indicates in his Foreword, everything that we do is situated and relational to values and beliefs. Fostering deep engagement with the values contexts to creativity forms a significant challenge for any parent or teacher.

This book raises some fundamental questions about mistaken assumptions we might make about stimulating creativity in education, and it uncovers numerous tensions and dilemmas. It is my hope that the book will both offer and stimulate some possible ways in which we might respond to these, and that it may set out a range of ongoing questions for scholars, educators and policy makers to continue to develop and to research.

Anna Craft
The Open University, January 2005

Acknowledgements

This book has benefited from many conversations with colleagues in schools, universities and policy bodies, in England and also in the United States. In particular, I would like to thank Bob Jeffrey and my many colleagues at The Open University, and also Howard Gardner and colleagues at Harvard University's Project Zero. The inspiration to write the book at all came in part from the direction into human creativity that Howard's work in particular took in the late 1990s. Thanks are due also to Penelope Best, Pam Burnard, Dawn Burns, Kerry Chappell, Pat Cochrane, Bernadette Duffy, Joe Hallgarten, Genie Gabel-Dunk and the Pupil Researchers at Monson Primary School, Teresa Grainger, Lois Hetland, Margaret Leese, Jean Keane, Lindsey Haynes and the Reception Class at Cunningham Hill Infants, Mara Krechevsky, Debbie Lee-Keenan, Ben Mardell, David Martin, Steve Seidel, Margaret Talboys, Katy Adje, Becky Swain, Bel Reid, and also Graham Jeffery and his colleagues at Newham Sixth-Form College in East London, Professor Christopher Bannerman and his colleagues at ResCen, Middlesex University, and Professor Peter Woods, formerly of The Open University. The inspirational work of Tim Smit and his collaborators at the Eden Project has given me hope that our imaginations can, collectively, be put to sound ecological and spiritual use in a world moving fast in other directions. I regard it as a real honour that Tim agreed to write the Foreword to the book. In addition, many other creative practitioners from within and beyond education have inspired and engaged me in thinking about the issues in this book; I hope they will forgive my not naming every one.

Thanks are also due to the National Endowment for Science, Technology and the Arts, Creative Partnerships Black Country, Creative Partnerships Hub, The Open University, the Qualifications and Curriculum Authority, the Economic and Social Research Council, the Calouste Gulbenkian Foundation, the Fulbright Commission and Arts Council England, for awarding funding grants which, whilst focused on specific areas of study, also afforded opportunities to explore many of the issues explored in the book.

I owe a special debt of gratitude to my family: my two patient children, Hugo and Ella, and my partner Simon, who encouraged my efforts despite the many family times forfeited in the final months and weeks of this book's gestation. Six-year-old Hugo's advice: 'think hard and be careful, but try your best' was invaluable; four-year-old Ella's drawings and notes to help me with my writing were a real tonic, as were the special times when the children joined me in my study with their own writing projects, complete with pencils, paper, toy laptop and their overflowing imaginations. My partner Simon's depth of thinking and commitment to a simplifying lifestyle, his own creative writing and some of his library, informed thinking in the later parts of the book.

Meanwhile, Angela Killick-Harris, Carole Munro and Keeley Elliott helped keep the household sane and functioning. Gill Bathurst provided inspirational respites through much-loved piano lessons next door, and Tora Wilkinson reminded me that walking through beautiful landcapes, dancing and making space for our children's 'best-friend' times are also important in a crowded life. David and Janette Stanley offered a place of refuge for us all when we needed it, and Naomi Craft and Saul Hyman, with their children Natasha and Isaac, helped put it all in perspective. My thanks are due finally to Maurice and Alma Craft, who in their different ways offered invaluable advice on the manuscript. It was through discussions with Maurice Craft in particular that I first became aware of the possibility of analysing the limitations, tensions and dilemmas inherent in promoting creativity in education. His gentle but regular prompting persuaded me to finish the manuscript.

Certainly, without all of these people's generosity of time and thought this book would not have been written. I hope each may be able to find aspects of themselves in it.

Anna Craft
The Open University, January 2005

Foreword

Don't come strutting in here Johnny Confident

Name a moment that has changed your perception of life. Romantically, one can name lots of them; but epiphanies, 'road to Damascus' moments, are very rare. When I was in the music industry I spent a short while making records with supermodels – their celebrity being thought (wrongly) a good guide to pop music success. I learned two things. First, supermodels are normally lonely, because most men are too frightened to ask them out. Second, when you gaze upon such physical perfection you soon get bored: there is such symmetry in the face that there is nothing to grab your interest. Picture-postcard topography of something ideal is bland.

Flaws create mystery, mystery creates fascination and fascination, in turn, leads to a desire to understand. Therein lies an important secret that all great musicians, artists and writers instinctively explore or exploit.

Name another moment. A friend asked me to give him 1 hour. He marked out 1 square metre of a field at the Lost Gardens of Heligan. Sit and look at this patch of grass for 1 hour, he said. I did. Life would never be the same again. As your eyes adjust to the micro-weave of the grass, you first notice the stems are all individual, scarred in different places and dead fibres randomly askew. A spider, ants, more spiders, different ants, beetles, insects of all shapes and sizes that I'd never knowingly encountered before. The noise of the birds – why didn't I hear them like that before? But... behind the birdsong, like a rumour of something distant, the murmur of the grass. What was once a field that I walked across on the way to something else was now a complete world of which I had been totally unaware. I could see literally hundreds of living things: some working in concert, like the ants; some doing their own thing. They were inextricably linked. This is ecology, I thought. Then, as I watched, I wondered whether I just wanted it to be linked, for each creature to relate to the next. Was this Celtic romance, 'a butterfly sneezes and it has an impact on the other side of the world' sort of thing?

At The Eden Project[1] we regularly have a beer in the local pub after work. What is Eden? I ask some of the new kids working with us for the summer holidays. Close your eyes, I say, and we play a strange version of Kim's Game (pelmanism). That beer in front of you. Where do the bubbles form? What colour is it? What jewellery is the person next to you wearing? What is on the table? Aghast, most realise they don't know, or they think they know but are wrong. All, that is, except the quiet girl who shyly nods in conversation, never volunteering anything save in answer to a direct question. She saw everything. She told me the colour of everyone's eyes and clothes, and even the perfume they were wearing. 'Life's so fast today,' they say. 'Oh, is it?' I reply. Maybe that's because they're skating over it, seeing nothing, understanding nothing. A series of undigested images and appetites. Maybe that's why most works of art choose as their focus the pain of isolation or, indeed, love. It is the pain that puts the brakes on this skating and makes you look at your emotional square metre of grass.

Emotional intelligence has its own creativity, its complex coping mechanisms and its surge for growth. It has been observed that, in many cases of autism, one finds abilities of extreme photographic memory and information assimilation married to emotional dysfunction. Does the search for the creative impulse lie here somewhere in the link between emotional development and the power of observation? Every good teacher is a catalyst to creativity, a liberator. Every bad teacher creates cages. Humans are superb escapologists when they can see and understand from what they are trying to escape. The impossible jail to escape from is the one where you cannot see the bars. That is why it is a great pleasure to have been asked to write the Foreword to Anna Craft's hugely important book. It is about creativity, but also about the chains that bind us all, and it does something hugely valuable. It describes what the bars might look like and the sloppy ideas to which we have signed up to too readily, and proposes some possible escape routes.

Creativity is a word that comes with baggage. In some circles it hints at genius, in others to dodgy accounting practices. Being creative is either praise or an inference of a character flaw. However it is used, the implication is that some kind of cleverness is involved, evidenced by some talent for conjuring out of nothing or problem solving. Most of us are suspicious of it being the Devil's work unless it is done in the name of a greater good, in which case divine intervention bestows a cod sanctity to the practitioner. Latterly, as it has become part of the educator's armoury, it has taken on a whole new meaning. It is something we all have, if only we could draw it out of ourselves. It is the defining element of the Ego, the essence of us, the self. We're all creative now, and this robs it of its exclusive sting. It is part of a

---

[1] The Mission Statement of The Eden Project, based in Cornwall, in the far south-west of England, is: 'To promote the understanding and responsible management of the vital relationship between plants, people and resources leading to a sustainable future for all.' It is the vision of Tim Smit and the project's co-founders.

universal quest for selfness, or so some would have us believe, but lurking in the undergrowth the snake of avarice is hissing, is sleething through the new world of intellectual property, ideas made real, consumer products that either are an end result of creativity, or will help you on the creative journey. Its close friend is Innovation, that other semantic impostor. New is good, but new that turns into something you can replicate for money is even better! I'm not a cynic, so I don't actually believe what I have just said – totally – but, in the Western World, creativity as an idea is horribly muddled with consumption, either in the thrill of the stimulation of the new for its own sake, or in the prospect that it represents a currency, soft at its source but as hard and cold as money when it enters the ocean in the big wide world.

Stand-alone creativity, unrooted in either experience or culture, is chaos. C. S. Lewis once said 'While science may lead you towards truth only the imagination can lead you to meaning.' Meaning is what we all seek in some shape or form, from understanding relationships between one another, or from a desire to be 'at one with the world'. In common with many of my generation, I haven't the comfort of religion, but a thread that runs through most of us is a desire for some kind of spiritual experience that gives us a sense of belonging or community in the widest sense of the word. I would argue that those who are most at one with the world have the least elemental drive to be creative in the sense of exploring the boundaries of the possible in a search for a language that reveals some 'truth' to them. It is rare to hear music or see works of art that are 'edgy' that are the creation of the contented. It is almost as if a necessary condition for masterworks is a rage within, a dysfunction of the soul, you might say. My youngest son once said in jest that he wished I'd been an abusive father so that he could be a credibly creative musician. All of us know that, by and large, this is a stereotype that doesn't bear very close inspection, but that there is a grain of truth in it. This is evidenced in part in our culture by awarding artists more latitude in behaviour than we would allow others. There is a wonderful irony that we will celebrate artists to whom we wouldn't give houseroom on a personal level.

It is in this notion of the artist as being somehow an outsider that gives the lie to creativity being a universal attribute. There appears to be an unconscious litmus test that distinguishes between 'showing off', craftsmanship and artistry. Of course, the distinctions are blurred. In my experience creativity is sparked by several influences. Take as a given, for a moment, that one has the technical ability to execute a particular piece of work or thinking. In the marketing world there is a famous phrase: 'Please give me the freedom of a tight brief' (a framework in which to create). Often, all it takes to liberate people is a sharply defined territory on which to focus their intellectual juices and away they go. The most disastrous technique is to say 'think of something', which often has the effect of producing despondency and inertia.

A friend of mine in São Paulo, Ricardo Semler (famous for his management books describing the revolutionary techniques used at his factories), has set up an educational trust. Children come to the school and they are watched as they play and explore their territory. One child, for instance, showed no interest in anything until he had lifted a stone and found a woodlouse underneath it. He was encouraged to draw it and, using this as a starting point, was encouraged to observe it ever more closely, which, as any good teacher knows, led him into writing about it, working out the mathematics of its carapace and studying its living habits. Before long he was fully assimilated into a recognizable 'curriculum', but one of his making.

Ricardo is inspirational because he takes a huge amount of time working up the right question. This is a technique I have borrowed from him, and it has changed my whole approach to developing ideas. He begins with the question 'What does great look like?' Time after time he exposes the fact that many of our actions or inventions are a response to a situation that we have accepted without ever going back to first principles. To give you a trivial example by way of illustration, I asked for the best waste management system possible for our restaurants at Eden, and I got it. Unfortunately, I had not asked, or framed the proposition correctly. I should have asked for the best waste management system possible that not only separated and minimised waste, but which also encouraged visitors to clear their own tables and in so doing learned about the waste processes in a way that would influence their behaviour at home. I cannot count the times that I have been told things can't be done, which on closer inspection reveal that no-one has actually tried.

The most inspirational example of this that I know is William Strickland, the principal of the Manchester School in Pittsburgh, in the heart of the roughest area of one of the roughest cities in the USA. Bill was a homeless child who put his nose up to the window of the Pittsburgh Arts College and watched an old man turning a pot on a wheel. The man spotted him and invited him in. To cut a long story short, the man took Bill under his wing and he eventually went to university, whence he returned to Pittsburgh with the ambition of providing the opportunities he had had to other poor people. His mantra is: 'If it's good enough for rich folks, it's good enough for poor folks too'. His other saying is: 'Give people world class facilities and you will get world class behaviours'.

He drew inspiration from Frank Lloyd Wright's architecture and searched out his best pupil, who he convinced to design a beautiful school bathed in natural light. His story of how he then persuaded people to donate money, so that today the Manchester School is one of the most famous in the USA, is remarkable. There is a fountain, there are works of art on all the walls, there is an art gallery as good as a national museum, except that it exhibits only the work of pupils; there is a concert hall paid for by some of the world's most famous musicians who have come there to play.

The refectory is full of hand-made furniture, and on open days all the parents come to share in the achievements of their children, something unthinkable when he began 15 years ago. What is the only constant in Bill Strickland's daily routine? Buying flowers. Every day he buys big bunches of flowers, which he places in the entrance hall and in the refectory. Why? Because if it's good enough for rich folks, it's good enough for poor folks too. In fifteen years there has been no vandalism, theft or violence at the school.

Talking to Bill, he tells you that his driving philosophy is that many of us have our creativity repressed as we get older. The crayons and paint are removed, and the things to bang and holler with are put in a box. He sees this as institutionalised arrested development. That is why all his pupils of whatever age are made to express themselves through art for their first year. They all choose to continue with it. He fundamentally believes that what is going on is 'self-expression' – finding a unique voice for each person. Once people have discovered their voices they can develop as human beings.

William Strickland is inspirational because he dared to put his beliefs into practice and has been vindicated by the results. He is also very fierce in drawing a distinction between self-expression and creativity. The former is as necessary as breathing; the latter, to him, is the interface between self-expression and the outside world. Language messes these distinctions up; I think there is something important in them, but what I'm not quite sure.

The battleground of creativity throws up much discussion about the appropriateness of defining creativity as if it were a universal attribute, recognised across cultures with the same weighting we give it. Like Anna Craft, I'm not convinced by this. Among Amerindian tribes the womenfolk are all accorded the status of 'creatives', in that they make and decorate most of the tradable artefacts which are exchanged for the essentials of the outside world, but the designs are dictated by tradition and symbolic meaning. To stray into self-expression outside their cultural framework would be thought of as madness. This attitude is common in many areas of the world. In fact, creativity that has broken the shackles of the culture whence it came appears to be a predominantly Western attribute. This, however, opens up the distinctions between creativity in problem solving (which is evident in all cultures of the world as they adapt to their environments and evolve new techniques to combat situations as they arise) and creativity in the arts (where we tend to interpret it to mean 'new' or previously unseen). It could be argued that creativity in the arts is in inverse relation to the power of the state or the atrophy within a culture. Most of the great artistic movements appear to coincide with either great social upheavals or realignments. This is as true for Pop Art in the 1960s as for the flowering of Chinese art in the Middle Ages.

The other major criticism of creativity as a universal attribute is that it has become associated with novelty and the 'throw-away' society, the inference being that the constant quest for the new by definition makes the old redundant, or that the pressure of the new encourages the assumption of inbuilt obsolescence into all that is made. Unlike Anna Craft, this I refute, for it confuses the act of creation by the Maker with the values of society which, while linked, are not connected at the hip: the Maker is aligned to creativity but not necessarily vice versa. Without the Maker, creativity still exists.

So many of us feel cowed in the presence of those who presume to have taste and an eye for the arts, those who are creative. Damn your certainties, we feel, but they set the cultural agenda in the face of our inability to express ourselves fully. A recent MORI poll (2004) found that 79% of Britons wished they were more cultured. This is either hugely exciting or terribly depressing; I'm not sure which. Louis Armstrong was once asked what Jazz was. 'If you have to ask . . . shame on you,' was the curt reply.

As I come to the end of my personal ramble exploring the nature of creativity I know exactly what he means: creativity is embarrassingly hard to pin down, and yet it is something that everyone should feel actively engaged in, free of fear – for their own health.

Tim Smit
Co-founder and Chief Executive, The Eden Project
26 January 2005

Introduction

This book has arisen from an awareness that the burgeoning discourse in policy, practice and research that serves to support the development of creativity in schools brings with it numerous implications. Many of these are positive, and, in general, creativity in the early twenty-first century has indeed carried a positive value. In terms of education, it has also brought together thinking about 'creativity', 'creative teaching', 'teaching for creativity' and 'creative learning' in such a way as to make them often indistinguishable. One of the purposes behind this book is to clarify some of the terms. As a practitioner, researcher and parent passionately committed to fostering the creativity of learners in schools, I believe that this is a part of our work in ensuring that we do the best we can to nurture learners' creativity.

However, the book has other purposes too. It is concerned with untangling some of the tensions, dilemmas and even possible limitations to promoting creativity in education. For if creativity is to be promoted in education, then we might ask ourselves what might be some of the possible implications of doing so.

The discussion is divided into three main parts. Part I uses a number of lenses associated with the school, to discuss creativity and learning, the development of a creativity language, curriculum and pedagogy. Part II takes a broader view, which encompasses *principles*. It explores creativity with reference to cultural specificity, environmental degradation and the destructive potential of creativity. Finally, in Part III, the implications of tensions and dilemmas in terms of pedagogy and principle are explored, and some resolutions proposed. A Postscript then lays out a range of possible onward journeys for development of, and research into, creativity in schools.

In Chapter 1, then, our attention first turns to setting the context, discussing why and how creativity has come to be such an important aspect of life in the twenty-first century, and the implications for education policies and practices. Recent education initiatives in England are discussed and the research context briefly touched upon.

Chapter 2 then discusses the problem of developing a creativity language. The chapter opens a discussion of the difficulties of terminology, analysing distinctions between creative learning, creative teaching, teaching for creativity, innovation, creativity, creativeness, imagination. Some of this discussion involves bringing together relatively long-standing thinking about these terms, e.g. creativity, innovation and imagination (discussed and written about for hundreds of years). Other terms are more recently in current coinage, such as creative learning, creative teaching and teaching for creativity (mainly in use since the 1990s, although with a history stretching back some 40 years). The chapter discusses some of the implications of such slippage in language, for what we claim to value within the classroom and school. Valuing 'creative learning' is distinct, for example, from valuing 'creative teaching'; each leads to different pedagogical strategies, environmental conditions and expectations of pupils.

Chapter 3 discusses issues associated with the curriculum, exploring the extent to which the existence of foundation disciplines constrains the fostering of learner and teacher creativity. It also asks to what extent is the fostering of creativity determined by its subject context. Some of this chapter, then, is concerned with the debate about creativity as subject specific, and creativity as cross-curricular. The role of knowledge is increasingly acknowledged within creativity research, for the domain provides a knowledge context within which to be creative. This means that teachers need to be sufficiently knowledgeable of the subject domain to bring learners to the edge of their knowledge, and to enable pupil creativity within the domain. But at the same time, there is a growing recognition of the need to be able to apply creative thinking in a wide range of contexts, which has led curriculum policy makers to codify creativity as a cross-curricular skill in, for example, the National Curriculum. The chapter attempts to reconcile these positions.

Another aspect of the curriculum and creativity is the extent to which individual subjects actually lend themselves to creativity. A brief examination is made of a number of subject areas, exploring and exemplifying the position that all subject areas in the school curriculum (or beyond) *are* conducive to the development of a learner's creativity. A further area that is briefly considered is the discontinuity provided by the curriculum statements themselves in the area of creativity. For example, in England, the conceptualisation of creativity in the early years curriculum (for the Foundation Stage) contrasts with the way it is conceptualised in the National Curriculum for primary and secondary school pupils.

One further dimension of curriculum and creativity is the possible tension between the existence of a curriculum with a great deal of content and the encouragement of pupil – and teacher – creativity.

Chapter 4 analyses the literature on pedagogical strategies and creativity. Drawing on empirical work from a number of curriculum areas, in both primary and secondary education, it discusses the extent to which pedagogy is limited by policy or other constraints (such as compulsory teaching frameworks or processes). The chapter proposes creativity as a specific teaching and learning approach and experience, one amongst others to be employed as appropriate. In this way it aims to further theorise the notion of teaching for creativity, and creative teaching – distinctions made in the NACCCE (1999) report.

Chapter 5 focuses on learning. To what extent is creativity a tool for 'coming to know', i.e. learning? If novelty and originality are elements of how creativity is defined, then in everyday creativity, or 'democratic' creativity, it could be said that an idea or action could be deemed novel or original within the terms of reference of the individual. Indeed, creativity could be seen as a way of expanding what one knows, understands and can do – in which case it could be said to be an aspect of learning. This conceptual tangle will be explored, and the chapter will argue that creativity, whilst being close to learning, is distinct because it is by definition generative. The chapter also discusses the notion of 'creative learning' from within the research literature.

Chapter 6 deals with a number of constraints/challenges, such as the individualisation of learning implied by the stimulating of learner creativity balanced against the collective needs of a group. It also explores the technicisation of teaching itself, and the way teachers exercise their own creativity as a response to this; and it revisits the distinctions between teaching creatively, teaching for creativity and creative learning.

Part II of the book deals with three fundamental limitations integral to the 'universalised' concept of creativity, all of which examine the separation of creativity from values. These are social (explored in Chapter 7), environmental (addressed in Chapter 8) and ethical (running through both).

Chapter 7 considers some of the *social* limits to fostering creativity, including its possible cultural specificity. Creativity, whether 'high' or 'ordinary', is often presented as if it were a universally applicable concept. But it may, by contrast, be quite culturally specific, in its strong emphasis on individuality and in the value it places on being able to think independently of social norms. This may reflect peculiarly Western values. It also may reflect a culture where the individual and the marketplace are held in high esteem. In a more repressive or conformist culture, creativity might be perceived to be less relevant and desirable. Clearly, cultural context may also affect people's experiences of creativity and their ability to manifest it, although this may not be a totally predictable relationship. Thus, in a social context where choices and personal autonomy are severely restricted, the drive to find alternatives may be quite strong. On the other hand, it may be that with socialisation emphasising submissiveness and involving continual strategising so as to avoid social or political sanctions, creativity would be suffocated. It is also possible that creativity may be imbued with social class-based assumptions, such as resilience, self-reliance, persistence and control over one's environment – also, future orientation and greater individualism.

All of these perspectives are considered and weighed up, arguing ultimately that the universalisation of creativity in the current world is both premature and inappropriate, advancing the argument that creativity is limited by its cultural specificity.

Chapter 8 reflects on environmental degradation. This is anchored in a discussion of the implications of 'innovation' as the norm. The case for fostering creativity in education can be seen as a response to the conditions and pace of life and the global market economy, as discussed in Chapter 1. But how desirable is the norm of innovation that the global economy demands? To what extent is it desirable to encourage and sustain the 'disposable' culture, where obsolescence is built in at the design stage of many consumer goods and where fashion dictates the need for constant change and updating? For there are clear environmental costs to giving high value to the market as if it were a divine force. To what extent do we, in the marketplace at any rate, encourage innovation for innovation's sake and without reference to genuine need? How desirable is it to encourage those values that present, via the market, 'wants' as if they were 'needs'? It could be said that a culture of 'make do and mend' might be something to be fostered, rather than looking to ways of changing what may be working perfectly well already, whether that be a system, a relationship, a service or a product. These issues, together with the spiritual, or existential, perspective on creativity, are explored, touching on the ethical and moral context to creativity and an analysis of creativity for destructive purposes. For creativity has, undoubtedly, a darker side. The human imagination is capable of immense destruction as well as of almost infinitely constructive possibilities. To what extent is it possible to generate systems that stimulate and celebrate creativity within a profoundly humane framework, and to encourage the critical examination of the values inherent in creative ideas and action? It is argued that the role of educators is to lead students to examine the possible wider effects of their own ideas and those of others, and to evaluate both choices and worth in the light of this. This inevitably means the balancing of conflicting perspectives and values – which may themselves be irreconcilable, as in the case, perhaps, of the creative act of destruction of 11 September, 2001.

The final part of the book considers the implications for what we might call liberal education, of the notion that creativity may be value- and culture-specific. It ultimately offers, however, a practical and theoretical framework for the acceptance of creativity as necessary to education. Chapter 9 explores dilemmas of principle posed by the argument in Part II of the book, that creativity is not a universal concept, and Chapter 10 explores dilemmas of pedagogy facing the educator posed by the practical issues raised in Part I.

Dilemmas of principle include the following problems:

- *If creativity is culturally specific, then how appropriate is it to encourage it within education?* Stimulating creativity involves encouraging learners to adopt a way of life that presents itself as universal when it is not; and the positive associations with creativity mask some possibly questionable values.
- *To what extent is the 'throw-away society' a given?* How appropriate is the implication that creativity is a good thing for the economy, for society and, therefore, for education? For implicit in this is the idea that innovation is of itself a good thing. How far is it appropriate for the fostering of creativity to occur without critical reflection on the environmental, social and other consequences there may be in treating the 'market as God' in this way?

Practical dilemmas include the following:

- *The curriculum.* How can the curriculum be both conceptualised and organised to stimulate creativity? A curriculum which is fixed, compulsory, which involves a great deal of propositional knowledge, and which takes up a great deal of learning time, may pose challenges to stimulating creativity – possibly more so than a curriculum which is more flexible.
- *Professional artistry within a centralised pedagogy.* The centralising not only of curriculum, but also of pedagogy, notably in literacy and numeracy, can be seen as posing a challenge to professional artistry – and in this sense may be seen as restricting potential teacher creativity, at least in some parts of the curriculum and in some phases. So, how does a teacher balance professional creativity and judgement against the requirements to teach in certain ways?
- *The distinctions and potential tensions between teaching for creativity, creative teaching and creative learning.* The distinction between teaching for creativity and creative teaching was made by the NACCCE (1999) report, which acknowledged that teaching for creativity may or may not involve creative teaching. The notion of creative learning is being theorised at present (Jeffrey 2004a, 2004b, 2005). The practical differences between each of these need exploration and articulation.

Chapter 11 proposes a framework for responding to the challenges raised in the book. This includes the role of active critical, intersubjective scrutiny, approaches to partnership, characterisations of apprenticeship learning, development of the notion of the teacher artist, the live ethical and social environment into which new ideas are born, and ways in which creativity can be conceptualised as core to being human and, therefore, the business of educators to foster. The chapter concludes with a call for deeper attention to be paid to LifeWork – the multiple perspectives involved in creative excellence that both 'faces in' and 'faces out'.

Finally, the Postscript proposes a number of areas for further development and research:

- *Learning and pedagogic practices.* Four areas of research and development are explored: progression in creative learning, assessing creativity, the balance between individual and collective creativity, and the nature of adult/expert engagement with learners in nurturing creativity.
- *Methodologies for investigating creativity in schools.* The shift toward capturing minutiae and complexity, in attempting to characterize lived experience, with less emphasis on measurement and causality, is explored, and recent and current studies of methodology discussed, calling for close scrutiny of the 'what', 'how' and 'why' of documenting creative learning.
- *Creativity and aspirations beyond school.* The inherent visibility involved in creative action, and the need to document and tease out young people's experiences of choice-making and, therefore, of becoming (more) visible, is laid out as an area for further exploration. Related questions of ethics and excellence are also discussed, together with underpinning implicit and explicit models of moral/ethical development. All of these are proposed as areas for onward development and research. Family and parenting patterns are also discussed, and proposed as an area for exploration: Where the adults in a home take on dual or multiple roles both within and beyond the home, what happens to the creativity of the children in particular (but also that of the adults)?
- *Framing, brokering and extending partnership.* The role of arts partnerships in fostering creativity in schools is expanding, at least in England. How well do we understand how it is most effectively done? A number of enquiry lines are suggested to help develop our understanding building on the recent work of researchers and classroom practitioners.

Finally the Postscript revisits the question of what it is all for, invoking again the study of LifeWork.

Getting it in perspective

As should be clear from the overview of the chapters, this book has been written out of a concern to step back and to ask some fundamental questions around the basis on which we see creativity as a good thing, and to explore some of the conceptual and practical tensions and dilemmas that arise from these questions.

Part I

Context: policy and practice

Part I

Introduction

Creativity is enjoying a renaissance of interest globally, in academic disciplines such as psychology, as well as applied domains such as education. In the United Kingdom, the revitalising of interest that had been relatively dormant since the work undertaken in the US and elsewhere in the 1950s and 1960s reflects social, economic, technological and political imperatives. Creativity has become viewed, since the late 1990s, as centrally relevant to education globally in a way it has perhaps never been before. This approach to creativity can be seen as significantly distinct from the era of educational research, policy and practice that preceded it. In many ways it may be seen as a revolution (Jeffrey and Craft 2001; Robinson 2001).

It is a complex revolution, with, as with all revolutions, a history and a trajectory. And, like any revolution, it brings with it changes and challenges. For teachers and schools this means making sense of and taking a stance on the contextual factors which have contributed to greater value now placed on creativity in education, both in nurturing the creativity of learners and in celebrating the creativity of teachers as professionals. It means developing the ways in which we describe and understand practice in schools, to construct and develop a language for understanding and promoting children's creativity. Developing a shared discourse, though, is a challenging process, and terms are often used interchangeably at the present time (Craft 2003b).

Other challenges are posed by the nature of creativity in relation to knowledge. The role of knowledge is increasingly acknowledged within creativity research, for the domain provides a knowledge context within which to be creative. This is emphasised in different ways by different researchers. For example, Weisberg (1986, 1988, 1993, 1995, 1999) proposes that creativity builds on knowledge, what he calls the 'foundation' view (Weisberg 1999: 226). How does this view relate to the notion advanced by the Qualifications and Curriculum Authority, of creativity as domain related in the foundation stage curriculum (DfEE/QCA 2000) and in the National Curriculum, of creativity as a cross-curricular skill (DfEE and QCA 1999a, 1999b)? Are there any aspects of creativity that are relevant across all areas of knowledge? How does the way that teachers and schools organise the curriculum relate to the promoting of children's creativity in specific areas of knowledge? What does this mean for teachers' own expertise in domains of knowledge, and what might a cross-curricular approach mean for developing disciplinary understanding and creativity? These and other questions are faced by schools wanting to promote children's creativity.

Integrally related to curriculum challenges, of course, are those stemming from the question of how we go about enabling learning; in other words, what kinds of pedagogical strategies may be appropriate to fostering creativity in the classroom. The report of the National Advisory Committee on Creative and Cultural Education (NACCCE 1999) proposed a number of distinctions, in terms, for example, of creative teaching compared with teaching for creativity. More recently, the notion of 'creative learning' has emerged as perhaps definitive of what we aim for in promoting creativity in the classroom. But how do teachers and schools integrate and attach meaning to these terms? How is creativity distinct from learning, and how is promoting creativity in the classroom distinct from good teaching?

These and many other questions are being addressed by policy makers, practitioners and researchers at present, and in Part I of the book we explore what is known and name some further tensions, dilemmas and challenges in the areas of policy development, a language for creativity, knowledge and the curriculum, pedagogy and learning. The last chapter of Part I brings some of these themes together in a discussion of some of the current tensions between policy and practice.

The argument that high creativity and everyday creativity are related is advanced by several researchers (Worth 2000), and the stance taken throughout Part I – and indeed throughout the book – assumes that they are indeed part of the same continuum.

1 Setting the context: policy, practice and constraints

This chapter explores some of the economic, social, political and technological context to the increased value placed on creativity globally, in particular with regard to education. It outlines ways in which creativity has become increasingly valued in policy and practice in education in England and ways in which this has been paralleled by interest from researchers. Finally, initial questions are posed about how appropriate the emergence of creativity in education may be.

Why the revolution?

The place of creativity in education has seen a revolution in value in the past 20 years. In many parts of the world, creativity has moved from the fringes of education, and/or from the arts, to being seen as a core aspect of educating. So why is this?

Politics, economics and social change are, of course, intertwined. To take economic and political change as an example, the globalisation of economic activity has brought with it increased competitiveness for markets, driving the need for nation states to raise the levels of educational achievement of their potential labour forces (Jeffrey and Craft 2001), which we return to later in this section.

Economic change is tied to politics, in that large, so-called multinational companies with global markets have become as powerful – in terms of wealth – as governments. Handy (2001) describes how, in November 2000, Shell and Vodafone each announced their profits for the previous quarter as being £2 billion. BP beat this, in the same quarter, at £2.5 billion. This compared with an announcement from the Chancellor of the Exchequer announcing that, owing to the successful British economy, he would be able to afford, over the coming year, to return £2 billion to the taxpayer in one form or another. The situation – whereby one multinational business alone can have the same amount of resources to play with over just one quarter of the year as a government presiding over the entirety of a country's social, medical, environmental, defence and other needs has over the course of a whole year – is an indication of the immense potential for powerholding in parts of the economy. Of course, this representation can be seen as fairly simplified; however, the fact is that many multinational companies do hold enormously high levels of resources.

A part of the complex picture of the economy is the changing structure of the workplace, so that an increasing amount of our economy is now made up of small businesses or organisations employing less than five people and with a turnover of less than £500,000 (Carter *et al.* 2004). Many of these have strong relationships with, i.e. are consultants or suppliers to, large companies/organisations, although a third of those surveyed sold their products and services direct to the customer in a local context. The Federation of Small Businesses Survey notes that a quarter of those surveyed in 2004 began their business in the last 3 years, and there is also a growing trend in home-based organisations (Carter *et al.* 2004). Handy (2001) notes that organisations have shifted from organising themselves as pyramids, to operating as networks and customised relationships, involving greater awareness of the 'customer' and a higher level of negotiation and contract to ensure satisfaction and continued business. As part of this, he describes the growing web of relationships between the individual and the multinational conglomerate, likening the relationship to one between an elephant (the multinational conglomerate) and a flea (the individual). He predicts that the life of the flea, or the independent worker, is the working life of the future for the majority – and this requires a different kind of attitude to work than previously. No longer is the 'till death do us part' analogy from marriage appropriate (except in the sense that marriage and partnership, too, have changed to become more itinerant, transient and network-based). For, at the start of the twenty-first century, employment in any one organisation is not for life. Even by 1996, only 40 per cent of the British labour force had indefinite contracts in full-time work. Education has a dynamic relationship with this shifting world of employment, for not only is the structure of work shifting in what has been described as a revolution 'comparable to the impact of the massive upheavals of the Industrial Revolution' (Robinson 2001: 4), but what also makes it so significant is the shift from manufacturing to a situation where 'knowledge is the primary source of economic productivity' (Seltzer and Bentley 1999: 9). Thus, what is significant in terms of educational achievement is changing accordingly.

So, what is the difference between educational achievement of the past and that of the future? It is not merely *excellence* in depth of knowledge about certain domains and knowledge how to undertake certain skills, together with knowing how to learn about new areas, that young people need. Critical to surviving and thriving is, rather, creativity. It is *creativity* that enables a person to identify appropriate problems, and to solve them. It is *creativity* that identifies possibilities and opportunities that may not have been noticed by others. And is it creativity which forms the backbone of the economy based on knowledge (Robinson 2001). In short, educational achievement is being 'reconstructed' and re-conceptualised.

In this reconstruction and re-conceptualisation, there are interesting tensions with what had existed previously. For, as documented elsewhere, since the late 1980s, educational structures, organisations, programmes, curriculum, pedagogies, accountabilities, conditions of teachers' work and their professional status have all been reconstructed (Woods and Jeffrey 1996). For the incoming New Labour government in 1997, education was the top priority. This was paralleled elsewhere in the Western world, where the reconstruction of education became of paramount importance. Interestingly, however, the directions of these reconstructions varied, and in some cases they went in opposite directions. For example, France loosened its central control, whilst in England it increased (Jeffrey and Craft 2001).

One of the common objectives, however, was to make education systems more effective in assisting the nation state to secure higher employment, and maintain economic performance. With manufacturing dispersing globally, new forms of wealth production have emerged, through increased marketing, the growth of service industries, electronic communications and e-commerce markets. This has been called the 'weightless economy' (Seltzer and Bentley 1999: 14). Many organisations began to maximise the intellectual and creative capabilities of the labour force, as well as its physical energy and general intelligence. Seltzer and Bentley (1999: 9–10) summarise this, and the challenge posed by these changes for education, as follows:

> While qualifications are still integral to personal success, it is no longer enough for students to show that they are capable of passing public examinations. To thrive in our economy defined by the innovative application of knowledge, we must be able to do more than absorb and feedback information. Learners and workers must draw on their entire spectrum of learning experiences and apply what they have learned in new and creative ways. A central challenge for the education system is therefore to find ways of embedding learning in a range of meaning for contexts, where students can use their knowledge and skills creatively to make an impact on the world around them.

As documented elsewhere, the fundamental shift from focusing on individual traits and abilities to concentrating on organisations, climates and cultures has had the effect of 'universalising' creativity (Jeffrey and Craft 2001). The shift has encouraged perspectives that suggest that everybody is capable of being creative, given the right environment. These perspectives contrast with earlier ones, where creativity was equated with 'genius' and 'giftedness' (Gardner 1993). The current competitive discourse has resulted in many institutions and organisations encouraging everybody to be creative in terms of improving the institution's performance and the creation of ways in which the organisation can diversify in order to expand.

Social change within organisations and beyond has accompanied the increased recognition of a need to encourage new ideas. By encouraging creativity and engagement through democratic cultures and rewards for innovation, organisations may elicit higher levels of commitment from employees and greater levels of job satisfaction, *and* enhance market share. One of the interesting features of the discourse in which creativity is 'universalised' is its curious culture-blindness (Craft 2003b; Ng 2003). Thus, strategies and approaches to increasing creativity of individuals, groups and organisations are, together with the discourse, universalised. The extent to which this is appropriate or effective will be explored in Chapter 7, where the possibility of the concept of creativity as being 'culturally saturated' will be examined.

Education arguably plays a role in the policy area as well as in the economic area. The promotion of collaborative practices and 'team work' prepares pupils and students for work in organisations that need to be creative and single-minded if they are to be effective in their highly competitive markets or in service industries that are underpinned by high levels of accountability.

In exploring why the need for greater creativity is emerging in Western society, we have so far touched only on the aspects of the economic context, and not the much wider social environment. Another significant influence is the decreasing level of certitude in lifestyles of the early twenty-first century. Roles and relationships, unchanging for centuries, are shifting fast. Women's entry into the workplace has altered the demography of the home, both in terms of the birth rate and also in terms of who cares for young children. A wider variety of contexts in which children are born, from single-parent families to those where couples choose not to marry, to second and subsequent marriages or families, and those where couples are same-sex, all represent a broadening of what we have come to think of as 'the family'. Expectations of continuity and commitment in family units have reduced as it becomes more 'the norm' for relationships to founder, to be replaced by new possibilities together with complex new family relationships. The gradual dissipation of organised religion, and the proliferation of religious and spiritual identity (including the option of Market as God), adds an additional factor to a previously predictable family and community structure and rhythm. All of these social factors combine to mean that a young person growing up and being educated in the twenty-first century has a much more active role than perhaps ever before in making sense of their experiences and making choices about their own life. We might argue that choice of identity is at the heart of twenty-first century living, for those who are enfranchised and empowered: choice of identity, played out through what we buy, what we believe, who we choose to be our friends and partners, and what we choose to spend our personal time and our working lives doing. We live in a world where young people can select who to be and can instantly 'belong', often through buying the trappings of that identity, but without the delayed gratification perhaps more common to traditional approaches to living.

But the economic, social and political are not the only contextual factors. The increasing role played by information and communications technology, arguably both requires greater creativity and also offers greater scope for it. The potential of information technology in particular is explored by Dewett (2003), who explores the potential it offers to the workplace; he summarises these as being that information technology:

- Links and enables employees.
- Codifies the knowledge base.
- Increases in boundary-spanning activities (can scan internal and external environment efficiently); networking out of hours and away from the workplace has increased, and this has the effect of creating greater autonomy. Autonomy is associated with creativity.
- Decentralises decision making and communication, thus overcoming hierarchies.
- Contributes to capacity to undertake efficient knowledge management, and thus to organisational learning.
- Encourages project work and collaboration bringing new perspectives and knowledge bases.

To an extent, Dewett's analysis is more relevant to what in the past might have been called 'white-collar' work. However, some of the arguments he makes would be true of mobile phone text messaging for workers who operate in 'manual' occupations, although it might be argued that the kinds of communication being sent through text messaging would be less likely to be focused on work than the white-collar worker's use of Web-based communication outside of office hours and from home.

However, if we pay less attention to the purpose and more attention to the extent to which activity is creative, some of the arguments made by Dewett could be applied beyond the workplace into lifewide experience. For example, the linking of people in synchronous and non-synchronous, and anything from dyadic to multiple interactions through Web-based e-communication systems, fosters dialogic collaboration – a fundamental, some would argue, to creativity (Wegerif 2004). Wegerif's work, which focuses on reasoning skills, draws on recent research by the Educational Dialogue Research Unit of The Open University, which has developed a dialogical model of reason. This involves interaction between people in building reasoning, and consists of an intersubjective orientation called 'exploratory' and a set of ground rules designed specifically to support collaboration in the classroom. Wegerif suggests that 'dialogical reason is characterised by the creation of a space of reflection between participants in which resonance between ideas and images can occur, as well as co-construction when participants build creatively on each other's proposals.' (Wegerif 2004: 26). Although Wegerif's work involves face-to-face interaction, the model of dialogic reasoning could well be applied in an electronic or Web-based environment.

Equally, e-communication offers potential for increasing autonomy, and also for making decisions and communicating efficiently. Indeed, because of its vast store of information and its instantaneous nature, it could be said that information and communications technology not only offers potential for creativity but that it actually demands it. Indeed, similar arguments are made by Levine *et al.* (2000) in their analysis of the relationship between the Web and business organisation of the future; they discuss in particular the importance of being in a relationship and of the significance of humanity, including having fun, through Web-based interactions.

Of course, many aspects of twenty-first century life are imbued with e-technology, and not all of these involve creativity at the point of use: for example, having barcodes on supermarket products or on library cards, interpreting data on the car dashboard display, or programming the video player to record a certain programme. But in many other ways, information and communications technology does offer opportunities for creativity.

The pace of change itself is both the outcome of creativity and, in an intensifying cycle, it demands more creativity. And within the global market economy, novelty and invention is in and make do and mend is out. Wants are substituted for needs; convenience lifestyles and image are increasingly seen as significant across cultures and socio-economic brackets. The speed at which the possibilities of choice multiply could be seen as demanding creativity to make adequate sense of these in order to choose appropriately; or to identify alternative possibilities which go outside of the framework on offer (as exemplified by electing *not* to do or buy something, as discussed by Lane (2001)).

In response to this external environment, then, which now both expects and demands greater creativity, education is being reconstructed, to encompass creativity in its curriculum and its pedagogy.

Policies and practices

It is ironic that, alongside the drive to reconstruct education to foster creativity, there has been a parallel drive toward technicisation and bureaucratisation, which, it has been argued, has had the effect of reducing creativity in the teaching profession (Jeffrey 2001a; Woods 1995, 2002; Woods and Jeffrey 1996; Woods *et al.* 1997).

Ironically too, the business world is now advocating that learning should take place through precisely those creative practices (projects, problem solving and different perspectives) that were being advocated by education-alists in the 1960s (Central Advisory Council for Education 1967a, 1967b) and which came in for such enormous criticism (e.g. Johnson 1971; Pinn 1969) that they were swept away under the tide of a statutory, knowledge-heavy, prescriptive, National Curriculum – so well documented in terms of primary education by Alexander (1995).

Elsewhere (Craft 2002), I have argued that the 'first wave' of creativity in education can be seen to have been in the 1960s, codified by Plowden (Central Advisory Council for Education 1967a, 1967b), but drawing on a long line of child-centred policy, philosophy and practice; the second wave being nearly 10 years after the introduction of the National Curriculum, in the late 1990s. During the mid- to late 1980s, immediately before the National Curriculum's introduction and during its immediate implementation period, creativity (along with many other worthy educational objectives, including educational research) was knocked off the agenda as 'oldspeak' (I remember this as a young project officer at the National Curriculum Council at the time). However, during the late 1990s, attention turned back to the fostering of creativity, alongside a resurgence of interest in psychology and education research. The revival of research interest can be seen, Jeffrey and Craft (2001) argue, as drawing in the role of social interaction in an unprecedented way.

The second wave was preceded by various structural changes at a policy level, demonstrating a much increased concern for creativity and its role in society and the economy. For example, in 1998, the National Endowment for Science, Technology and the Arts (NESTA) was established, by Act of Parliament. Funded through the interest on an endowment fund made available through the National Lottery, NESTA's mission was to identify and fund creativity and innovation across knowledge boundaries, and also carry out research and evaluation focusing on these. Another significant change was the establishment in the 1990s of the Department of Culture, Media and Sport (DCMS), bringing these three areas into unprecedented focus.

These perhaps provided a suitable backdrop for the curriculum initiatives that were then spawned. During the second wave, there were three major curriculum-based initiatives:

- the inclusion of 'Creative Development' as one of the seven Early Learning Goals for early years children (QCA 2000);
- the commissioning of the NACCCE, which reported in 1999;
- the Qualifications and Curriculum Authority (QCA) and Department for Education and Employment (DfEE) identified 'creative thinking skills' as a key skill in the National Curriculum (DfEE and QCA 1999a, 1999b).

Let us briefly examine each of these.

First, the inclusion of 'Creative Development' as one of the six Early Learning Goals in the Foundation Stage Curriculum. 'Creative

Development' encompasses art, craft and design and various forms of dramatic play and creative expression, all of which have traditionally formed a core part of early years provision. It emphasises the role of imagination and the importance of children developing a range of ways in which to express their ideas and communicate their feelings.

Second, the commissioning of the NACCCE, which reported in 1999. The committee gave advice on what would need to be done at a range of levels, including policy making, to foster the development of pupil creativity within school education. It linked the fostering of pupil creativity with the development of culture, in that original ideas and action are developed in a shifting cultural context. It suggested that the fostering of pupil creativity would contribute to the cultural development of society and that creativity rarely occurs without some form of interrogation of what has gone before or is occurring synchronously.

The report distinguished between different definitions of creativity, proposing the 'democratic' definition as the one perhaps most appropriate to education, suggesting 'all people are capable of creative achievement in some area of activity, provided the conditions are right and they have acquired the relevant knowledge and skills' (NACCCE 1999: Paragraph 25).

Thus:

- pupils' self-expression is valued;
- all people are seen as capable of creativity.

One of the recommendations of the NACCCE report was the establishment of much greater activity in building creative partnerships to raise achievement across the curriculum. This eventually turned into the Creative Partnerships initiative that involves an investment, mainly by the DCMS and the Department for Education and Skills (DfES), of some £114.5 million across the first two phases, which involve 25 regional projects, each involving around 20 or more schools together with local creative practitioners. In 2005–6 a further 11 regions are set to join the project.

Third, the QCA and the (then) DfEE identified 'creative thinking skills' as a key skill in the National Curriculum, proposing a *cross-curricular* role for creativity in the aims of the school curriculum, saying that 'the curriculum should enable pupils to think creatively... It should give them the opportunity to become creative...' (DfEE and QCA 1999: 11). This perspective on creativity as a cross-curricular thinking skill reflects the notion proposed by some that creativity is not the preserve of the arts alone but that it arises in all domains of human endeavour.

The QCA also initiated a creativity curriculum project, *Creativity: Find it, Promote it!* Various findings came out of that project, and it began its dissemination phase in 2004. Perhaps the most significant of these is the

QCA (2005a, 2005b) creativity framework, which says that creativity involves pupils in:

- questioning and challenging
- making connections, seeing relationships
- envisaging what might be
- exploring ideas, keeping options open
- reflecting critically on ideas, actions, outcomes.

All kinds of other policy initiatives have flowed from these major developments. These include the following:

- Excellence in Cities, a scheme replacing Education Action Zones and designed to raise achievement, particularly in the inner city, the first phase of which was launched in 1999. Initially targeted at secondary schools and then introduced to primary schools, this programme was widely believed to have led to higher attainment in both GCSEs and vocational equivalents for pupils whose schools were in the scheme. The programme had seven main strands:

  o in-school learning mentors;
  o learning support units for difficult pupils;
  o programmes to stretch the most able 5 to 10 per cent of pupils;
  o city learning centres to promote school and community learning through state-of-the-art technology;
  o encouraging schools to become beacons and specialists;
  o action zones, where a cluster of schools work together.

Excellence in Cities includes some schools and action zones focusing specifically on creativity (DfES 2005a).

- For several years at the end of the 1990s and start of the 2000s, DfES Best Practice Research Scholarships and Professional Bursaries for teachers were funded to encourage teachers' creativity and thinking, disseminated through Teachernet on the DfES Website (DfES 2005b). From 2004 the theme was continued through the Creativity Action Research Awards offered by Creative Partnerships and the DfES.
- Ofsted (2003a, 2003b) taking a perspective on creativity through two reports published in August 2003.
- The DfES (2003) publishing the document *Excellence and Enjoyment*, for primary schools, in May, exhorting primary schools to take creative and innovative approaches to the curriculum and to place creativity high on their agendas.

- The DfES establishing the Innovation Unit as a sub-unit of the department, with the brief to foster and nurture creative and innovative approaches to teaching and learning; the DfES also embarked on funding a number of research, development and continuing professional development (CPD) initiatives, including a series of creative citizenship conferences throughout 2004; also, a research programme that explored the application into education of Synectics, a business model for creativity (Synectics Education Initiative *et al.* 2004).
- The Arts Council and the DCMS being integrally bound in to the delivery of Creative Partnerships and associated activities (Creative Partnerships 2005).
- The establishment of a creativity strand within the Department of Trade and Industry (DTI) from the end of the 1990s (DTI 2005).
- QCA developing creativity CPD materials for Foundation Stage through to KS3, and making these available to teachers from Spring 2005 (QCA 2005a, 2005b).
- National College for School Leadership developing the notion of Creative Leadership for fostering creativity in pupils (NCSL 2005).
- The introduction of the 'personalised learning' agenda (DfES, 2004a, 2004b, 2004c).
- The Creative Action Research Awards programme to promote exploration of creative learning, funded through Creative Partnerships.
- Various policy makers from the UK Treasury downwards taking an interest in how best to stimulate creativity in higher education, including creativity in initial teacher education.

There was a matched growth in interest within the UK research community. Following a relatively fallow period from the 1970s until the late 1980s, the last part of the century saw a burgeoning of interest in creativity research as applied to education. Research foci included: the conceptualising of creativity (Fryer 1996; Craft 1997, 2001a, 2002); exploring how creativity could be fostered and maintained (Jeffrey 2001a, 2001b); investigation of creativity in specific domains, such as information and communications technology (Leach 2001); documenting creative teaching (Woods and Jeffrey 1996) and exploring creative leadership (Imison 2001). A major direction of research into creativity, both within education and beyond it, has been to contextualise it into a social psychological framework that recognises the important role of social structures in fostering individual creativity (Jeffrey and Craft 2001; Rhyammar and Brolin 1999).

During the 1990s, under the influence of the perspective from developmental, cultural and social psychology, research into creativity became more comprehensive, and began to focus more on the creativity of ordinary people within aspects of education. At the same time, the methodology for investigating creativity in education also shifted, within a general trend, from large-scale studies aiming to measure creativity, towards ethnographic, qualitative approaches to research focusing on the actual site of operations and practice, as well as towards philosophical discussions around the nature of creativity (Craft 2002).

The aspects of creativity being investigated at this point, in the early years of the twenty-first century, are quite distinct from those emphasised in the mid to late twentieth century. Earlier approaches were influenced by the emphasis, from the 1950s, particularly in North American research, on the psychological determinants of genius and giftedness. Many would argue that this era of research was launched by Guilford's (1950) examination of the limitations of intelligence tests and his investigation of 'divergent thinking'. There followed many studies which attempted to test and measure creativity, to pin down its characteristics and to foster it through specific teaching approaches, both within education and beyond. An influential figure in the classroom was Torrance (1962), who developed many experiments and tests for creativity.

The recent burgeoning of interest in creativity in education does not have the same emphasis on measurement. The 1950s work led to three major lines of creativity research:

- personality
- cognition (including work on psychometrics and psychodynamics)
- how to stimulate creativity.

A feature that each of these lines shared in common, was the defining of creativity as connected with a 'product outcome' – a distinct position from more recent views of creativity (Elliott 1971).

One way in which current creativity research connects with that of the 1950s is the tendency to see creativity as a 'generalised' phenomenon, and not tied purely to a particular area of knowledge. But, in general, the current climate, in the UK in particular, is quite distinct from the earlier one in its changed emphases, which include foci on:

- ordinary creativity rather than genius
- characterising, rather than measuring
- the social system rather than the individual
- encompassing views of creativity which include products but do not see these as necessary.

So, creativity research in education burgeoned again in the latter part of the twentieth century. As to policy, there are numerous themes that run across many of the policy initiatives named earlier, such as social inclusion, the role of the arts, the raising of achievement, the exploration of leadership and the place of partnerships.

A positive agenda?

There is, of course, an obvious tension between the burgeoning of a culture of supportive interest around the concept of creativity, and the fact that this in itself can be questioned. The very idea of the concept of creativity being at all limited is paradoxical in itself, for it would seem that creativity is an open-ended concept. It is concerned with the development and application of possibilities – and thus is inherently *un*limited. This book sets out to analyse creativity from a number of perspectives, all of which question this notion.

2   A language for creativity

This chapter considers some of the difficulties of terminology in the study of creativity in education. It discusses core terms such as creativity, innovation, and imagination. It goes on to explore the use of classroom-related terms such as creative learning, creative teaching and teaching for creativity. Finally, it deals with some of the implications of such slippage in language, for what we claim to value within the classroom and school, arguing that the language of creativity needs precision.

Introduction

In the current era, creativity and associated capacities are highly regarded as a life capability, both for the individual and society (Bentley 1998). The case for fostering creativity is made at the level of the individual (Craft 2002) and also for society, by commentators (e.g. Seltzer and Bentley 1999; Handy 2001) and by policy makers (e.g. NACCCE 1999; NESTA 2003).

But it is common to find slippage between these words, with consequences for what is then valued in any applied context, including education. This chapter examines two separate sets of terms: first, some which might be described as 'core', in other words 'innovation', 'creativity', and 'imagination'; second, some terms situated in the context of education, in other words, creative teaching, teaching for creativity and creative learning. Finally, it considers some implications of the terms and the slippage between them for pedagogy.

The analysis draws on literature and values found predominantly in northern Europe and North America, which means that the conclusions drawn may have elements of cultural specificity embedded within them; some issues related to creativity and cultural specificity will be explored in Chapter 7.

Untangling three core terms

The study of creativity and imagination extends far back into human history. It is a massive area to characterise, as the composer Aaron Copland said in a lecture delivered at Harvard University in 1952: '[the concept of human creativity] goes back so far in time, so many cogent things have been written and said – acute observations, poetic reflections, and philosophical ponderings, that one despairs of bringing to the subject anything more than a private view of an immense terrain' (Copland 1980: 40).

The Greek, Judaic, Christian and Muslim traditions all contain the notion of 'inspiration' or 'getting an idea', founded on the belief that a higher power produces it (Rhyammar and Brolin 1999: 260). The Romantic era in Europe brought a major shift in focus, starting to see the source of inspiration as the human being, accompanied by the artistic expression of it. During this era, originality, insight, the creative genius and the subjectivity of feeling were highly valued. From the end of the nineteenth century, the question of what fostered creativity began to be investigated, particularly in psychology.

Since the first systematic study undertaken by Galton in 1869, which focused on 'genius', a long history of investigation has unfolded. Most of the systematic work started at the turn of the twentieth century, when four traditions can be seen to have been adopted in psychology, these reflecting the changing terrain of the discipline itself: psychoanalytic, cognitive, behaviourist and humanist.

Alongside psychology, philosophers, sociologists and anthropologists were also making sense of this most human characteristic. And in applied fields such as education, the ways in which creativity could be understood provided a backdrop – and for some a foundation – for pedagogical practices.

Against the context of this mass of literature we might try to make some simple (but hopefully not simplistic) distinctions between creativity, imagination and innovation.

Imagination: in 1980, a tripartite distinction was made by the philosopher Passmore (1980) between imaging, imagining and being imaginative. Imaging, he took to mean a variety of forms of mental representation or image, including visual, olfactory, auditory, kinaesthetic, gustatory, and so on. Imagining he took to mean 'supposing' that something be the case, as one would in hypothesising, or as a child might do when 'pretending', and as one might do in empathising with another's perspective. Being imaginative, he suggested, referred to the generation of a novel outcome. Scruton (1974) has pointed out that imaging and imagining are mental acts and also that they may be conjured at will, whereas being imaginative may not always be either a mental act, or conjured at will. It has been argued (Craft 2002) that everyday, or 'little c', creativity necessarily involves being imaginative, and may at times also involve imagining. It could be argued that this is true of all creativity whether everyday or not. So, put simply, some aspects of imagination are implicit within creativity.

Creativity: creativity and approaches to studying it have varied enormously over time and also reflect the values context of those researching it.

One significant distinction made by psychology scholars is between 'high' creativity (Csikszentmihalyi 1990; Gardner 1993; Feldman *et al.* 1994; Simonton 2003) and 'little' c creativity (Craft 2001a).

High creativity has been described by Feldman *et al.* (1994: 1) as

> the achievement of something remarkable and new, something which transforms and changes a field of endeavor in a significant way... the kinds of things that people do that change the world.

This reflects the view that high and little c creativity are part of a continuum (Amabile 1990). By contrast, little c creativity has been suggested to be the ordinary but lifewide attitude toward life that is driven by 'possibility thinking' but is about acting effectively with flexibility, intelligence and novelty in the everyday rather than the extraordinary (Craft 2002: 43):

> a sort of 'personal effectiveness' in coping well with recognising and making choices....A creativity of everyday life, or what might be called 'little c creativity'...[and] in identifying and making choices, a person is inevitably self-shaping.

Another set of distinctions is that which distinguishes approaches to creativity that focus on the individual (e.g. Sternberg and Lubart, 1995b) and those that focus on collaboration/processes between people, and also the important role of motivation, notably marked by the work of Amabile (1983, 1988, 1989, 1990, 1996, 1997).

Yet another way of examining the question of creativity is to explore the sub-disciplinary perspective brought to conceptualising it. For example: *psychoanalytic* (this included Freud's discussion of creativity as the sublimation of drives and Winnicott's work on development, which makes creativity central and intrinsic to human nature); *cognitive* (this grew on the foundation of Galton's work and included Mednick's exploration of the associative process and also Guilford's exploration of the divergent production of ideas and products); *behaviourist* (this included Skinner's conceptualisation of creativity as chance mutation in the repertoire of behaviours); *developmental* (including Feldman's work on the development of creativity and the spectrum between low and high c creativity); and *humanistic* (theorists here included Rogers, May and Maslow, whose discussions focused on the self-realising person acting in harmony with their inner needs and potentialities).

Creativity, then, may be interpreted in many different ways, some emphasising the locus (person, collective or process), others emphasising the product (idea or physical outcome) and others emphasising impact (global or local), but all see creativity as involving the *generating of novel ideas*. The definition proposed by the NACCCE, and which has currency in education, reflected this. The committee's definition of creativity was 'Imaginative activity fashioned so as to produce outcomes that are original and of value' (NACCCE 1999: 29).

Perhaps one further useful dimension is that described by Nolan (2004), who distinguishes between:

- Creative thinking, i.e. generating new ideas, concepts, wishes, goals, new perceptions of problems. Nolan suggests that this can be fostered through a variety of processes – and what is generated is 'new thoughts, which in themselves do not change anything in the real world until they are implemented in some way' (Nolan 2004: 1).
- Creative behaviour, i.e. those behaviours which facilitate the creative process. Nolan suggests that the first step in creative behaviour is suspension of judgement; following this, many other strategies may follow.
- Creative action, i.e. actually doing new things. Nolan includes here doing things for the first time, as well as doing 'things which are new to the world' (Nolan 2004: 1). He sums up creative action as 'experiment and innovation'.

Nolan's perspective is that creative behaviour is the cornerstone of creative thought and creative action, and that it can perhaps be understood best as 'constructive behaviour', which emphasises generativity in thought, rather than position adoption (which can lead to unconstructive, unresolved argument). What is highlighted by his recognition of the ways in which creativity can be separated is that it enables us to examine some of the assumptions we may hold about the ways these different elements of creativity interact.

Innovation by contrast, may be seen as *the implementation of new ideas to create something of value, proven through its uptake in the marketplace.* An innovation can be seen as a new idea being launched on the market for the first time. Five characteristics of an innovation have been identified which influence how rapidly it is likely to diffuse (i.e. succeed in the marketplace). These are discussed in a classic text by Everett Rogers (2003) as being:

- relative advantage (being perceived to offer advantages relative to comparable products);
- compatibility (being perceived as being compatible with the existing values, skills and past experiences of potential customers and users);
- complexity (the extent to which potential customers perceive it as being difficult to understand and use);
- observability (the extent to which it is visible to others);
- 'trialability', i.e. whether an innovation may be tried out before purchase.

In addition, characteristics of the market, the innovator and of regulation, legislation and government policy can influence both the creation of innovations and the speed at which they diffuse.

The Innovation Network, a spin-off of the virtual Innovation University created in 1996, brings together innovators to reflect on their processes and to learn from one another. It offers what it calls a 'DNA (trademark)' of innovation principles, which demonstrates that creativity is a necessary precursor to innovation, which is about application and implementation. The DNA structure of innovation was developed in the last years of the 1990s by the Founding Fellows of Innovation University and has been field tested annually since then. The principles, which have been revised over time, are:

- Context: the world. Innovation occurs in the context of suppliers, competitors, customers, the economy, government, communities and families, and world events.
- Culture: the 'playing field' for all innovation projects/activities. In other words, organisations that foster innovation are flexible, welcome ideas, are empowering, tolerate risk, celebrate success, foster synergy and encourage fun. The four components in a creative culture are: leadership (role models who see possibilities for the future); people (the source of innovation); basic values (the backbone that defines an organisation); and innovation values (the mindset that makes the impossible possible).
- Ideas, change, passion and trends – entryways to innovation: these are the innovation drivers, providing the impetus/stimulus needed to move away from the status quo.
- Outcomes lead to another cycle: renewal change reinvention trends.

The Innovation University offers what it calls a 'roadmap' of the seven operational dimensions (source: www.thinksmart.com):

- challenge: the pull
- customer focus: the push
- creativity: the brain
- communication: the lifeblood
- collaboration: the heart
- completion: the muscle
- contemplation: the ladder

This 'roadmap' demonstrates at least two important points. Firstly, that innovation is here seen as a group process. Secondly, that innovation is seen as encompassing creativity, but that this is only a part of what innovation is.

Put simply, then, creativity may be seen as encompassing imagination, and innovation may be seen as encompassing both creativity and imagination.

There is no direct causal line between creativity and imagination and innovation, since there are potential obstacles to innovation, which include the technical, financial and organisational. For it has been noted that 'Creativity is not enough to ensure a successful innovative product. Success requires that the *technical, financial* and *organisational obstacles to innovation* and the *obstacles to diffusion* are overcome' (Roy 2003).

It may be noted that this attempt to untangle core terms drew for imagination on philosophy, for creativity on psychology, and for innovation on the applied fields of design of products and organisations. The choice of these foundations will have its own implications for how we make sense of the terms; however, with this caveat, let us consider the applied field of education.

Untangling terms applied to education

In this section, the three terms *creative teaching*, *teaching for creativity* and *creative learning* are explored, in that order.

In its characterising of creative teaching, the NACCCE (1999) report made a distinction between *teaching creatively* and *teaching for creativity*.

Creative teaching was seen as 'using imaginative approaches to make learning more interesting and effective' (NACCCE 1999: 89). Creative teaching approaches, at least in primary schools, have been well documented by Woods (1990), who proposes the properties or features of creative teaching to be innovation, relevance, control and ownership, returned to later in the book, particularly in Chapter 10.

Teaching for creativity, by contrast, was seen by NACCCE as forms of teaching that are intended to develop young people's own creative thinking or behaviour. The terms, then, appear to be distinct, at least in the NACCCE formulation. It has been suggested (Jeffrey and Craft 2001) that creative teaching may be interpreted as being perhaps more concerned with 'effective teaching', and teaching for creativity may be seen as being more concerned with 'learner empowerment' as its main objective.

However, more recently, it has been argued (Jeffrey and Craft 2004a) that the dichotomy which is implied by this distinction may be both false and also unhelpful, in that teaching creatively is implied in, and often leads to, teaching for creativity (notwithstanding some evidence of creative reactions to constraining situations (Fryer 1996)). Indeed, the NACCCE report itself suggests that 'teaching for creativity involves teaching creatively' (NACCCE, 1999: 90), noting that: 'Young people's creative abilities are most likely to be developed in an atmosphere in which the teacher's creative abilities are properly engaged' (ibid.). In addition, Jeffrey and Craft (2004a) argue that pedagogic practices may be more usefully interpreted and understood if the emphasis of enquiry and analysis is on both the teacher and the learner's perspectives.

An aspect of this involves conceptualising the third term in this applied section, i.e. 'creative learning', a feature of the current decade. The National

College for School Leadership names creative learning within its programme, Creative Partnerships has become increasingly focused on it, and Bob Jeffrey's ten-country European study, Creative Learning and Student Perspectives (CLASP), is addressing the learner's experience of creative pedagogies, asking numerous questions, including:

- What does creative teaching and learning consist of?
- What is learned, and how?
- What difference does it make to the learner?
- What feelings, as well as cognition, are involved, and what is the relationship between feelings and cognition?
- What is to be gained by bringing student perspectives into a creative pedagogy?
- How far do students act creatively to make their learning meaningful (CLASP 2002)?

Early characterisations of creative learning suggest that it involves learners in using their imagination and experience to develop learning, that it involves them strategically collaborating over tasks, contributing to the classroom pedagogy and to the curriculum, and it also involves them critically evaluating their own learning practices and teachers' performance (Jeffrey 2001b).

And it has been argued (Jeffrey and Craft 2003; Craft 2003c) that, in order to research creativity in the classroom effectively, the relationship between the teacher and the learner must form the focus of the study, and that what is needed is empirical work which seeks to further characterise and analyse creative learning, creative teaching and teaching for creativity. In doing so it may be useful to explore ways in which Nolan's (2004) creative thought, creative behaviour and creative action may interrelate. Some recent literature on pedagogical relationships and strategies around these three terms is explored in Chapter 4, and further discussion of the notion of creative learning will be found in Chapter 5.

But to return to the question of language, with which this chapter is concerned: put simply, it has been suggested that creativity involves imagination, and that innovation involves both creativity and imagination. It has been suggested that creative teaching, teaching for creativity and creative learning may be seen as different aspects of the same process, although further empirical work is needed to demonstrate some of the ways in which these distinctions and relationships are played out.

But what could be the implications for pedagogy of using these different core and applied terms?

Implications for pedagogy

Clearly, the name that we give an activity or process acts as a 'frame' for how we then put it into practice. The very fact that we might distinguish between our use of the terms creativity, imagination and innovation could alter how we go about emphasising activities in the classroom. And similarly, the value that we place on the three elements of pedagogy discussed here, i.e. creative teaching, teaching for creativity and creative learning, seems likely to influence the way a classroom is organised and executed.

There are many permutations; after all, I have briefly discussed six terms, which is too many possible combinations to play out here. However, let us take two starkly contrasting thought experiments to underline the point. They are based on recent observations that I have made in fieldwork, but they are fictional.

Benjamin teaches modern languages in a boys' secondary school. He values imagination very highly and organises much of his teaching in such a way that boys have to imagine themselves in new situations, in order to use and develop their written and spoken language skills. His focus alternates between interaction, where collective creative thought, behaviour and action are usually called for, and individual work, where imagination is often but not always required. His own interactions with students are very significant in the way that he teaches, and his teaching often encourages and celebrates creative learning and learner creativity, while being being creative teaching. The following is an extract from a report of a lesson observation in a Y9 German lesson that Benjamin was teaching (Craft 2003c):

> In this lesson, a role play game was introduced using a telephone and music, with an element of chance designed to encourage students to speak in German using a script presented via the interactive white-board. [Benjamin] nudged the role play exercise, although scripted, into improvisation of voice and intonation, and eventually the students began to improvise the words too, having an impromptu but totally appropriate and very funny conversation in German, leaving the whole class plus researcher and teacher in hysterical laughter.

Benjamin's classroom, then, provides examples of creative teaching and learning and also teaching for creativity. In other words, his pedagogy is creative in itself, and students are drawn into the learning (thus, their learning is 'creative') and his practice also fosters their creativity (thus, he teaches for creativity). In Benjamin's pedagogy, there is a strong emphasis on using imagination to apply language creatively.

Joyah teaches dance in a sixth-form college. She values innovation highly and organises much of her own teaching to cross disciplinary boundaries and to encourage student engagement in making (i.e. choreographing, producing and performing) pieces live and on film. She is herself a professional dancer and choreographer. Her own skills and expertise as an artist provide a model for her students. She is certainly creative herself and teaches creatively. Most of her students find the way she teaches to be an empowering experience, which feeds their own creativity; however, some find themselves awed by her skills, and so experience blockages in their own creativity.

Joyah's classroom provides a contrast to Benjamin: first, in that the subject matter is different; but second, that her approach to teaching is extremely creative. Implicitly, she aims to foster creativity (therefore, to 'teach for creativity') and to foster creative learning, but it is not always apparent in her practice. She uses a mentoring model in her practice, being a teacher–artist, thus encouraging students to model their creativity on hers. Her work always moves students toward performance (an end 'product'), and often has built into it ways of monitoring impact on an audience (an aspect of market awareness). Thus, her work can be described as demonstrating creative teaching and encouraging innovation in students.

Clearly, the domains from which the examples come are contrasting ones, and this may explain some of the differences in approach. However, hopefully, these vignettes may serve to begin to show how the difference in emphasis on imagination or innovation and a difference in pedagogical style – one encompassing creative learning and teaching, and teaching for creativity, and the other focusing very heavily on creative teaching – may result in pedagogically contrasting classrooms. They may also be associated with differences in different learning.

The NACCCE (1999) definition of creativity was 'imaginative activity, fashioned so as to produce outcomes that are original and of value'. We may think that, because we have this statement for creativity as applied to education that many of us might unify behind, our task in fostering student creativity would be straightforward. However, what this chapter suggests is that if we are to foster student creativity effectively, we need precision in associated terms too.

3   Creativity, knowledge and the curriculum

This chapter discusses the extent to which the existence of foundation disciplines constrains the fostering of learner and teacher creativity. To what extent is the fostering of creativity determined by its subject context? What does this mean for how we organise time and content?

Context: creativity, knowledge and the curriculum

In Chapter 2 we explored the meaning of interrelated terms such as creativity, imagination and innovation. In this chapter, it is creativity that we focus on, and some of the relationships between creativity, knowledge and the curriculum.

Chapter 2 discussed approaches to creativity, noting that some emphasise the locus (person, collective or process), some emphasise the product (idea or physical outcome) and some emphasise impact (global or local). All, however, see creativity as involving the *generation of novel ideas.* In considering creativity in education, and in relation to knowledge and the curriculum, it is appropriate to draw on the NACCCE (1999: 29) definition also introduced in the last chapter, i.e. creativity as 'Imaginative activity fashioned so as to produce outcomes that are original and of value'. How does creativity in this sense relate to knowledge? And to curriculum? As context to exploring the answers to these questions, a thumbnail sketch of the difference between the two is presented.

We can think of knowledge as the building blocks of understanding, organised in domains that overlap in focus and style but which have distinct priorities, values, codes of engagement and forms of expression. Learning can be seen as enculturation into the working practices of a domain. Thus, mathematical knowledge is distinct from musical knowledge, and knowledge in the biological sciences is different from theological knowledge, although in the case of each pair there are overlaps between them in terms of focus and expression. This could also be described as disciplinary knowledge – i.e. knowledge of the discipline; disciplinary knowledge, being developed by experts in the area (usually as a result of years of immersion within the discipline, domain or craft) (Gardner 1999, 2000). Gardner even describes the immersion as being rather like an apprenticeship; indeed, in some cases it may actually involve an apprenticeship. He describes the period of becoming an expert as involving the discarding of irrelevant habits of thinking and tools for doing, and also 'the construction of habits and concepts that reflect the best contemporary thinking and practices of the domain' (Gardner 2000: 123).

Curriculum, by contrast, can be seen as the way in which domains of knowledge are made available in a learning environment; in some ways, therefore, it is the 'what' of learning. Clearly, there are different levels of curriculum from the formal, explicit, curriculum statement through which implicit messages can be detected, about what is valued. Equally, the informal curriculum, which may have no codified curriculum statement, is a key part of any learning environment. Thus, the ways in which adults interact with children and with other adults would form a part of the informal curriculum, and could have an effect on children's learning and yet may not be codified officially. We might be tempted to assume that curriculum and knowledge are the same thing, but they are clearly not, as the curriculum involves selection of certain topics for inclusion while others are excluded. A significant aspect of the curriculum is *how* it is made available to children. The teacher, team and school have an influence, in different ways, on what is included and how, within a wider framework of statutory or non-statutory guidance. And clearly, the selection and organisation of knowledge is underpinned by values and beliefs about how children learn. We will examine the dimension of approaches to learning later in the chapter. But first, what is the role of knowledge in creativity?

Knowledge and creativity

The role of knowledge is increasingly acknowledged within creativity research, for the domain provides a knowledge context within which to be creative. This is emphasised in different ways by different researchers. For example, Weisberg (1986, 1988, 1993, 1995, 1999) proposes that high creativity builds on knowledge, what he calls the 'foundation' view (Weisberg 1999: 226). By contrast, although also with regard to acts of 'high creativity', Csikszentmihalyi (1999), Feldman (1999) and Gardner (1999) emphasise the significance of experts in a given field of knowledge recognising work as creative. For something to be creative at this level means a departure from what is generally accepted to be conventional knowledge or approaches within the field – which means that both creator and judges must know what is conventionally accepted in order to know whether something new is creative.

A number of questions arise when we translate the implications of the need for knowledge in order to be creative to the school setting, whether we are talking of very young children or teenage learners. These include:

- How do we conceptualise different kinds of knowledge in being creative?
- How significant is depth of knowledge in being creative?
- What roles do judgement of knowledge play in creativity?

Kinds of knowledge

Ryle's (1949) distinction between two fundamentally different kinds of knowledge provides a useful framework here. He suggested that there is a difference between 'knowing how' and 'knowing that' as follows.

- *Knowing how*: procedural knowledge – the kind required for riding a bike, to fit the right shapes through holes in a toy, to turn a door handle, or to navigate around a computer game.
- *Knowing that*: conceptual knowledge or knowing *about* something. It is the kind of knowledge you need to plan a balanced meal for a child, to make sense of symbols on a map, or to understand that it is impossible to shop at a certain supermarket outside of certain hours.

Often, however, knowledge is a mixture of the two sorts, and is developed through engagement with the world. For example, a child learning to draw develops both procedural and conceptual knowledge. The child develops an understanding that it is possible to represent, as well as developing the procedural knowledge of how to hold a pencil/use the materials to hand. Often, the knowledge which young children accumulate is bound up with procedural knowledge, and even begins with more know-how than knowing-that. Gradually, they acquire the underpinning 'knowing that', or background knowledge, that helps to explain how things work, and why. Similarly, a teenager learning to cook develops procedural knowledge about how to combine and heat or cool ingredients, but will also develop some conceptual knowledge about the properties of different ingredients. An older child may acquire some of the conceptual knowledge before the procedural, i.e. in the opposite order from the young child. Nevertheless, each experiences both, and one informs the other. Indeed, some would go much further and argue that, to demonstrate the understanding of knowledge, some kind of 'performance of understanding' is necessary; thus, in some way, procedural and conceptual knowledge need to be brought together (Gardner 1999, 2000; Blythe *et al.* 1998; Perkins 1999). These writers argue that understanding can be demonstrated, and interrogated, publicly in any learning context through a performance of that understanding through varied media and through other learners plus the teacher interrogating that performance of understanding. This particular performance view of understanding was developed by a team of researchers at Harvard University's Project Zero in the 1990s. It grew out of a long history of research at Project Zero, particularly in arts education, which opened up a 'discipline-based' approach to it (rather than a purely 'creative self-expression' approach). This shift is described by Clark *et al.* (1987). Even relatively recently, it has been argued that the shift among teachers and schools to valuing the significance of the disciplinary understanding from which creativity may evolve was still in progress in the UK (Cunliffe 1998).

The performance view of understanding developed at Project Zero involves the identifying of 'understanding goals', the exploration of these through a 'generative topic' or 'essential questions', the performance of understanding and 'ongoing assessment', or the continuous feedback from peers and teachers around shared criteria (Blythe *et al.* 1998). The idea is that *understanding can be demonstrated through performance* and this can itself, in turn, be interrogated by other children and by the teacher. This process could be described as having both the potential to bring together conceptual and procedural understanding, and also offering the opportunity for creativity, for synthesis, in doing so.

In fostering creativity, we need to be engaging with both conceptual and procedural knowledge: know how and knowing that. As NACCCE argued, learners and teachers should critically scrutinise the outcomes of creative thinking, for both originality and value. Without both kinds of knowledge, this critical scrutiny is impossible. For example, teenagers who work creatively with food technology to produce an unusual and nutritious combination would need some knowledge of conventional combinations as well as basic nutrition to be able to judge how creative this was, in terms of originality and value.

Depth of knowledge

Does a learner have to have, in any sense, 'expert' knowledge in order to be creative? The line we adopt in response to this question will reflect the spectrum of novelty seen as relevant to creativity. In other words, if we hold an inclusive perspective, as I have argued for (Craft 2000, 2001a, 2001b, 2002) and as NACCCE (1999) proposed, which says that all people are capable of creativity from early childhood onward, then we would accept a spectrum of knowledge. We would, accordingly, expect differing depths of knowledge according to experience and capability. So, we would expect a 16-year-old's creativity in drawing to involve a much greater depth of knowledge in order to demonstrate creativity than that of a 5-year-old. This is a perspective held by Piirto (1992), who argues that a learner who is still mastering the discipline may nevertheless be creative.

Judgement

Where is judgement located? In other words, how are 'originality' and 'value' judged and by whom? In the case of 'high' creativity, or the work of exceptional people, the field of experts would judge the extent to which work is original or of value. But in the case of everyday creativity, can the 'field' be as narrow as the individual themselves? It has been argued (NACCCE 1999; Craft 2000, 2002) that it can indeed be this narrow. In other words, the individual learner, and/or their teacher, may be the judge of the originality and value of the work. Clearly, the depth of knowledge that teachers bring to judging the originality or value of a creative outcome, such as the representation of some relationships in an algebraic formula, is likely to be greater than that of a learner; however, they may not have the depth of expertise that a field-acclaimed expert (say, in mathematics) would have.

Knowledge, learning and the curriculum

As indicated earlier, our perspectives on learning will influence the ways in which we organise the curriculum, i.e. the opportunities for creativity that we offer learners. Perspectives on learning which currently dominate practice, either explicitly or implicitly, tend to focus around socio-constructivist views of learning – of children as active, competent learners who 'co-construct' knowledge with a more able expert, often an adult. Learning and development have been described over the years through different dominant theories, reflecting beliefs about what learning involves. Theories that have dominated early years, primary and secondary school education have included:

'*Learning as growth*'. In this view of knowledge, children's growth and development (including their learning) is seen as unfolding in response to their physical environment from a blueprint which is laid down as though it were in a seed. The theory has its roots far back into the nineteenth century in Europe. Froebel (1887, 1895), the prominent thinker who brought this idea into being, also invented the idea of the 'kindergarten' – the 'child garden', an idea which still influences early years practice worldwide. It included the idea that indoor and outdoor learning spaces are significant for small children, but also the notion of the teacher – or early years practitioner as we would now say – as 'gardener', i.e. responsible for tending these young growing beings. Other well-known early years thinkers whose ideas would form part of a 'learning as growth' approach include Montessori (1914), and also, perhaps, Steiner (1922).

If a model of 'learning as growth' underpins our approach to the curriculum, then we are likely to offer opportunities for learners to explore in their own time and space, and to avoid frameworks that could move learners into identifying questions or answers before they may be ready.

We are equally likely to give them control over 'closure' in a creative activity. For example, rather than placing a time limit on, say, generating ideas for a design, we may offer space to 'park' ideas until they are ready to be expressed in a formalised or even semi-formalised, way.

'*Behaviourism*'. Behaviourism, of whom perhaps the most well-known proponent was B.F. Skinner (1960, 1974), is often seen as offering a useful framework, particularly for supporting children with behavioural and learning difficulties. The approach, which was immensely popular in North America and Europe until the 1960s, is based on a system of positive and negative reinforcement. The idea is that learners learn to remember and to do certain things by associating rewarding behaviour on the part of adult experts, and that they learn not to do things that bring negative responses. Translated into the classroom, the theory goes that students respond to praise and avoid behaviours that lead to negative feedback.

If a behaviourist view of learning underpins our practice in a dominant way, then approaches to the curriculum in terms of fostering creativity are likely to involve conditioning, rewarding creative behaviours and indicating high expectations for creativity.

'*Learning as construction*'. Perhaps the first person to write about constructivism, in the 1920s, was Piaget, the Swiss developmental psychologist. He suggested that learning occurs by the child organising, sorting and developing ideas about the world around them. His theory was that all children go through the same stages of development and that it is important for them to have access to practical experiences where they can manipulate the physical world around them in order to construct their own ideas about it. It was immensely influential in the way that early years provision and primary education came to be organised. A very important direction taken more recently by constructivists has been to see the social as equally important, and hence the approach known as 'social constructivism' adopted by the Russian psychologist Vygotsky (1965, 1978), who first began publishing his ideas in the 1930s. His work has continued to be influential in helping us to understand ways in which children relate to people around them as they develop ideas about the world. Other thinkers who have taken Vygotsky's ideas further include Rogoff *et al.* (1998), who worked on learning as culturally situated, through studies of guided participation; also, there are the Reggio Emilia pre-schools in Italy, whose approach to learning has proved influential in the UK and elsewhere (Magaluzzi 1996; Project Zero/Reggio Children 2001). We could also see Athey's (1990) idea of 'schemas' as constructivist, as it involves the child actively constructing meaning in their environment. Although the majority of these writers have influenced or been concerned with learning in the early years and primary years of education, the principles of constructivism are also appropriate and relevant to older learners.

Clearly, if our dominant model of learning is a constructivist one, then the organisation of the curriculum is likely to offer opportunities for learner engagement. It will offer opportunities for pupils to ask questions, identify problems, determine lines of enquiry, generate their own ideas and draw thoughtful conclusions. It will offer opportunities to construct and co-construct knowledge, as well as opportunities to use it to develop outcomes which may be novel. It will also emphasise exchanges of perspectives, collaboration and co-construction. Attention will be paid to ways in which adults and others with more expertise and experience can intervene to nudge creativity forward with reference to the learner's perspective in particular.

Although the reality is that in all practice there will be a variety of underpinning perspectives on learning, it could be argued that greater awareness of the values underpinning practice is likely to be fundamental to developing further opportunities for learners to express their creativity across the curriculum.

Creativity as shaping new knowledge

Whichever approach to learning one adopts as dominant in the foundations of one's practice, we can see creativity as, effectively, offering pupils opportunities to shape new knowledge. It is important to recognise and celebrate this, as it emphasises the significance of pupil engagement with existing and possible knowledge. Shaping new knowledge cannot occur without some understanding of what already exists, and without opportunities to engage with this and take it to a new place.

This could involve a range of levels of engagement and support. To take music as a domain, at one end of the age spectrum we might see Reception children participating in putting a well-known folk or other story – such as 'The Three Little Pigs' – to sound, rhythm and music. They might be scaffolded to pose questions, to select possible responses and to evaluate one another's sounds. Further up the age spectrum, we might see Y9 pupils constructing drums and other acoustic instruments from found objects, and then making a soundscape with them. In this case, we would expect far less scaffolding to occur and a greater level of learner-initiated construction. But in both cases pupils are working from the known (in the case of the younger children, a known story and a set of known instruments; in the case of the older children, knowledge relating to finding, designing and modelling, as well as knowledge relating to rhythm, pitch, tempo, etc.), together with knowledge of one another, which they would draw on in co-constructing sound. In each case, learners would take their existing knowledge on to a new place, in the making of something which for some of the learners, and possibly in a wider context too, would be novel.

So, having explored some approaches to knowledge and discussed creativity as a form of knowledge creation, what kinds of scaffolding are offered by the curriculum framework and how consistent are they?

Curriculum frameworks

As we saw in Chapter 1, there have been a number of initiatives in the past few years that have embedded creativity in the formal curriculum of schools and early years settings, including school-based nurseries. This means that practitioners in each phase of education have access to a framework and structure for fostering creativity in the curriculum.

However, the different parts of the curriculum's scaffolding are not unproblematic, as each can be subjected to critique. In addition, there are inconsistencies between the curricula which are problematic. We now take these one by one.

Content-based critiques

In the Foundation Stage, Creative Development encompasses art, craft and design and various forms of dramatic play and creative expression. It emphasises the role of imagination and the importance of children developing a range of ways of expressing their ideas and communicating their feelings. It reflects traditionally accepted norms in early years practice, and thus many have welcomed the codifying of creativity in some form within the early learning curriculum. Nevertheless, several problems may be detected.

First, the formulation of 'Creative Development' implies that creativity involves only specific parts of the curriculum and certain forms of learning. But, it could be argued (Craft 2000, 2002; Duffy 1998) that problem finding and solving, using imagination and posing 'what if?' questions, could (and do) occur within a whole range of domains.

Second, conceiving of creativity as something that may be 'developed' also opens it to the standard criticisms of developmentalism. For there is an implication that there is a static end-state or even ceiling, the implication being that, given the appropriate immediate learning environment, children will 'develop'. The presuppositions of a ceiling and of natural development are each problematic.

Third, the implication is that play and creativity are the same. But are they? Play may be, but is not necessarily, creative. 'Snakes and Ladders', for example, is dependent upon a mix of chance and a set structure, and thus may not involve much creativity, but 'Hide and Seek' may well involve a great deal, demanding the consideration of options and possibilities for hiding places and seeking strategies. Pedagogical strategies, of course, inevitably have a role to play in the extent to which children's free play is creative (Beetlestone 1998; Duffy 1998).

By contrast with the Foundation Stage curriculum, the *National Curriculum Handbook* for primary schools proposes a *cross-curricular* role for creativity in the aims of the school curriculum, saying that 'the curriculum should enable pupils to think creatively.... It should give them the opportunity to become creative...' (DfEE and QCA 1999a: 11).

Creativity is defined as a cross-curricular thinking skill. This reflects the notion proposed by some that creativity is not the preserve of the arts alone but that it arises in all domains of human endeavour. As we saw in Chapter 1, QCA has developed a creativity framework to help practitioners to identify and promote creativity in the classroom, involving five elements:

- questioning and challenging;
- making connections, seeing relationships;
- envisaging what might be;
- exploring ideas, keeping options open;
- reflecting critically on ideas, actions, outcomes.

Yet identifying creativity as a skill could be seen as an oversimplification, for to operate creatively must necessarily presuppose an understanding of the domain, and thus creativity cannot be seen as a knowledge-free, transferable skill. Although the curriculum framework itself, being knowledge-heavy, does provide the potential knowledge base within which creativity is to operate, it is left to teachers to make the connection.

Coherence critiques

It can be argued (Craft 1999, 2002, 2003a, 2003b) that there is currently discontinuity in the curriculum statements themselves, at least in England, as follows. The conceptualisation of creativity in the early years curriculum for the Foundation Stage contrasts with the way it is conceptualised in the National Curriculum for primary and secondary school-aged pupils in the following ways:

> *Definition.* The Foundation Stage seems to define creativity as encompassing the interaction of the arts and aesthetics, with play and self-expression in child development. By contrast, the National Curriculum definition seems to be a skill-based one, to do with how pupils approach learning in the different subject areas. This is borne out by the QCA guidance that emerged from the Creativity Curriculum Project (QCA 2005a, 2005b).
> *Focus.* Born of the different definitions, the focus of each curriculum is distinct. The Foundation Stage Curriculum focuses on creativity as imaginativeness, self-expression, dramatic play, art, craft and design. This contrasts with the notion of creativity in the National Curriculum as a cross-curricular thinking skill as relevant in science, mathematics, history and modern foreign languages as it is in English, design and technology or music.
> *Detail.* The detailed discussion of creativity in the curriculum for different age stages in 'Creative Development' contrasts with the

National Curriculum. For, despite the work done by the QCA Creativity Project, which has generated lots of examples (QCA 2005a, 2005b), the National Curriculum does not yet in detail map creativity in each subject area.

Our discussion has focused, so far, on the problematising of the explicit, formal and stated aspects of the statutory curricula in England, and the inherent difficulties in the content and coherence of the scaffolding that they purport to offer. However, it is also important to note some of the *implicit* messages in the curriculum.

These include the fact that creativity, albeit in different forms, is valued sufficiently to be seen as a significant aspect of the curriculum entitlement of all children and young people. Another implicit message concerns models of learning. It could be argued that the model that appears to underpin the two curricula is a constructivist one, as it appears to be assumed that children and young people will engage actively in creative learning opportunities, and be encouraged to do so.

Of course, the formal curriculum is not the only dimension, for the informal aspects of curriculum provision also speak volumes about the valuing of creativity. However, the formal curriculum is defined by statute and organised by practitioners and institutions, and the extent to which students are encouraged to think and generate ideas for themselves is a marker of low creativity is regarded.

Is creativity transferable?

There is, however, one significant further question that *is* raised by the model of creativity as a cross-curricular skill, adopted in the National Curriculum. What does this mean for the role of knowledge? If creativity is not domain specific, but a 'transferable skill', then where is the knowledge base on which it draws?

It has been argued (Craft 2000, 2002) that at the heart of all creativity is possibility thinking – which drives creativity in different ways in different domains. The thesis is that possibility thinking involves a continuum of strategies, with at one end the question 'What does this do?', to 'What can I do with this?', both of which have the potential to encompass both problem finding and problem solving. Thus, although musical creativity may be *expressed* in different ways from mathematical creativity, it is nevertheless driven by the same underpinning curiosity combined with imagination.

Taking this stance would mean that we accept the heart of creativity as a transferable skill, but not necessarily its expression, which requires knowledge of the domain. This would seem to reflect the position held by Feldman, much of whose work has focused on creativity and development (Feldman 1989, 2003). Indeed, this kind of stance has been described as a 'middle-ground' position (Plucker 2004) characterising creativity as both content (i.e. domain) specific with some 'transferable', or 'content-free', elements. Perseverance may be another transferable component, according to Sternberg and Lubart (1999).

Can we say that some subjects lend themselves more readily to creativity than others? It has been argued (Craft 2000, 2002) that *all* subject areas in the school curriculum (or beyond) are inherently conducive to the development of a learner's creativity.

But there is an even more fundamental question concerning creativity and knowledge, and that is the increasing role played in 'knowledge production' by thinking that comes from more than one discipline or domain. For much new thinking at the level of 'high creativity' does involve the merging of ideas from two or more disciplines.

The interdisciplinary nature of much high creative thinking could be seen as a justification for cross-curricular, or interdisciplinary, work in school. This assumes that there is a continuum between high creativity and little c creativity. This case is argued by both Feldman (2003) and Gruber (1980) who, in doing so, acknowledge a link between creativity and cognitive development. The interdisciplinary nature of high creative thinking also disguises the fact that there are many different ways in which subject areas can be brought together.

Interdisciplinary and transdisciplinary work

The notion of interdisciplinarity is starting to pose interesting questions, both for work that brings two or more domains together and for how the school curriculum is itself defined. Work in this area, particularly in North America (Boix-Mansilla *et al.* 2003; Klein, 1996; Nikitina and Boix Mansilla, 2003), has explored the ways in which domains of knowledge are brought together by experts to interrogate fundamental and other questions facing human beings. The work of Boix-Mansilla and colleagues is focused in particular on the implications for school curricula (Boix-Mansilla and Gardner 2003; Gardner 1999, 2000; Nikitina and Boix-Mansilla 2003).

The ways in which disciplines are brought into articulation with one another can be differentiated into those which are 'transdisciplinary', i.e. where a common issue is examined through multiple perspectives (for example, evolution could be explored through archaeology, palaeontology, biology, theological studies, and so on), and those which are by contrast 'interdisciplinary', i.e. where two or more disciplines are brought together to form new knowledge (Boix-Mansilla and Gardner 2003).

Boix-Mansilla *et al.* (2003) suggest that interdisciplinary thinking is moved forward by either collaboration (i.e. where the frontiers of knowledge are moved forward by two or more experts working closely together sharing their expertise), or by people who they term 'hybrids', i.e. individuals who have mastered two or more disciplines. It is unlikely that in schools, given the expertise required to move forward interdisciplinary thinking in this way, we would either as teachers or learners achieve such a transformation. However, transdisciplinary work in schools may be both far more possible and appropriate.

In terms of the curriculum in schools, there are many ways in which transdisciplinary work can be achieved. This, in part, depends on the subject areas concerned. Nikitina and Mansilla (2003) propose that in the case of, for example, high-school mathematics and science, three strategies can be used to bring the subjects together: *essentialising*, *contextualising*, and *problem centering*.

Essentialising explores fundamental concepts and helps establish *internal* connections within science and mathematics.

Contextualising involves creating *external* ties between the scientific and mathematical theories and their historical and cultural roots.

Problem-centered integration brings different disciplinary tools toward the solution of a pressing problem.

Each has its strengths and weaknesses and is also, they note, only a first step – teachers may create hybrid versions of these models. The point, though, is that generating creativity in schools involves both drawing deeply on and deepening disciplinary understanding.

We have so far examined some relationships between creativity and knowledge production, both domain-specific and transdisciplinary; we have explored models of learning which may underpin provision in learning environments for expressing these processes, and we have considered some aspects of curriculum. In the last part of the chapter, we consider, briefly, a fundamental challenge in schools or other educational settings, where curriculum and time are in tension with one another.

Curriculum and time

There are potential tensions between the existence of a curriculum with a great deal of propositional knowledge, and the encouragement of pupil – and teacher – creativity. These are related, in part, to having the time and space to internalise propositional knowledge and to having access to what might be called possibility space, or to a kind of 'dreaming time', to take it into what may be a potential transformation, through engagement, whether that is performance (using it) or some other form of expression. There is much evidence from studies of the development of high creativity that time is a fundamental ingredient in the development of talent. In the case of high creativity this first means time to play around with the ideas, processes and procedures of that domain, then to develop technical mastery, and then to move into finding one's own voice in the domain (Starko 2001; Gardner 1993; Gruber and Davis 1988; Gruber and Wallace 1999; Perkins 1981). Although the provision of time on the part of the educator and the exercising of persistence on the part of the learner do not necessarily lead to high creativity, it is nevertheless unlikely that talent will develop without time being available. This is recognised in the QCA's current creativity framework (QCA 2005a, 2005b); however, the challenge for teachers and schools is to find ways of making time available in a curriculum which remains crowded. Loveless (2003) offers a model for using Information and Communications Technology (ICT) to support learners' creativity in the creative subjects of the primary curriculum. In her formulation, the ICT forms a lens or framework for developing what could be described as disciplinary understanding as a foundation to creative activity in subjects such as music, art and English.

Summing up

This chapter has argued that creativity is situated in knowledge, both conceptual and procedural, and that creative action and thought are possible in any area of knowledge on the basis that at its heart is 'possibility thinking'. It has suggested that if creativity is to be demonstrated then it may require a performance of understanding that brings the conceptual and the procedural together. Creativity requires differing degrees of depth of knowledge and differing loci of judgement, depending where on the spectrum from novice to expert a learner is operating.

Knowledge organised in the curriculum frameworks that are currently in use in England were discussed and their potential and shortcomings in supporting learner creativity explored. It was suggested that opportunities for creativity offered through the explicit and implicit curriculum are influenced not only both by the nature and limitations of such curriculum scaffolding, but also by our approaches to learning. The extent to which we encourage disciplinary or transdisciplinary engagement may have a bearing on creative thinking and action, for transdisciplinary study may encourage and model knowledge production. However, this assumes both a depth and a grasp of knowledge. An aspect of developing this is providing adequate time, a particular challenge where the curriculum content is heavily specified.

4 Pedagogy

This chapter focuses on pedagogical strategies and creativity, starting with conceptual distinctions, and exploration of the relationships between teaching creatively, teaching for creativity and creative learning; the first two of these being distinctions made in the NACCCE (1999) report. Drawing on empirical work from a range of contexts from primary through to further education, it discusses the extent to which pedagogical strategies are limited by policy or other constraints (such as compulsory teaching frameworks or processes). The chapter closes by proposing creativity as a specific teaching and learning approach and experience, one amongst others to be employed as appropriate.

Pedagogy and creativity: distinctions

As already discussed, in recent years, distinctions in the language of pedagogy and creativity have begun to be recognised by policy makers, practitioners and theorists. Throughout this chapter, and indeed this book, pedagogy is seen as encompassing appropriate and defensible professional judgements about how teaching is undertaken and learning nurtured. This chapter forms a foundation for later discussions, particularly in Chapter 7, and we begin with the conceptual distinction made in the NACCCE (1999) report: teaching creatively and teaching for creativity.

Teaching creatively and teaching for creativity

Creative teaching is focused on the teacher's practice. The NACCCE (1999: 89) report suggests that it is characterised by 'using imaginative approaches to make learning more interesting and effective'. As noted in Chapter 2, it has been suggested (Jeffrey and Craft 2001) that creative teaching could perhaps be interpreted as being focused towards 'effective teaching'. This interpretation may also be borne out by the recommendations in the government policy document *Excellence and Enjoyment* (DfES 2003) for primary schools to foster excellence through myriad innovative opportunities for children to express and develop their creativity.

In contrast to creative teaching, *teaching for creativity* was seen by the NACCCE (1999) report to be focused on the learner and to encompass forms of teaching intended to develop young people's own creative thinking or behaviour. Jeffrey and Craft (2001) intimate that teaching for creativity may be more focused on 'learner empowerment' than on 'effective teaching'. Personal agency can be seen as being at the heart of teaching for creativity, with the locus of creativity residing in the individual as well as being simultaneously universalised (ibid.).

As acknowledged in Chapter 2, the NACCCE report suggests that teaching creatively is implied in (although not necessary to) teaching for creativity. It often leads to it, although there is also evidence (Fryer 1996) that constraining situations do not necessarily inhibit successful teaching for creativity.

More recently, Jeffrey and Craft (2003) have analysed the distinctions between these terms through empirical work in the early years and primary sector, which indicates that *teaching creatively* involves:

- using imaginative approaches;
- making learning more interesting;
- being effective.

Teaching for creativity, by contrast, it is suggested, involves:

- the passing of control to the learner and the encouraging of innovative contributions;
- teachers placing a value on learners' ownership and control, when innovation often follows;
- encouraging children to pose questions, identify problems and issues;
- offering children the opportunity to debate and discuss their thinking;
- encouraging children to be co-participant in learning, resulting in further control for learners over appropriate strategies for their learning
- being at the least learner considerate and ideally 'learner inclusive', thus prioritising learner 'agency';
- encouraging 'creative learning', the construction of 'creative learners' and ultimately the 'creative individual'.

We argue that the distinction has been useful in highlighting the significance of *teaching for creativity*. However, in making the distinction we also suggest there is a danger that a new dichotomy becomes institutionalised in educational discourse, similar to those in the past, such as formal and informal teaching or instruction and discovery learning. These past dichotomies have been criticised as responsible for the development of restrictive pedagogic ideologies (Alexander *et al.* 1992; Alexander 1995). It could be argued that the dichotomising process has already begun with regard to creativity in education; indeed, our exploration of the different foci of teaching creatively and teaching for creativity could be seen as an example of just this. While we used these characteristics to highlight the positive nature of both *teaching creatively* and *teaching for creativity*, there is, nevertheless, a danger that pedagogic practices may be dichotomised in such a way as to be unhelpful to the development of creativity in education.

Interconnections and lessons for pedagogy

So, what might the interrelationships be between creative teaching and teaching for creativity, and what can we say about pedagogy in exploring these? This is a challenging question, which the NACCCE (1999) report perhaps anticipated in recognising the close relationship between the two. The report notes that 'Young people's creative abilities are most likely to be developed in an atmosphere in which the teacher's creative abilities are properly engaged' (NACCCE 1999: 90).

In order to avoid a creativity dichotomy, the nature of this relationship needs exploring. There has been a great deal of research and conceptual analysis, mainly, although not exclusively, from North America, over the last 20 years or so, which has examined aspects of pedagogical approaches that foster pupil creativity (Balke 1997; Beetlestone 1998; Craft 2000; Edwards and Springate 1995; Fryer 1996; Halliwell 1993; Hubbard 1996; Jeffrey and Woods 2003; Kessler 2000; Shallcross 1981; Torrance 1984; Woods 1990, 1993, 1995; Woods and Jeffrey 1996).

From these studies, we know that pedagogical strategies that foster creativity include:

- developing children's motivation to be creative;
- encouraging the development of purposeful outcomes across the curriculum;
- fostering the study of any discipline in depth, developing children's knowledge of it, to enable them to go beyond their own immediate experiences and observations;
- using language to both stimulate and assess imaginativeness;
- offering a clear curriculum and time structure to children but involving them in the creation of new routines when appropriate, reflecting on genuine alternatives;
- providing an environment in which children can go beyond what is expected and are rewarded for doing so;
- helping children to find personal relevance in learning activities;
- modelling the existence of alternatives in the way information is imparted, while also helping children to learn about and understand existing conventions;
- encouraging children to explore alternative ways of being and doing, celebrating where appropriate their courage to be different;
- giving children enough time to incubate their ideas;
- encouraging the adoption of different perspectives.

However, none of these studies has explicitly examined the relationship between teaching creatively and teaching for creativity in the classroom. An examination of the relationship between these two facets is possible through focusing on some established features of creative teaching, such as those developed by Woods (1990): innovation, ownership and control and relevance. Research begun in 1990 initially dealt with the creativity of the teacher and the nature of their creative teaching (Woods 1993, 1995). More recently, the research has shifted to the impact of creative teaching on learners, its effectiveness, the creativity they bring to the learning context and the creativity they are encouraged to develop by being part of a creative teaching context (Jeffrey and Woods 1997; Jeffrey and Woods 2003). As part of this research programme, long-term ethnographic studies were carried out between 1999 and 2001 in what has been recognised as a creative English first school. The ethnographic, empirical research provides detail of how the relationship between *teaching creatively* and *teaching for creativity* in education is constructed.

From analysis of this data, it has been proposed (Jeffrey and Craft 2003) that:

- teachers who work creatively employ both *creative teaching* and *teaching for creativity* according to the circumstances they consider appropriate;
- *teaching for creativity* may well arise spontaneously from teaching situations in which it was not specifically intended;
- *teaching for creativity* is more likely to emerge from creative teaching contexts.

It is suggested that creative teaching does not necessarily lead to learner creativity. However, it may provide suitable contexts for both teacher and learner to be creative, in a number of ways. For example, when teachers use their own creativity, learners may use the spaces provided to maintain and develop their own creative learning. Also, as teachers model the expression of their own ideas, this in itself may encourage children's creativity.

A pedagogy which fosters creativity depends on practitioners being creative to provide the ethos for enabling children's creativity; in other words, one that is relevant to them and in which they can take ownership of the knowledge, skills and understanding to be learnt. A pedagogy that fosters creativity may also actively involve the child in the determination of what knowledge is to be investigated and acquired, and ensuring children a significant amount of control and opportunities to be innovative.

An inclusive approach

Creative teaching, then, may, but does not necessarily, lead to learner creativity. It is proposed that teaching for creativity may be more likely to succeed where learners are included; i.e. where the approach is a learner-inclusive one.

The NACCCE (1999) report proposed that in *teaching for creativity* teachers need to address three related tasks:

- encouraging young people to believe in their creative identity;
- identifying young people's creative abilities;
- fostering creativity by developing some of the common capacities and sensitivities of creativity such as curiosity, recognising and becoming more knowledgeable about the creative processes that help foster creativity development, and providing opportunities to be creative, a hands-on approach.

Jeffrey and Craft (2004a/b) suggest that a *fourth* task in teaching for creativity is

- adopting an inclusive approach to pedagogy, inherent in which is passing back control to the learner and in which teachers and learners enter a co-participative process around activities and explorations, posing questions, identifying problems and issues together and debating and discussing their thinking.

Jeffrey and Craft (2004a/b) make the argument about an inclusive approach to pedagogy based on empirical data from first and primary school education. All themes, though, may be relevant in secondary and post-compulsory education.

Indeed, this last theme in particular is taken up by recent research undertaken in a sixth-form context (Jeffery *et al.* 2005). Through in-depth analysis of the practices of one department in a sixth-form college in East London, where teaching for creativity is highly successful, Jeffery *et al.* (ibid.) identify a range of pedagogical strategies which characterise the teaching. These include:

- An inclusive approach to pedagogy (which reflects the strongly inclusive college perspective), where students are welcomed to co-participate with their peers and to co-create with their teachers who, as well as modelling creativity in their domain, also provide, as one would expect, expert knowledge, experience and advice. The adoption of a model of near-peer mentoring is a further inclusive practice, where ex-students are invited to lead parts of courses and extra-curricular activities in a variety of ways, including being artist-in-residence for a short spell, thus fostering the ex-students' skills and those currently studying in the college.
- A weave of formal and informal learning, both within the formal curriculum and beyond it; staff regularly offer extra-curricular opportunities for students to participate in, and these often draw explicitly on students' lives beyond the college, as exemplified by Parkes and Califano (2004).

In addition, this particular case study identifies a number of structural factors that contribute to the success of the department in fostering the creativity of its students. These include:

- The inclusion of artists in the teaching team, the teacher–artist being an evolving model within the college; the teacher's role is informed by their expertise in the field beyond the classroom, and in return there are elements of symbiosis in the way their art is informed by their teaching of the form. It adopts, thus, an approach to the teacher as cultural intermediary/social entrepreneur.
- A management model where as much as possible is devolved to the delivery teams.
- A commitment to working in partnership with a variety of relevant agencies in the community, united around a common theme (in this case urban regeneration).

Aspects of the ways in which this particular team works, in particular those involving partnership with arts professionals, are explored further in Chapter 11.

An important aspect of a learner inclusive pedagogy, it is argued (Jeffrey and Craft 2003, 2004), is that the learner's experience and imagination forms an important part of the process of investigating knowledge. These are expressed and fostered through devices such as possibility knowledge (Woods and Jeffrey 1996) and possibility thinking (Craft 2002). This approach is similar to that proposed in other research (Lucas 2001; Lucas et al. 2002; Pollard et al. 2000; Woods and Jeffrey 1996; Emilia 1996). The approach highlights and prioritises the 'agency' of the learner in the teaching and learning process and might be contrasted with a 'child considerate' approach (Jeffrey 2001c), which views the child as an organism that needs nurturing, rather than being democratically included. This locus of inclusivity in nurturing learner creativity – engaging the learner as a co-participant – may lead to creative learning, i.e. learning which excites learners and encourages their agency and generativity.

It should be seen from the above discussions that teaching creatively and teaching for creativity are interrelated, and that the apparent dichotomy between the terms may be a false one. For example, it is suggested that it would not be possible to prove through empirical evidence that a teacher's creative practice was devoid of an intention to teach for creativity – or that the development of pupil creativity was a causal outcome of an intention to teach for creativity. Rather, it is suggested that it may be more illuminative to explore creative pedagogic practices if the focus is on the teacher *and* on the learner.

To this extent, the notion of 'Creative Learning' and the pedagogical strategies associated with this may be seen as occupying a middle ground between the two overlapping categories of creative teaching and teaching for creativity. Chapter 5 explores the notion of creative learning further; the final part of Chapter 4 discusses pedagogical aspects of creative learning environments.

Features of inclusive learning environments

A feature of 'creative learning' is the surrounding inclusive learning environment (Jeffrey and Craft 2003, 2004). An aspect of this is the framework devised by Woods (1990) describing 'creative teaching' and which can be used to explore creative learning. It could be argued that creative learning occurs in environments which foster the following for both teachers and learners:

- innovation
- ownership
- control
- relevance.

These features can also be seen in pilot-study material collected by Craft (2003c) on behalf of the QCA. In the most impressively creative classroom observed in the pilot, *innovation* was demonstrated by:

- opportunities for pupils to suggest, invent and propose ideas;
- encouragement of pupils in making connections;
- provision of an atmosphere of fun, enjoyment, exploration and possibility;
- the use of humour in encouraging invention.

Ownership was perhaps encouraged and demonstrated by:

- learners not being interrupted whilst they were expressing ideas;
- teachers adopting an acknowledging manner toward learners;
- teachers adopting a varied and appropriate pace;
- students being seen as a resource in the room, with their ideas being valued;
- respect for one another being valued.

Control was perhaps demonstrated by:

- celebration of students' work and offering them a significant role in doing so;
- different forms of learning being offered within the same session, e.g. acting out, role play, group work, working in pairs, plenaries, individual work, using whiteboards and interactive whiteboards, miming;
- teachers being prepared to acknowledge the boundaries of their own knowledge.

Relevance appeared to be demonstrated by:

o   the fact that students' interests informed some of the content of lessons as vehicles for conceptual and procedural knowledge;
o   teachers' engagement with students' interests;
o   teachers differentiating their responses to individual learners;
o   the fact that student and teacher talk was all on task.

In addition, further pedagogical features (based on field notes in October 2002 and June 2003) included:

o   no raised voices; control was often gained by lowering the voice;
o   clear instructions and structure;
o   praise given appropriately;
o   relationship; every child seen as an individual, called by name;
o   teachers manifested and expected high energy;
o   discipline was low-key but firm.

Schools, pedagogy and creative learning

The QCA (2005a, 2005b) suggests that schools which are successful at stimulating creative learning:

- value and celebrate pupils' creative and innovative contributions;
- work collaboratively with creative and innovative individuals and groups, within and beyond the school;
- provide opportunities for pupils to experience and contribute to a stimulating physical environment, within and beyond the school;
- manage time effectively, providing opportunities for pupils to explore, concentrate for extended periods of time, reflect, discuss and review.

The QCA perspective reflects research work done in the last 10 years or so on organisational creativity; three major studies are relevant here. One was in Europe (Ekvall 1991, 1996) and two in the USA (Amabile 1988; Isaksen 1995). They explored the organisational climates that seem to stimulate and support creativity. The results from these three programmes have converged at several major points, suggesting that, in a creative climate, the participants in the organisation:

- feel challenged by their goals, operations and tasks;
- feel able to take initiatives and to find relevant information;
- feel able to interact with others;
- feel that new ideas are met with support and encouragement;
- feel able to put forward new ideas and views;
- experience much debate within a prestige-free and open environment;
- feel uncertainty is tolerated and, thus, risk taking is encouraged.

Amabile's (1988) model suggests that individual creativity may be affected by even very minor aspects of the immediate social environment. Creativity may be impeded where rewards are determined in advance, where there is undue time pressure, oversupervision or competition, or where choices are restricted in terms of approach or working materials, or where evaluation is expected.

The artistry of fostering creativity

One of the interesting features of the emerging discourse and practices in fostering learner creativity is the curriculum policy context. For it is one in which contrasts can be detected. These emerge, in part, out of a dual emphasis on excellence on the one hand and on creativity on the other hand. Although on one level these are not in tension, some of the ways in which these agendas are being resourced and fostered result in a tension between the emphasis on performance, targets and accountability (what some have called a 'performativity' discourse) and the contrasting emphasis on innovation and creativity. One aspect of this tension, in terms of pedagogy, is the introduction of what might be described as prescriptive practices, such as the National Literacy Strategy and the National Numeracy Strategy, that appear to remove teacher judgement and artistry to a considerable degree. Yet, as literature cited in this chapter demonstrates, there are schools and teachers who are succeeding in fostering creativity through inclusive practices, even within this wider context (Jeffrey and Woods 1997; Craft 2003c).

It could be argued that teaching creatively, teaching for creativity and fostering creative learning all involve a high level of pedagogical sensitivity and skilfulness in being alert to the meld of environment, learner engagement and experience, moment, domain and so on, as well as adopting appropriate strategies to support creative learner engagement. To be able to do this implies a high level of professional artistry, whatever the context. In some ways we might argue that creativity could be seen as a highly skilled approach to teaching, which draws out the very best of learners. Some of the lenses through which this notion of artistry can be articulated and implemented are discussed in Chapter 11, which addresses, among other notions, the 'teacher as artist'.

Acknowledgements

This chapter draws on ideas developed in a variety of different pieces of work. These include a joint paper by Jeffrey and Craft, presented first at a symposium of the British Educational Research Association Special Interest Group Creativity Education, February 2003, and published in *Educational Studies* in Spring 2004. It also benefited from the commissioning by the QCA in early 2003 of a pilot study in primary and secondary classrooms, exploring creative teaching and teaching for creativity, and from discussions and written exchanges with Graham Jeffery and the research team at Newham Sixth-Form College, who, with a grant from the National Endowment for Science, Technology and the Arts, undertook a 3-year study investigating their own practices and the creative achievements of their students (Jeffery *et al.* 2005). Finally, the chapter draws on many other classroom visits and conversations.

5 Learning and creativity

How do creativity and learning connect? A term in common currency in the early years of the twenty-first century is 'creative learning'. What is meant by this? This chapter seeks to untangle some distinctions and similarities between creativity and learning and seeks to theorise a little further, the notion of 'creative learning'.

Consider the following two vignettes.

Going to the seaside

Two girls are in a nursery classroom of a school. Evie is 4 years and 7 months and Holly is 3 years and 11 months. They are both sitting on the chair used by their teacher at the start and end of sessions. With them is the class teddy bear, which they are dressing in a new outfit. As they work together exploring his possible clothing options they come across some swimming shorts. A conversation evolves, in which Evie suggests they take him to the seaside and Holly agrees, safely strapping him in. Together, and taking up suggestions made by two onlooking girls, they transform the chair into their car using books (windows) and two pieces of cloth from the dressing up box (road and roof). They invite the two onlooking girls to join them and set off, with Evie leading the group with invitations to tip in one direction and then another as they take the corners.

Learning the meaning of a word

6½-year-old Jacob overhears his teacher mention the word 'syllable' to another adult. He asks what the word means, and his teacher explains by clapping the syllables in first his name, and then the names of other children in the class, as well as her own name. Jacob starts to do the same, exploring the sounds and commenting on what he notices. Other children sitting in his group listen, and start to clap the syllables in their own names, experimenting, listening to one another and talking. Conversations emerged about how to mark the syllables and how many syllables were in each person's name.

Which of these examples involved creativity? Which involved creative learning? Our answers to these questions depend on what we understand 'creativity' and 'creative learning' to mean. But first, a little more about creativity and learning as potentially connected terms.

In some ways, creativity and learning may be seen as closely related. For if novelty and originality are elements of how creativity is defined, then in everyday creativity, or 'democratic' creativity, it could be said that an idea or action could be deemed novel or original within the terms of reference of the individual. Indeed, creativity could be seen as a way of expanding what one knows, understands and can do – in which case it could be said to be an aspect of learning.

When we learn something new (at whatever age) we are making new connections between ideas and making sense of them for ourselves. We are constructing knowledge, and in this sense we could perhaps describe what we are doing as being creative. The more we are engaged in the meaning-making, the fuller and more fully owned by ourselves is the map that we are constructing. This is perhaps the most engaged space we can be in when we are in the process of imaginative playfulness.

Vygotsky, an influential figure in constructivist theories of learning, has been described as having had a dialectical approach to imagination (Lindqvist 2003), in unpicking its meaning in relation to play and learning, through logical investigation. Lindqvist notes that Vygotsky (1995: 249) discusses 'play as imagination in action: a creative process that develops in play because a real situation takes on a new and unfamiliar meaning', seeing play as a 'dynamic meeting between the internal and the external' (ibid.). We can see this in the vignette of the girls going to the seaside at the start of this chapter. They are engaged in imagination-in-action, and they also provide us with evidence of the significance of the social context in the construction of possibilities: although Evie suggests and leads the group, they each make their own contributions to the overall 'journey', Holly putting the bear on her lap and strapping him in, and the other two girls suggesting the need for a roof and windows, which are then wound down by Evie. The internal worlds of each child meet the external and shared world of the 'car' on its journey to the seaside.

Vygotsky's notion of inner speech and its dialogical character also give a basis for an interpretation of a dynamic relationship between consciousness and the world. Vygotsky's approach emphasizes personal sense and the creative process of knowledge. It is a generative process (i.e. involving the making of new connections). And fundamental to it is agency, or self-direction, which both require and demand this dialogic relationship. It could be argued that what he is describing, when he describes learning in this way is, in fact, creativity. But is it?

Creativity in education has been described in Chapter 2, drawing on the definition of the NACCCE (1999) as involving the imaginative generation of outcomes that have both originality and value. Perhaps this is where differences may exist between 'learning' and 'creativity', if in order for something to be creative it must involve both originality and value. And yet, even this does not help us, if we take what NACCCE called a democratic interpretation of creativity. For according to NACCCE, the 'field of judges' can be as narrow as the agent themselves. This reflects positions adopted by others (Craft 2000, 2002; Feldman 1974, 1989, 2003). So, a new connection – for example, Evie's idea that the chair is now a car – does not need to be original to anyone other than oneself. Likewise, the idea (such as the one of winding the windows down on the journey) needs to be of value, but if it is of value only to Evie and yet rejected by the other children, it would still, according to NACCCE, Craft and Feldman, be deemed creative. Similarly, as Jacob clapped out the syllables in his own name, and those in the names of the children sitting near him, he was making the connections for himself. So, it seems that 'creativity' and 'learning' in education are not distinguishable if we take a constructivist approach to learning, unless we take a harder line on what counts as 'original' and 'of value'.

If, on the other hand, we were to adopt another approach to learning, such as behaviourism, then we may be able to see learning (which we would see as occurring through conditioning) and creativity (which is concerned with breaking out of conditioned responses) as quite opposite to one another. In the Jacob example, we see how behaviourism, or conditioning, may play a part in creativity: Jacob mimicked his teacher initially as she modelled the clapping out of the syllables; however, Jacob then went *beyond* this to creative activity in constructing his own understanding, in large part through experimentation. Thus, Jacob was ultimately constructing; making sense through engagement rather than conditioning. So, although we can acknowledge a possible behaviourist element to this vignette, ultimately the frame is a constructivist one.

Creative learning

If, then, within a constructivist framework, creativity and learning are taken to be the same thing, then what can we understand by the term 'creative learning'? Before exploring this term, a word about what Gardner (2000) refers to as 'entry points' to understanding. As more or less a reflection of his stance on intelligence as 'multiple' and as a way of enabling learners to find pathways to disciplinary content, Gardner proposes seven different paths to engaging students with the core activities of any generative topic. He uses the metaphor or a room with a number of possible doorways through which to enter it. The seven entry points are:

- *Narrational*, i.e. access to a topic through story or narrative.
- *Quantitative*, i.e. use of quantitative methods, e.g. measuring, comparing.
- *Logical*, i.e. use of logical reasoning to understand the topic, e.g. working with hypotheses, which are then tested.
- *Existential/foundational*, i.e. considering philosophical aspects, e.g. considering questions about value, purpose and meaning.
- *Aesthetic*, i.e. emphasising appreciation of properties through beauty, forms and relationships.
- *Hands-on/experiential*, i.e. using practical investigations.
- *Interpersonal*, i.e. allowing access to a topic through a social experience, such as working collaboratively on a design or a presentation.

It would, of course, be possible to explore the meaning of creative learning through any of these entry points. Indeed, during a recent visit to Harvard University's Project Zero with practitioners engaged in Creative Partnerships, artists from the Black Country (an area in the West Midlands of England) worked on representing creative learning through the aesthetic entry point, work that it is hoped will be written up in due course. However, this chapter approaches the question mainly through the existential entry point, exploring meaning through textual discussion. The narrational entry point also forms a small element of the exploration, through the occasional use of small vignettes.

In the early years of the twenty-first century, the policy, practice and research discourse has expanded to include the 'middle ground' of Creative Learning, which has been proposed as a lens for understanding the middle ground between 'Creative Teaching' and 'Teaching for Creativity' (Jeffrey and Craft 2004a). It has certainly become common currency in much of the discussion and project work designed to promote the creativity of children and young people in England, and possibly beyond.

Attempts to conceptualise it include work by the QCA (2005a, 2005b) and Creative Partnerships (2005). At the time of writing, both bodies broadly see creative learning as any learning that stimulates learner creativity. Such conceptualising occurs against the background of a particular approach to recognising and assessing creative achievement, which might be described as a situated approach.

Evidence of creative learning: pupil behaviours

In contrast with earlier approaches to finding evidence of creativity, which were developed in a psychometric framework and involved testing using de-contextualised tasks (Torrance 1966, 1969, 1974, 1984), practitioners are now much more concerned with assessing pupil behaviour on tasks which are contextualised and relevant to them (Fryer 2000).

Policy-level thinking around what pupil behaviours might provide as evidence of creative learning is in evolution. In parallel with the development of the Creative Partnerships (2004a) definition of creative learning, which is not yet in the public domain, the QCA (2005a, 2005b) had developed the following evidence of children's behaviours from their 3-year 'creativity across the curriculum' project. At its root is the NACCCE (1999) definition of creativity, as 'Imaginative activity fashioned so as to produce outcomes that are original and of value'. And although the QCA framework refers to 'creativity' rather than 'creative learning', it seems to offer a useful approach to defining this latter.

The QCA proposed the following five areas of evidence of learner creativity, as discussed in earlier chapters

1 questioning and challenging;
2 making connections, seeing relationships;
3 envisaging what might be;
4 exploring ideas, keeping options open;
5 reflecting critically on ideas, actions, outcomes.

As mentioned earlier, the Creative Partnerships framework for describing creative learning is in evolution alongside the QCA one (Creative Partnerships 2005). Although developed in isolation from one another, it is possible that these two frameworks could (and should) be brought together in the next phase of promoting creativity in schools. Implicit in both the Creative Partnerships and the QCA models is the child as generative; a quality taken up by researchers. For example, it is proposed that a core aspect of 'creative learning' is enabling children's possibility thinking (Craft 2002; Jeffrey and Craft 2004a/b). In other words, facilitating the evolution, expression and application of children's own ideas forms the heart of 'creative learning', which, it is proposed, engages children powerfully in knowledge production. What this core element of 'possibility thinking' means in terms of different domains and at different phases of development is only in the early stages of being documented, and a pilot study is under way (Craft *et al.* 2004a) with an international dimension (Craft and Martin 2004, Craft, Burnard and Grainger 2005) to explore this element further.

In some contexts, e.g. those where 'improvement' is part of the contextual agenda, creative learning has taken on a meaning which is concerned with the impact on learners of deep engagement. Thus, it may be that in some school contexts of deprivation and underachievement, one marker of success in creative learning may be described and measured not only in terms of knowledge and understanding, but also around raised achievement, engagement with school, motivation, behaviour and reduction in unauthorised absences. These kinds of criteria seem to be concerned with how young people relate to both school and their potential for agency within and beyond it; indeed, there is evidence that these criteria are being addressed through the work of Creative Partnerships. One region, Slough, interviewed nearly 400 young people who had been involved in Creative Partnerships activities since the autumn of 2003, and found that motivation, self-confidence, achievement and working well with teachers and peers were all reported by the young people as having been improved by the experience (Creative Partnerships, Slough 2004a).

It could be argued that 'creative learning', however, must, by definition, have more to do with the generation and initiation of new possibilities (what might be called *generativity*) than with motivation and engagement, which could be seen as necessary to, but not sufficient for, creativity. Indeed, it has been suggested that the creative learner is at the heart of a successful economy in the twenty-first century (Cropley 2001; Robinson 2001; Seltzer and Bentley 1999).

What other kinds of pupil behaviours might be seen as evidence of creative learning, with the emphasis on generativity? Others we could consider might include those collated by Stein (1974), which are derived from personality characteristics identified in various research studies:

- achievement within a domain of knowledge;
- seeking of order;
- curiosity;
- assertive, self-sufficient, dominant and even aggressive;
- tendency to be less formal, less conventional, to reject repression and to be less inhibited;
- tendency to like work, to be self-disciplined and to be persistent;
- independence and autonomy;
- capacity to be constructively critical;
- tendency to be widely informed;
- openness to emotions and feelings;
- personal judgement influenced by the aesthetic dimension;
- capacity to adopt values which fit with the wider environment;
- capacity to manifest masculine interests if female, and vice versa if male, without inhibition;

- tendency not to require social interaction;
- self-fulfilled and self-realised.

Although these are all personality characteristics, they all translate into behaviour. To these we might add Torrance's (1965) personality characteristics:

- having the courage to hold a strong opinion;
- curiosity and search approach;
- independent judgement;
- independent thinking;
- intuition;
- capacity to become preoccupied with tasks;
- unwilling to accept things without being convinced with evidence;
- idealistic and visionary;
- risk-taking approach.

Others we might name might include:

- goal-directedness;
- fascination for a task;
- orientation toward risk taking;
- preference for asymmetry and complexity;
- willingness to ask many (unusual) questions;
- capacity to display results and consult other people;
- a desire to go beyond the conventional.

Person characteristics are notoriously difficult to pin down or measure (Fryer 2000). Indeed, apparent contradictions can be found in the literature: Shallcross (1981), for example, identifies a range of person characteristics associated with creativity which include acceptance of disorder, which contrasts with Stein's tendency to prefer order. On the other hand, there could be explanations for this (such as a capacity to tolerate alongside a tendency to create order could result in creative activity). Equally, there is, in fact, a surprising degree of overlap in such attempts to define personality characteristics.

Given the difficulty of defining creative learning behaviours, one way of trying to determine what is going on for learners is to capture and interpret evidence from the classroom (such as the small vignettes at the start of this chapter). Thus, we might say that in those vignettes that opened this chapter, Evie and Holly demonstrate their independence and flexibility in developing the imaginative play around the 'trip to the seaside'. This process of evidence-capture, to help refine as well as exemplify what we may mean by creative learning, is perhaps one of the significant challenges with which we are faced in schools at the current time.

Another way of making sense of pupil behaviours is through the processes involved.

The process of creative learning

Creative learning also implies within it *something about the way in which the learning occurs*, as witnessed by the pilot stage of the ten-country European project, CLASP (Jeffrey 2004a), which suggests that creative learning involves students in:

- using imagination and experience;
- strategically collaborating over tasks;
- contributing to pedagogy/curriculum;
- critically evaluating their own learning practices and teachers' performance.

The European study reflects themes that emerge from a one-school case study (Jeffrey and Woods 2003) which attempts to articulate the concept of 'creative learning', and encompasses pupils' reactions to some creative teaching; the second half of this chapter will explore pupil and teacher perspectives further; but for now, let us focus on ways of characterising the process or processes of creative learning.

Additional analysis of data from the Jeffrey and Woods (2003) study was done by Jeffrey (2004b) and Jeffrey and Craft (2003) to explore features of creative learning, including pupils making relevant connections and relevant contributions, developing relevant strategies, and offering pupils 'adventurous control', or control in decision making, as demonstrated in this excerpt from Jeffrey (2004b: 25):

> I asked the Year 5 group why they chose such complex constructions for their Aztec nets. Will said 'I wanted a challenge'. Patrick said 'I prefer the challenge and failing. I've failed a few times and now it is easier'. A challenge appears to be part of the school culture, not as a euphemism for working hard but an opportunity to control the learning activity. One of the challenges during the Maths trail around different classes was to see how far the learners could get doubling numbers, without calculators. Daniel [Yr 5] starts at 110 'because I like a challenge. It doesn't matter if I don't finish'. In this case the finished product is not a requirement nor a focus, the process itself is seen as enough of challenge to engage learners and Daniel used his control over the process to take ownership of the task by starting where he wanted to and to determine its success criteria.

Creative learning could contain learning tasks set by the learners themselves, discussions of and perhaps records kept of the reasons for decisions taken to show how learning is constructed by learners in the pursuit of experimentation and adventure.

Making learning 'fun' includes handing back control in different ways, one of which is by providing a variety of tactile mediums, which in Emily's [Yr 3] case was seen as an adventure: 'You could think it was boring at first but then you learn that it is fun...The patterns on the string looked boring but the sticking made it fun'. The use of different mediums for investigating shape enhanced experimentation and adventure but at the same time it increased the confidence of learners who take control of the medium and use it competently for their own ends as is exemplified by these Foundation learners producing a firework on the Dazzle software in the ICT suite.

Similar processes are emerging from a Think Tank project with secondary pupils in the Creative Partnerships region mentioned earlier in this chapter. Pupils highlighted approaches to learning that enabled them to become engaged, to get inside the domain for themselves, as creative learning. This was characterised by some as 'learning by doing', by others as 'learning by seeing,' e.g. in the case of seeing a theatre production rather than just reading the play script (Creative Partnerships 2004b).

Much work in the area of identifying processes of creative learning has been concerned with primary education; however, a significant development project launched in late 2004 by the Specialist Schools Trust in England sought to characterise, evidence and nurture creative learning across the secondary curriculum, in both individual subject areas and through collaboration across the subjects. At the time of writing, the project had just launched, but the findings that come out of it may help to inform the forms of engagement and expression experienced by pupils aged 11–18, at least in a small group of schools in England (SST 2004).

Clearly, there could be many ways of expressing engagement, and questions begged by the question of engagement include the role of pedagogical strategies in supporting creative learning processes.

To this end, the QCA (2005) discusses pedagogical strategies in the process of learning, suggesting that practitioners need to

- set a clear purpose
- balance freedom and constraint
- fire imaginations through the Other or the unfamiliar
- enable children to work together
- establish success criteria
- expect the unexpected
- review work in progress regularly.

Other pedagogical strategies include Murphy *et al.*'s (2004) features of:

- *active engagement* (i.e. teachers adopting strategies which enable pupils to engage actively in their learning as autonomous problem solvers and learners);
- choosing tasks which are *culturally authentic* (i.e. reflect activity in the world beyond school);
- selecting tasks which *offer children personal authenticity* (i.e. enable pupils to find personal relevance and meaning, and to have some control and autonomy in their learning);
- *integrating conceptual and procedural knowledge* (rather as discussed in Chapter 3, bringing together knowing that and knowing how into what the learner can then *do* with their understandings, and carefully monitoring individual pupils' need for further conceptual and procedural clarification and content).

Although specifically identified within the DTI's Electronics in Schools programme for pupils in Key Stages 3 and 4, these pedagogical strategies may also be generalisable to other phases and domains.

Other features of pedagogy which appear to foster creativity, include

- quality of interaction, leaving students with decision making authority;
- the role of 'locus of control' (Jeffrey and Craft 2003).

As explored in Chapter 4, Craft has put together findings from a range of sources that suggest learning opportunities that foster children's creativity do some or all of the following:

- they develop children's motivation to be creative;
- they encourage purposeful outcomes across the curriculum;
- they foster in-depth knowledge of disciplines;
- they use language both to stimulate and assess imaginativeness;
- they offer a clear curriculum/time structure, but they involve children in creating new routines when appropriate, reflecting on genuine alternatives;
- they encourage children to go beyond what is expected and reward this;
- they help children to find personal relevance in learning activities;
- they model the existence of alternatives in the way information is imparted, whilst also helping children to learn about and understand existing conventions;
- they encourage children to explore alternative ways of being and doing, celebrating where appropriate their courage to be different;
- they give children enough time to incubate their ideas;
- they encourage the adoption of different perspectives.

Additional strategies are identified by Craft (2003d):

- encouraging the adoption of different perspectives;
- modelling the variety of ways in which information is discovered and explored and imparted.

All of these approaches to learning are designed to foster learner confidence in the capacity to generate, express and carry through their own ideas, with a joy in generative activity of this kind.

Summing up

So far, then, we have explored the relationship between creativity and learning, arguing that, in a constructivist frame, learning and creativity are close, if not identical. We have explored creative learning in terms of learner behaviours and the process of learning. Perhaps one way of conceptualising creative learning, then, is to separate the learning process from the outcomes. Thus, creative learning could be seen as both learning creatively and learning to have confidence in being creative. And these two – learning creatively and learning to be creative – can be interrogated and evidenced both at individual and collective levels.

In the second half of the chapter we look at the kinds of outcomes we might be capturing as evidence of creative learning, and also children's and teachers' perspectives on creative learning.

Outcomes from creative learning

The outcomes we name as relevant from creative learning may be a mixture of process and behaviour. Processes we would look for might include

- capacity to take risks
- originality
- daring/effective combinations.

But the separation between processes and behaviours is not clear-cut, as the QCA framework demonstrates. The five areas identified as pupil behaviours by the QCA can also be seen as processes: questioning and challenging, making connections and seeing relationships, envisaging what might be, exploring ideas and keeping options open, and reflecting critically on ideas, actions and outcomes.

Essentially, when we are looking at outcomes, we are looking at evidence of children's inter-mental generative connections with their own and others' ideas. In other words, our attention is focused on how children share their own ideas and relate to those of others.

Coming from an 'improvement' perspective on creative learning, and with the cultural agenda also in mind, we might name yet other outcomes, proposing that the following could be possible outcomes from creative learning:

- improvements in practice and learning;
- reconceptualising partnerships, moving beyond the 'cultural provider' model to approaches which prioritise creative development;
- an increased emphasis on long-term sustainable partnerships;
- schools and cultural practitioners increasing their own creativity to apply knowledge and skills in new ways as valued goals evolve.

This latter set of outcomes is tied in both to cultural education and creativity, and is also a concern with improved learning and pedagogy. These outcomes are less about the behaviour of individual children and more about the ways that teachers teach, and the ways that schools and the cultural sector operate in partnership. Where children's achievement is referred to it is not tied to creativity in particular, but rather to learning generally. The framework, it could be argued, is concerned with pupil and adult *engagement*. It could certainly be said to reflect the suggestions made in the policy document for primary schools, *Excellence and Enjoyment* (DfES 2003), which exhorted schools to adopt innovative practices in organising and delivering the curriculum. The document suggests that 'Promoting creativity is a powerful way of engaging pupils with their learning' (DfES 2003: 3). But whilst engagement may be necessary to creativity, it is not equivalent to it. Thus, it could be argued that to connect the creative learning agenda with the improvement agenda in both pedagogy and learning implies a relationship between them that is non-existent.

Partly as a consequence of the NACCCE (1999) report, which linked creativity with culture, and which also proposed the establishment of the organisation Creative Partnerships, the cultural agenda is also implied in some of the criteria discussed above. But while creative learning may encompass partnership and engagement with the cultural sector and with the development of cultural understanding and appreciation, this is, it could be argued, only a part of the picture, for overemphasising this relationship is to reduce creative learning from lifewide to being seen as domain, discipline or sector specific.

Children's and teachers' perspectives on creative learning

One feature of current empirical research work exploring creative learning, perhaps unsurprisingly, is the documenting of children's own perspectives.

A major project focusing on children's experiences is the ten-country European study CLASP, which explored the central research question,

'What characterises creative learning for children aged 3–11?' Data were collected on:

- creative learning contexts
- social interactions
- cognitive explorations
- the subjective experience of learning
- the learning processes of teachers and learners.

The project addressed a number of research questions relating to student experiences of creative pedagogies. These included:

- What does creative teaching and learning consist of?
- What is learned, and how?
- What difference does it make to the learner?
- What feelings, as well as cognition, are involved, and what is the relationship between feelings and cognition?
- What is to be gained by bringing student perspectives into a creative pedagogy?
- How far do students act creatively to make their learning meaningful? (CLASP 2002)

The relationship between teacher and learner is the focus of the empirical work, exploring the creative agency of each. Findings from the students' perspective show that students use their imagination and experience to develop their learning, they collaborate over tasks strategically, they contribute to the classroom curriculum and pedagogy, and they evaluate critically their own learning practices and teachers' performance.

The project has generated some tentative inter-national characteristics of successful creative learning experiences (Jeffrey 2004b). They include:

- learner's interest in extending time and interest over projects;
- the satisfaction in engaging in challenges and risk taking;
- a high level of social enthusiasm;
- the advantages to be gained from manipulating technology;
- the importance of appropriate teacher intervention tactics;
- the relevance of learner inclusivity in pedagogy, encouraging learners to make suggestions and to evaluate learning activities with one another and with teachers in a co-participative framework;
- the importance of everyday life and learning as a resource, building on learners' experiences and existing relationships with places and people;
- the value in teachers creating investigations, tasks and problems;
- the relevance of autonomy, choice and responsibility for learners;

- the prioritisation of humanitarian relations by teachers and learners in the process of engaging with knowledge (i.e. working within a stance of care and interest in recognising the learner's histories, interests, feelings, anxieties and fears).

These strategies that have emerged from CLASP research demonstrate creative learning occurring across a wide age range of pupils, from primary through to secondary. Perhaps most importantly, there is no one model that determines the existence of creative learning, but there are some common features.

Data collected in both primary and secondary schools in England for a pilot project on behalf of the QCA, mentioned briefly in Chapter 4 (Craft 2003b), this time exploring both teachers' and pupils' perspectives on 'creative learning', add to the interim CLASP findings. The Craft (2003b) study included observation of a wide range of practitioners and their pupils. Practitioners ranged from student teachers, to newly qualified teachers and those in the early stages of their careers, right the way through to very experienced, senior and expert practitioners as recognised by Advanced Skills Teacher status. Data were collected (through observation, informal and formal interviews and focus group discussions) from pupils and teachers in several mixed and single-sex State primary and secondary schools, covering the age span 7–16, and across a small number of subject areas (English, mathematics, modern foreign languages, science, music). Students were interviewed where possible, and asked about their own creativity and that of their teachers. The data, from a limited range of schools in one region of England, provide pilot case study material from which to propose possible generalisations.

Dominant themes identified in the pilot from the pupil perspective were as follows:

- *Being given some knowledge as a foundation before being asked to do anything with it.* Several secondary students commented on the difference between primary and secondary schools, saying that teachers with specialist knowledge seemed able to help students to plug gaps in their learning more effectively than primary teachers had been able to. For example, from one 13-year-old boy: '[in primary school] We never used to learn how to do words, she used to expect us to know how they were spelled and what they meant. Mrs X teaches us.' And from a Y6 boy of a mathematics lesson: 'Mrs Y explains things nicely.' The teacher's own knowledge was sometimes cited as significant in being offered a foundation for one's own creative thinking, as demonstrated by this comment from a 13-year-old boy about his English teacher 'she knows a lot about literature from New Zealand ... it is fun so it helps you relax' [extract from transcript]; and a 14-year-old commented that, in secondary school, the teacher's own knowledge was itself both inspiring and important: 'primary school was like more laid-back . . . like you had one teacher who teaches everything . . . whereas you get a specific teacher who like teaches that subject, they go into more depth, they know what they're on about . . . so like in primary school you got one teacher who knows like a bit about everything . . .' [extract from transcript, June 2003].

- *Being intellectually challenged and stretched.* An 11-year-old Y6 girl said, of a creative mathematics lesson: 'When it is very challenging to start with it feels like you are trapped in your brain, but when you've got the answer you feel free!' [extract from transcript, June 2003]. There was a balance for several students interviewed between being challenged and feeling 'safe', however. Several commented on collaboration and group work as facilitating their confidence: e.g. 'You could help each other . . . it made the story a lot easier . . . it was a lot easier than following videos, 'cos you could like talk amongst yourselves with some of the quotes but using your own language, whereas watching the video or doing some of the work in class, you couldn't because it was all in old English' (girl, 14); 'If you got stuck and things, you could always ask someone to help you out' (boy, 14); and 'in like a normal class, if you wanted to read it out, some people would feel embarrassed to read in case they made mistakes but in a smaller group with about six people it was easier to read out . . . people helped you and corrected you' (girl) [extracts from transcript, June 2003]. Others commented on how interesting it was to work with others on a given task: 'it sort of broadens your mind listening to what other people think it is' (boy, 14) [transcript, June 2003].
- *Being 'seen'.* This included differentiation. As one 13-year-old boy said, commenting on a maths teacher: 'In this school I am given the work I need. I struggled in my primary school cos it was all long division and stuff. I was given the same work as everyone else. This is better.' Being 'seen' also meant feeling that teacher knew individuals and cared about them. A 13-year-old girl commented, of her English teacher, 'She knows us all really well'; another said 'She talks to you as if you are her friend, as if we are people'. It also included being aware of praise when given with humanity, as this boy commented, of his English teacher: 'She compliments us quite a lot, whereas a lot of teachers kind of use sarcasm . . . it is more of a nice way of doing it' [extract from transcripts, June 2003]. Jeffrey and Woods (2003) document primary children's delight in being taken seriously, as co-participants, as peer-participants, as leaders and as learners. Similarly, the Think Tank project in Creative Partnerships, Slough (2004), referred to earlier in this chapter, revealed how important secondary pupils felt it was to be seen and recognised. One pupil said that they had a sense that their teacher would 'stop her whole life to listen' (Creative Partnerships 2004b: 1).

- *Acknowledging the boundaries in discipline and behaviour.* Noting that teachers need to hold these: 'She does obviously have to be a tiny bit strict, which is useful, cos she won't take anyone like being completely ridiculous' (13-year-old boy, talking about English teacher) [extract from transcript, June 2003].

- *Being 'in relationship'.* Students often commented that they saw the relationship as two way: 'You get to talk to her individually...you actually get to know her' (girl, 13, talking about English teacher); and others talked about the interactions as fun, e.g. this 13-year-old boy talking about the same English teacher: '...some teachers never even talk to the kids, they just say something and you have got to write it down but it's not like that...you do learn in those lessons but with Mrs X you learn a lot AND you have fun at the same time...so you are looking forward to it' [extracts from transcripts, June 2003]. Occasionally being in relationship meant working collaboratively on tasks. One 14-year-old commented on a collaborative English task, 'you kind of worked as a team, but thought as an individual' (girl) [transcript, June 2003]. The Think Tank project in Creative Partnerships, Slough (2004b) yielded secondary pupils' perceptions of certain teachers learning alongside them, as well as being dynamic performers in the act of teaching and learning. They commented on the significance of body, voice, and space in engaging students.

- *Being inspired by the teacher's love of the subject.* Comments made by students of a highly creative English teacher included these: 'At the moment, English is probably my favourite subject, not just because of the subject, but because of the teacher mainly...'; 'When you ask the person next to you "what lesson have we got next" and they say "English", it's just like a sigh of relief – and it's like a positive thing, 'cos you know you can just like enjoy the lesson and relax' (boy, aged 13). 'I find my favourite subjects are my favourite teachers, as well' (girl, aged 13); 'Quite often I find when I come out of English and I am really happy...and then you go and ask your friends and they have all had English as well, and they say "Oh, it was alright but a bit boring though" and you're just like really excited...' (boy, aged 13); and 'I think when I don't have Mrs X any more in a way I think I will go off English, I don't think I will enjoy it as much' (boy, aged 13) [extracts from transcripts, June 2003].

- *Wanting to please the teacher.* This was a common theme, summed up by one 13-year-old boy who said, 'You want to try hard in her lessons. You want to try and get really quite a good mark' [extract from transcript, June 2003].

- *Feeling the learning to be fun, less formal.* As one 13-year-old boy said, of a mathematics lesson that had combined mathematics, technology and art: 'If it's boring you don't want to learn. If it is fun you do', and a girl of 14 who is often excluded from lessons due to behaviour difficulties, said with enthusiasm of this lesson: 'It's better than the other maths... it's funner... I hate all the normal stuff, drawing all angles out... this thing is easy but you have to concentrate, if Mrs Y explained clearly I could just do this and not those sheets – you have to concentrate so you can get the lines...' [extract from transcript, June 2003]. This sort of learning seemed often to involve a mix of subjects and also student engagement in constructing something of their own. For example, an observation of a teacher training student's Y9 science lesson was passed on to the researcher in which the trainee had dressed up as Lavoisier and used storytelling techniques to explore how scientists use evidence to arrive at an explanation. The class then divided into groups to discuss a card-matching activity and then to develop their own material based on the theme [extract from data file, June 2003]. In another school, several Y9 students, interviewed about a board game which their teacher had invented for learning about Macbeth, which involved learning the play through adopting roles and speaking the lines of the play aloud through a collaborative, yet competitive process, commented on how much fun it was to work together, as demonstrated by the following: 'It makes it much more interesting than sitting down and doing written work,... the more interested you are in what you do, the more you learn.... It's a bit overwhelming with just normal reading work cos if you are just given a booklet and think, Oh God, I gotta go through it all... whereas in the game it's in different stages so it's spaced out, so it gives you time" (girl, aged 14) [transcript, June 2003].

- *Approaches and materials often led children to have their own ideas about how to develop them.* As witnessed by this 14-year-old boy's comment, on a Shakespeare board game devised by a group in collaboration with the teacher and then played for literally months afterwards, 'I think it's really useful for remembering cos you'll like remember the quote cos you laughed about something when you were playing the game... when you are just reading it all you don't normally take it all in' [transcript, June 2003]; and by this quote from his classmate: 'It was a really cool way to go around... cos then it helps you – when you do things in class, it would help you remember all the famous quotes – cos the big quotes in the end of year exams, we needed some of those and they were in the game' (boy, aged 14) [transcript, June 2003].

In the Craft pilot study, each of these teachers was seen by the pupils as working them hard, offering them stretching work and expecting them to think for themselves. As one 13-year-old, commenting on mathematics, said: 'this maths is more challenging... it is nice to have a go at more challenging things, to have a go at it... I am just more comfortable if they just explain and then I try to do it myself... I do care if I get it wrong but

I like to have a go to show the teacher that I've tried' (girl) [transcript, June 2003].

Turning to the teachers, themes in the teachers' own perspectives on their promoting of creative learning included:

- *Having genuine enjoyment of the subject, or of teaching, or both.* This was illustrated vividly by one teacher of English who said: 'I know I can get more out of myself and out of them if I am relaxed enough to be myself...though sometimes the students cross the professional boundaries a little bit sometimes... BUT I hope that what we get more than anything, is just mutual respect ... they are here to learn, not to be told off, ... I just really enjoy it' [field note, June 2003].

- *Providing opportunities for learners to take risks.* This was illustrated in Benjamin's German Y9 lesson cited in Chapter 2, where a role-play game was introduced using a telephone and music, with an element of chance designed to encourage students to speak in German using a script presented via the interactive whiteboard. In a primary school, a steel band was observed, involving around 15 children aged 8 to 11. The teacher held the rhythm with tom-tom drums, whilst the children first played a set piece on steel pans and drums, and then were encouraged in the moment to experiment with developing it. The result was an impressively professional-sounding performance [based on field notes, June 2003]. This risk-taking is recognised as significant by pupils too, as notes from the Creative Partnerships Slough Youth Think Tank document testify (Creative Partnerships 2004b).

- *Willingness to take a risk in their own pedagogy.* One example of this came from a student teacher of English who found herself teaching 'in role' (i.e. using a different persona, in order to make a language point) from time to time, and creating a collaborative activity which had the potential to backfire, but in fact was a roaring success [based on interview notes, June 2003].

- *A commitment to 'being in relationship'.* This included being unafraid of negotiating meaning and reasons, as indicated by this field note from a Y8 English lesson on different 'voices' of English. 'One student said he thought the Canterbury Tales sounded boring, and she [the teacher] asked "Why?" – taking that conversation quite a long way, hearing what he and several other children thought it was about. Engagement with the students was confident, joyful, two-way, dynamic. She modelled perspective sharing powerfully and effectively' [field note, June 2003].

- *Hoping that students would do something different with their knowledge and skills.* For example, a newly qualified teacher was observed encouraging a large mixed ability Y7 group of boys to write poetry in French, taking their understanding and command of the language several steps further than previously and scaffolding their capacity to apply their knowledge and skills in a new context [based on field notes, June, 2003].

- *A willingness to take on the learner role at times.* For example an English teacher was observed discussing the history of the Oxford English dictionary. She engaged as a learner herself, also as this extract from field notes indicates. 'When they were discussing the Oxford English dictionary, she put her own hand up in answer to her own question, "who thought that the OED had always been there?" She was unafraid to express her own weaknesses, e.g. drawing. During an activity where students were using Egyptian and Greek alphabets to form their own name she acknowledged one pupil's struggle to copy accurately by saying, "Did you notice I didn't put my own name up there on the board?"' [field note, June 2003]. This approach was also recognised by pupils who formed part of the Slough Youth Think Tank within Creative Partnerships (Creative Partnerships 2004b).

- *Aiming to draw on students' interests.* For example, the Head of Modern Foreign Languages in one school was observed referring to girls and music in French and German lessons, alongside the formal curriculum content, to encourage conversation in the language. This seemed to be welcomed by the students. An English teacher in a mixed secondary school was observed drawing on one particular 14-year-old boy's knowledge of and interest in Chaucer, for the benefit of the whole class [drawn from field notes, June 2003].

- *Aiming to 'capture the imagination', and enabling children to 'use their imaginations'.* For example, a mathematics lesson was observed in which two gifted Y6 girls who had been working on calculations for scale models of the Earth and the sun, suddenly realised what the significance of the models was. Looking at the models they had made, one said to the other, 'I can't believe we live on that, we just walk around on it' [drawn from field note, June 2003].

- *Seeing creativity as 'an enabler', 'to enhance learning' and to 'raise motivation and, therefore, achievement'.* This was often apparent within relationships, as this field note from a Y8 English lesson may illustrate: 'She [the teacher] gave a great deal of encouragement – mixing leadership and student engagement/responses. She laughed a great deal – sometimes mixing discipline with laughter (e.g. "Kirsty, your face is so much nicer than the back of your head..."), and clearly had a good relationship with the students. She checked out understanding and assumed that pupils would draw on knowledge across subject boundaries, making that explicit – e.g. "think about what you may have learned elsewhere, for example in History. Make sense of ALL of the information you have access to"' [extract from field note, June 2003].

- *Being willing to 'leave the script'.* As one teacher of English put it, following a particularly creative presentation in which students had developed some creative work of their own: 'I was thinking on my feet a little bit ... some planned but some extemporising – this is very typical. The mood and the temperature in the room has got to be right for the plan...' [extract from transcript, June 2003].

These vignettes perhaps serve as a small step in moving forward our understanding of teacher perspectives on creative learning. The penultimate point perhaps illustrates yet another aspect of 'creative learning', which is the relationship between different parts of the curriculum. It could certainly be argued that some of the practices documented here are skilful pedagogy and not specific to *creative* learning in particular; however, several other practices, such as risk, relating, aspirations for utilising the knowledge and skills, and capturing imagination, may be specific to fostering creativity.

Summing up

The notion of 'Creative Learning', then, is still in the process of being theorised. An approach has been proposed here where both process and behaviours are recognised as part of how creative learning is conceptualised. However, the term 'creative learning' already obscures a variety of other related, interconnected and conflicting ideas. These have been explored during the chapter and include improvement/'effectiveness' discourse, the culture agenda and engagement versus generativity.

Returning to the two vignettes at the start, perhaps we can conclude that, from a constructivist perspective, each one involved creativity, since each documents learning; and, within a constructivist framework, creativity and learning may be seen as identical. However, our response to whether the girls going to the seaside or Jacob learning the meaning of syllables represent *creative learning* or not depends on what we think creative learning is. This is, without a doubt, an important and significant area for future work by teachers, policy makers and researchers.

6 Tensions between practice and policy

In many ways, policy scaffolding and research findings support increased activity and commitment to teaching for creativity and fostering creative learning, in curriculum and pedagogy. But how unproblematic is this? It could be argued that there are constraints and tensions in the translation of policy into practice, and the formation of policy from practice. This chapter explores a number of these.

Evolutions in policy

As we know, education (together with other social provision) is deeply affected by government policy and, in the United Kingdom, by an election cycle of approximately 4 years. Earlier chapters have discussed the evolution of curriculum policy since the last part of the twentieth century, moving towards an increasingly significant role for the fostering of learner creativity. By mid 2004, the notion of 'personalised learning' was added to the emphasis on creativity (DfES, 2004a, 2004b, 2004c).

A backdrop of personalised learning

Placing children's holistic experience of school, and life beyond it, at the heart of provision for their learning, the DfES called for schools and teachers to consider how to use technology to support learning personalised around the needs and talents of every child (DfES 2004b). In a press release in January 2004, the Secretary of State for Education said (ibid.):

ICT transforms education and the way that children learn. Every child matters, and I want a system of personalised learning that allows each of them to learn at their own pace, in ways that suit them best ...effective use of the latest technology is absolutely vital in realising this vision. It is not about technology, it is about what technology can do to meet the personal needs of every learner, raising their aspirations and achievement.

In January 2004, the Minister for State for School Standards, David Miliband, told the North of England Education Conference that personalised learning involved supporting all pupils in achieving highly, through tailoring their education to individual interests, aptitudes and needs. As he put it, it would mean (DfES, 2004b)

> High expectations of every child, given practical form by high quality teaching based on a sound knowledge and understanding of each child's needs. It is not individualised learning where pupils sit alone. Nor is it pupils left to their own devices – which too often reinforces low aspirations. It means shaping teaching around the way different youngsters learn; it means taking the care to nurture the unique talents of every pupil.

The Government department responsible for this initiative, the DfES, was keen to emphasise that this was not a new initiative, in that successful schools have done this for many years. However, as with so many initiatives in education, the Department's hope was to universalise such practices so that all children have access to them 'so that across the education system the learning needs and talents of young people are used to guide decision making' (DfES 2004b).

Stemming from the central principle that each child should be offered high-quality learning experiences enabling them to do their unique best, it was acknowledged that this would involve taking into account different perspectives: those of pupils, parents and carers, and of teachers. The Innovations Unit within the DfES quotes David Miliband, 18 May (Innovations Unit 2004), as follows:

> We need to engage parents and pupils in a partnership with professional teachers and support staff to deliver tailor-made services – to embrace individual choice within as well as between schools and to make it meaningful through public sector reform that gives citizens voice and professionals flexibility.

By the end of 2004, what it could mean for schools, local authorities, the DfES and for the system overall was also coming under scrutiny as follows (DfES 2004b):

For pupils it means:

- having their individual needs addressed, both in school and extending beyond the classroom and into the family and community;
- coordinated support to enable them to succeed to the full, whatever their talent or background;
- a safe and secure environment in which to learn with problems effectively dealt with;
- a real say about their learning.

For parents and carers it means:

- regular updates, that give clear understanding of what their child can currently do, how they can progress and what help can be given at home;
- being involved in planning their children's future education;
- the opportunity to play a more active role in school life and know that their contribution is valued.

For teachers it means:

- high expectations of every learner, giving the confidence and skills to succeed;
- access to and use of data on each pupil to inform teaching and learning, with more time for assessment and lesson planning;
- opportunities to develop a wide repertoire of teaching strategies, including ICT;
- access to a comprehensive CPD programme.

For schools it means:

- a professional ethos that accepts and assumes every child comes to the classroom with a different knowledge base and skill set, as well as varying aptitudes and aspirations;
- a determination for every young person's needs to be assessed and their talents developed through diverse teaching strategies.

For the DfES and local authorities it means:

- a responsibility to create the conditions in which teachers and schools have the flexibility and capability to personalise the learning experience of all their pupils;
- a system of intelligent accountability so that central intervention is in inverse proportion to success.

For the system as a whole it means:

- the shared goals of high quality and high equity.

Beyond education, the implications of personalising public services were explored by Leadbeater (2004) on behalf of DEMOS. A major aspect is individualising services to be tailored to the much more active consumer. Personalisation was linked by the DfES with citizenship issues more generally (DfES 2004c: 4): 'personalisation ... is about putting citizens at the heart of public services and enabling them to have a say in the design and improvement of the organisations that serve them'.

In terms of education, this individualised learning agenda seems to fit closely with the policy impetus to promote learner creativity, in the sense written about elsewhere, that creative children are self-directed and manifest agency in finding their way through opportunities and challenges, lifewide (Craft 2000, 2002). The personalised learning approach seems to emphasise the potential for children to be foci as clients, in determining their modes of learning, and their routes through these. The emphasis in personalised learning is, of course, to support the learner as an individual, with unique preferences in styles and content of learning. This raises interesting questions in terms of fostering creativity in practice, as we go on now to explore.

Relating the personal to the collective in pedagogy

The notion of personalised learning is carefully distanced from the notion of 'individualised' learning in being about learner engagement and learners having a stake in, and taking responsibility for, their own learning, particularly as they get older. Individualised learning is defined by the DfES as being focused around individualised tutoring; as they put it: 'Personalised learning is not individualised learning. It is about focusing on the individual within a group. Pupils are still taught in classes' (DfES 2004b).

Clearly, one particular dilemma for the educator in promoting creativity is the need to balance the creative needs of the individual against the collective creative needs of a group, in at least two senses.

First, what impact do children's ideas have upon one another? How should they be evaluated, weighed up, followed through? How might they affect other people? These are important questions, however large or small pupils' ideas may be, and beg a pedagogical response. So, whether they are generating ideas about how to develop the outdoor area, suggesting an idea for a game, coming up with ideas for testing the properties of an object, or planning arrangements for a performance or installation, their individual ideas will have potential impact on others.

Second, there are times when it is appropriate for children to be creative collaboratively or collectively and not simply as individuals. Children may, for example, be invited to undertake some musical composition together, or to solve a mental maths problem by working in pairs. In each of these examples the children may generate their own ideas but have these tempered, checked, extended, elaborated and celebrated by others with whom they are working.

In these different ways, then, the individual meets the collective in terms of creativity and it could certainly be argued that the extension of nourishment and support for the individual must be set in the wider context of others. In practice, this means encouraging children to evaluate their own ideas and the ideas of others. This could involve children giving one another verbal, written, dramatic, symbol-based and other forms of feedback, which may also be extended to include negotiation of both what the evaluator meant and how feedback might be used. This notion of interactive feedback, which serves both to express and deepen disciplinary understanding and to strengthen the pupil's foundations for creative engagement, can be usefully informed by the notion of the 'performance of understanding' (Blythe 1999). This is an aspect of the Teaching for Understanding framework developed by researchers at Harvard University's Project Zero, in which the adoption of clear understanding goals, taught through generative topics and assessed and developed through performances of understanding (Blythe *et al.* 1998; Perkins 1999), discussed in Chapter 3. The engagement of individual with collective in creative activity is also assumed and explored by others (Lunn *et al.* 2003; McNiff 2003). Using a model proposed by Weisberg (1986, 1988, 1993, 1995, 1999) which acknowledges the interaction of tacit and new knowledge, Lunn *et al.* (2003) explore this in the context of a design-and-technology classroom, demonstrating ways in which the collective and the individual mesh inevitably, such that the individual's pathway is not clearly identifiable. McNiff (2003), drawing mainly on adult creativity in various contexts including sport and business, argues that dialogic relationship with others nurtures the flow of individual creativity and that creative potential can be unleashed through interactions, in teamwork. In the case of Lunn *et al.* (2003), the suggestion is that influences from others may not be easily tracked in a class or workshop. In the case of McNiff (2003), he proposes approaches to nurturing collective creativity that place the participants or learners in an executive position, and the teacher in a less visible, but nevertheless active, role.

The process of stimulating creativity in education poses other additional and perhaps fundamental challenges, however, which could be described as conflicts of perspective (Craft 2003a, 2003c, 2003d, 2003e). Let us consider these in terms of how policy and practice connect in terms of pedagogy and the curriculum.

Conflicts of perspective?

Conflicts of perspective in the relationship between creativity in education policy and practice will be taken up further in Chapter 10, but in this chapter the fundamentals are laid out. First, let us consider a few definitions.

The word *pedagogy* is chosen here advisedly, since, as indicated in Chapter 4, what is at issue is not purely practice but, rather, the making of 'rationally defensible professional judgements' (Hirst 1979: 16), drawn from knowledge 'grounded in different kinds of evidence, together with principles which have been distilled from collective understanding and experience' (Alexander 2004: 8). As Alexander notes, the meaning of pedagogy can be debated, and has been variously represented in England, from what could be described as the Bernsteinian perspective, setting pedagogy in the context of reproduction of culture (Bernstein 1990), to the much narrower approach which essentially sees pedagogy as the practice of teaching. Somewhere in the middle of that continuum (if indeed it can be described as such) we might place 'reflective practice', where pedagogy is seen as the combination of beliefs, attitudes and reflections on practice, *and* practical classroom work in teaching and facilitating learning (Soler *et al.* 2000). Alexander (2004: 11) offers a further perspective which could be seen as occupying the middle ground, i.e. 'the act of teaching together with its attendant discourse'. In this chapter, what is under scrutiny is the 'middle-ground' approach to pedagogy, or the practices and discourse that encompass both the 'how' and the 'what' of teaching.

This middle-ground perspective perhaps has most in common with the northern, central and eastern European continental approach to pedagogy, which is to draw together the practice of teaching with its underpinning knowledge, argument and evidence. On the other hand, as Alexander (2004) notes, the engagement of pedagogy with curriculum tends to be lacking in continental approaches to pedagogy.

So, what about the 'what' and the 'how' of teaching? In terms of *curriculum*, this we might describe, very simply, as discussed in Chapter 3, as the 'what' of learning. As Alexander (2004) acknowledges, curriculum has dominated English educational discourse, placing pedagogy as being of lesser importance. However, we could argue that curriculum is more than a list of knowledge or a range of experiences that we expect to offer learners, as, aside from the overt and (for teachers in England) prescribed and government-determined curriculum, every teacher and school works with and creates a hidden curriculum too. This is made up of the values of teachers and schools which are conveyed to children in many ways, from the extent to which their home life (including their interests, parents and caregivers) is engaged in the life of the school, to the way classrooms, corridors and other communal indoor and outdoor areas are laid out and resourced, to the ways that people communicate with one another. These hidden curriculum areas are closely bound up with pedagogy, because they are about how teachers individually, and teams and schools collectively, go about their work. This craft of teaching has been documented by many researchers (Brown and McIntyre 1993; Gage 1978; Galton *et al.* 1999) and is, effectively, the study of where pedagogy and curriculum meet.

Earlier chapters have affirmed that policy for fostering creativity in the pre-school and compulsory school sectors exists and is in evolution. However, tensions in perspective can be detected between policy on the one hand, and how creativity is being translated into practice in learning contexts on the other hand. These tensions in perspective might be summed up as, first, paradoxes in 'scaffolding', second, disconnected curricula, and third, curriculum organisation.

Paradoxes in scaffolding

As discussed in Chapter 1, there have been numerous moves in England toward scaffolding the promotion of children's creativity in education. However, some of this scaffolding has occurred in paradoxical contrast to other, parallel, policy moves.

One of these paradoxes is the tightening of control. This is evidenced in both pedagogy and the curriculum, as well as other aspects of the management and financing of schools in England (Craft 1997; Woods *et al.* 1997). For, whilst creativity is being encouraged, the means by which this and other educational goals are being achieved can be constraining for teachers.

Alexander has undertaken a searing critique of the recent policy document mentioned earlier in this book, *Excellence and Enjoyment* (DfES 2003), which formed an early statement about the Government's 2003 Primary Strategy designed to continue the work on raising standards while emphasising teachers' and schools' professional judgement in doing so. Although the document has a great deal to say that is of relevance to creativity (as discussed briefly in Chapter 1), Alexander (2004: 15) argues that the document offers 'ambiguity of content', which he suggests belies 'a desire to be offering freedom while in reality maintaining control. Applying this to creativity: on the one hand, teachers and schools in England face encouraging codification of creativity in the curriculum and exhortations to be more innovative in their practices, as well as nurturing pupil creativity; on the other hand, they are subject to strategies such as the National Literacy Strategy and National Numeracy Strategy, which provide a teaching plan as if practitioners were to be understood as technicians rather than professionals.

The challenges posed by holding creativity as a goal may be greater than those posed by other curriculum areas. This is because the establishment of an appropriate organisational climate for stimulating creativity, we are told, includes enabling pupils and teachers to feel (Amabile 1988; Ekvall 1991, 1996; Isaksen 1995):

- that new ideas are met with encouragement and support;
- able to take initiative and to find relevant information;
- able to interact with others;
- that uncertainty is tolerated and thus risk taking encouraged.

The establishment of these strategies in a policy climate which at times appears to treat teachers like technicians rather than artists (Jeffrey and Craft 2001; Woods *et al.* 1997), and which attempts to control both content and teaching strategies centrally to an increasing degree, is challenging (Gabel-Dunk and Craft 2002). Thus, it may be that the fostering of teaching for creativity, creative learning and teaching creatively is limited by a centrally controlled approach to pedagogy in some school years or contexts.

There is certainly evidence that for some people, in response to the tightening framework within which teachers' work, creativity has become a way of achieving personal and institutional survival (Craft 1997; McCarthy 2001; Safran 2001). Woods and Jeffrey have explored ways in which teachers have maintained their own teacher creativity, and also continued to foster the creativity of children, against the odds (Jeffrey and Woods 2003; Woods 1990; Woods and Jeffrey 1996). This is explored further in Chapter 10.

Disconnected curricula

Other limitations to creativity produced by the application of policy to practice are the discontinuities in the curriculum. For example, the differences in approach to creativity as conceived of in the early years curriculum, compared with the National Curriculum and the NACCCE (1999) report, are striking. The latter two are more concerned with the development of creativity as a cross-curricular skill, and the first is heavily focused on the creative arts and play (Craft 1999, 2002, 2003e). The positioning of creativity as a life-skill (Craft 2002), or as a cross-curricular skill (DfEE, and QCA 1999a, 1990b; QCA 2005a, 2005b), needs to be reconciled with the positioning of creativity as associated with the arts, and with self-expression (QCA and DfEE 2000). In addition, as noted in Chapter 5, the background policy work being developed through Creative Partnerships, to offer a cultural and creative entitlement to children and young people needs to be brought into articulation with these different conceptions of a curriculum for creativity.

Curriculum organisation

To what extent is the fostering of creativity limited by its subject context? There has, over recent years, been much debate about creativity across the curriculum (NACCCE; 1999; Craft 2000, 2002; QCA 2005a, 2005b). It has been argued that it is both possible and necessary to promote creativity in different curricular areas, and efforts have been made by the QCA to exemplify how. This perspective is tied to the view that creativity is not subject specific, although it is manifest distinctly in different subjects.

Thus, creativity in physical education may involve constructing a dance or gymnastics sequence within a framework of moves or intended impact, or collaboratively inventing a new ball game on the athletics field, given certain equipment and games rules to encompass within it. Creativity in music may involve individual or collaborative composition using keyboards, which provide some framework; creativity in ICT may involve inventing a database that could answer questions about a particular topic that children have already researched; creativity in English may include story or other writing with an element of originality. Mathematical creativity may involve both the identifying and the solving of number or other problems, i.e. using mathematics to think with.

Although creativity is often associated with the creative and performing arts, it has become much more recognised in recent years that opportunities for developing learner creativity exist across the curriculum. It has been argued that this different manifestation does necessarily imply any *limitation* in the fostering of creativity, rather, in principle, the opposite (Craft 2003a).

It could certainly be argued that the way in which the curriculum policy framework is translated into the time available in a school day may offer greater or fewer opportunities for fostering learner and teacher creativity. For it might be argued that where the curriculum is taught as discrete subjects this may constrain learner and teacher creativity, in discouraging thinking about themes which cross the subject boundaries. Rowe and Humphries (2001)), offer an example of how time and subject boundaries can be dissolved and melded to give a primary dominance to connecting themes of study where, at different times, different foundation subjects may take the lead. The school, Coombes Nursery and First School in Berkshire, is a living example of an approach to stimulating the creativity of children and teachers, across the curriculum, which is achieved, in part, by a project-based approach. Similarly, at Cunningham Hill Infant School, featured in the QCA training materials for creativity (QCA 2005a, 2005b), working across the curriculum is a key feature of the school's approach to learning. It is, perhaps, much more common to find this approach in the nursery and lower end of the primary school. We do also find it, albeit less commonly, in the upper primary school. Prince Albert Primary School in Birmingham, also featured in the QCA creativity materials (QCA 2005a, 2005b), offers an example of ways in which disciplinary learning is at times integrated through project work and also supported by information and communications technology through appropriate use of whiteboards in the classroom and across the school.

But in considering ways in which the subjects of the curriculum can be organised to promote creative thinking, behaviour and action, we need to avoid at least two pitfalls. One is to avoid confusing the subjects of the school curriculum with domains or disciplines; the curriculum is a form of representation of the domain, but it will only ever represent a selection, both in content and also often in representing a particular point in time. The other, which is linked, but perhaps is more significant, is that an integrated curriculum needs to have clear *understanding goals* in terms of the subjects that it brings together. So, cross-curricular work with 4- and 5-year-olds that offers children the chance to explore the well-known rhyme 'Hickory, Dickory, Dock', for example, may offer children opportunities for creativity in English (e.g. making their own rhymes, constructing a collective story around time, inventing a mystery that has occurred at a particular time, or designing riddles around times on the clock face), design and technology (e.g. designing a clock with moving parts, to encompass a moving mouse) and mathematics (e.g. constructing and solving problems involving counting on and back up to 12, and also working with time and time intervals). Some of these may overlap, e.g. making riddles that focus around the times on a clock face could link up with constructing and solving problems using time intervals. However, it is important that the understanding goals are clearly routed in the underpinning subjects and that the linking activities are born of these goals, not the other way around.

It is this that is the fundamental point. If it is the understanding goals that drive the organisation of curriculum, then a flexible approach will perhaps always be the most successful, rather than a strict adherence to any one particular approach, such as subject-separated or subject-integrated. For there may be times when it suits one's understanding goals to integrate some subjects together and other times when it is necessary to separate them.

It is suggested, then, that the naming (and also separating) of subjects is not of itself, necessarily, a limitation on the fostering of creativity; however, it *is* necessary to be clear about what understanding is sought in each subject area so that children's creativity is fostered specifically in that context. And the current formulation of creativity as connected with one part of the curriculum only, in the 3–5 Foundation Stage curriculum and as a cross-curricular skill for children aged 5 to 16 in the English National Curriculum, lays the challenge to connect creativity with the subject areas at the door of the practitioner.

Putting policy in perspective

The chapter has so far explored three major challenge areas in the translation of creativity policy into practice: paradoxes in 'scaffolding', disconnected curricula and curriculum organisation. Areas of professional dilemma and judgement have been identified and discussed, in the context of evolving curriculum frameworks (in England) that attempt to enable both learner creativity and the creativity of the practitioner in promoting this.

The wider policy context poses dilemmas for practitioners. These, together with the relationship between knowledge, the curriculum and creativity, will be taken further in Chapter 10, as will some of the issues arising from the finer distinctions between teaching for creativity, creative teaching and creative learning.

Having identified some of the challenges inherent in translating policy to practice, the next two chapters move to some broader social and ecological considerations.

Part II
A broader view

Part II

Introduction

Creativity as universalised and marketised

Part I of the book explored what kinds of tensions, dilemmas and challenges are faced by teachers and schools in promoting creativity. In Part II the focus becomes a little wider, to consider some of the fundamental values contained in the notion of creativity in the curriculum.

The context of the current drive to foster and value creativity has been described as a universalised one (Jeffrey and Craft 2001; Ng 2003), where creativity is seen as both relevant and necessary in a very wide variety of social, economic, cultural and political contexts. It has been argued (Jeffrey and Craft 2001) that a dominant discourse informing the universalisation of creativity has been 'creativity for empowerment', driven by the increasingly symbiotic relationships between creativity and work, where work increasingly both demands and produces creativity. An aspect of this has been the switching of responsibility for social change from large global forces, including governments, back to the individual, in whom conflicts and dilemmas of power within society are realised (Mills 1959), with concomitant demands on the education system to ensure that young people are appropriately supported in rising to this challenge (Cropley 2001; Craft 2000, 2002; Seltzer and Bentley 1999). At the same time, there has been a paradoxical and fundamental shift from focusing on individual abilities and traits in realising creative potential, to organisations, cultures and climates, such that much policy and research around creativity focuses on how to maximise creative performance to maintain competitive advantage (Jeffrey and Craft 2001).

This drive to see creativity as anchored in the marketplace has influenced much recent policy on creativity in education in different parts of the world (DfEE 1997; NACCCE 1999; Scottish Executive 2004; The Ministry of Education, Singapore 1998; Woods 2002). We might call this the 'marketising' of education. The reasons for it are logical.

However, what implications does this approach to creativity, as both universalised and marketised, bring with it? What does it mean in terms of the relationships between culture and creativity? How does the universalised notion of creativity reflect differences in socio-economic context, and in political context, experienced by individuals and communities? What might be some of the consequences of accepting a view of creativity as anchored in the global marketplace?

In Part II of the book, these and other questions are discussed, together with some of the dilemmas that consequently face teachers and schools. Questions are raised about the appropriateness of a model that has been described as culture 'blind' (Ng 2003) and which is tied to environmental and spiritual degradation (Lane 2001). Thus, fundamental questions are raised about some of the foundation assumptions that form the bedrock of the renaissance of creativity in so many societies in the twenty-first century.

7 The social context to creativity

Creativity, whether 'high' or 'ordinary', is often presented as if it were a universally applicable concept. But it may, by contrast, be quite culturally specific. This chapter explores some aspects of this. Creativity has also been linked to the development of culture within a society; indeed, the creativity agenda in England has been taken forward on a dual platform of both creative and cultural development. The chapter, therefore, also discusses aspects of this very specific linking of the wider social context to creativity and the outcomes of creative activity. It also explores some other aspects of the possible social and political context to creativity, discussing some of the implications for educators.

Context: liberal individualism?

The universalisation of creativity discussed in the Introduction to Part II is, by definition perhaps, what might be called 'culture blind' (Ng 2003). Creativity is called for in the context of liberal individualism closely tied to the marketplace, therefore the form of creativity called for is one that represents that political stance of liberal individualism. In other words, the discourse around creativity is one in which high value is placed on individuality and being open to thinking generatively outside of social and other norms. 'Thinking outside of the box' is a phrase frequently used at a lay level. As Ng (2001) puts it, creativity represents a form of individuated behaviour. Essential to it, he argues, is critical thinking, i.e. rejection of some sort of norm. Ng (2001: 225) argues that 'culture has a strong influence on whether and to what extent the person engages in creative and individuated behavior, as opposed to uncreative and conforming behavior'. Perhaps most importantly, he argues that the East, in particular, brings a different and contrasting perspective to the creativity discourse. This is echoed by Yeung (1999), who notes that despite analysts who describe the 'globalised' society as 'borderless' (Ohmae 1990, 1995; O'Brien 1992; Horsman and Marshall 1994; Chen and Kwang 1997), there is evidence of Asian models of capitalism, in particular, characterised by business remaining distinctly tied in to political and economic alliances (Berger and Dore 1996; Hefner 1998).

And yet, to return to the theme of creativity in particular, the call for creativity is one that is often both universally described and applied, through the argument which goes something like 'people need to be more creative to survive and thrive in the twenty-first century' (Craft 2004), without regard for cultural or sub-cultural values and approaches to life, with evident implications. This chapter attempts to explore some of the issues involved in framing creativity as universal in this way.

Creativity and cultural context

So, what evidence is there that creativity is manifest differently according to culture, or that adopting a universal vocabulary toward creativity is inappropriate?

In one recent study, Ng (2003) investigated differences between two groups of undergraduate students, representative of 'Eastern' or Confucian values, and of 'Western' or liberal individualist values. He used a questionnaire with 158 white undergraduates from Australia and 186 Chinese undergraduates from Singapore, to explore the extent to which creativity is culturally saturated. His hypothesis was that these two populations would represent two different value sets.

The Singapore students in the study represented Confucian values where, as Ng (2003: 224) put it: 'Confucian societies of the East put a greater emphasis on the social group *vis-à-vis* the individual. In such a tightly organized society, there are many social rules and regulations to govern the behavior of the person who is socialized from when young to fit in with the in-group. Failure to do so will result in social sanctions. Conflict with the in-group is strenuously avoided to maintain social order and harmony. Instead, discipline and conformity to tradition are emphasized, and children are expected to respect and obey their elders.'

By contrast, the Australian students in the study represented Western individualism, with a much greater emphasis on the individual over and above the social group (Bellah *et al.* 1985). In such a loosely organised society, Ng suggests, members are socialised from youth to develop their uniqueness as a person and to stand on their own feet instead of becoming psychologically dependent on the in-group. They are expected to pursue their own interests and passions in life, rather than complying with the in-group. In support of this, he reports that Chao (1993) found that 64% of Euro-American mothers emphasised that an important goal of child rearing was to emphasise and nurture the unique self of the child. This contrasted with just 8% of Chinese mothers emphasising that particular goal in bringing up their children.

Ng suggests that individuated behaviour is typical of liberal individualism and cites Markus and Kitayama (1991, 1994), who argue that those living in individualistic and collectivistic cultures construed themselves differently due to differences in socialisation, such that individualistic socialisation involves

- self construed as independent
- self as separate from social group
- personal feelings and opinions expressed in direct ways
- 'individuated behaviour'.

By contrast, collectivistic socialisation involves

- self being construed as related to group; as interdependent
- self seen as part and parcel of social group
- compliance with in-group
- 'conforming behaviour'.

Markus and Kitayama suggest that the individual's need for validation is tied culturally, such that in a collectivistic society the need for validation is toward conformity with the social group, whereas in an individualistic society the social pressures are toward differentiation and difference, leading to behaviour that is individuated to a much greater degree. Ng (2003: 225), citing Ho (1994), argues that: 'the Chinese way of raising a child, which emphasizes the importance of filial piety, encourages the development of cognitive conservatism, a constellation of attributes that lead the person to adopt a passive, uncritical, and uncreative orientation toward learning; to hold fatalistic, superstitious, and stereotypical beliefs, and to be authoritarian, rigid and conformist.' This reflects empirical work done by Dunn *et al.* (1988) and Boey (1976).

Ng's empirical research bore out his hypothesis, although he also noted traces of a pressure for acculturation to occur in the direction of cultural individualism rather than in the direction of cultural collectivism (also a suggestion made by Smith and Bond (1993)). Lim (2004: 4), discussing Ng's work, suggests 'the Asian view traditionally emphasizes control by the environment so that the individual adapts; the Western view emphasizes the individual so that the individual changes the environment'. Lim also notes that, in the Western model, there is a large emphasis on encouraging the individual to 'become themselves', where uniqueness is identified and celebrated. By contrast, and like Ng, he suggests that the traditional Eastern model is collectivist, and conformist, tending to weed out attributes that could prevent social cohesion and fitting in with the social group. It is a social approach which, he suggests, 'draws attention to a person's shortcomings, problems or potentially negative features that need to be corrected to meet the expectations or norms common in a social relationship. As a result, self-esteem can be greatly dampened and creativity subdued' (ibid.: 4). Lim (2004) provides a summary of the differences between East and West offered by Ng (2001); these are given in Table 1.

Table 1 Comparing and contrasting of Eastern and Western cultures. Adapted from Lim (2004) and Ng (2001).

East	West
Tightly organised, with social rules and norms to regulate behaviour.	Loosely organised, with few social rules and norms.
Collectivistic, with emphasis on social group.	Individualistic, with emphasis on the individual.
Hierarchical, with distinctive ranks and status.	Egalitarian, with less distinction between superiors and subordinates.
Great emphasis on social order and harmony in the family and society.	Great emphasis on the open and democratic exchange of ideas between individuals.
More concern with face or in gaining the social approval of the group.	More concerned with realising one's creative potential in life.

Ng and Smith (2004, in press) explore ways in which teachers in the Eastern tradition find difficulty in valuing creativity in the classroom, seeing creative children as more disruptive than other children. They suggest that this paradox can be accounted for by the dominant conception of learning in the Confucian tradition, which emphasises the moral cultivation of the learner. As a consequence, the teacher serves as a moral exemplar to students and the appropriate response from students is to demonstrate respect through obedient behaviour. They note that, in the creative classroom, there is an increase in student responses which run counter to the Confucian model of docile learner, submissive and conforming, such that instead students are encouraged to be argumentative, individualistic and sceptical. For teachers who are socialised into the Confucian tradition, this poses actual and perceived challenges in classroom management and class control.

Ng's (2002) empirical work suggests that the teacher's attitude toward learners has an impact on their effectiveness in fostering creativity in the classroom, such that 'conservative-autocratic' teachers who expect obedience and respect, rather than challenge, from their students, and who see themselves as the ultimate authority, place little emphasis on developing students' individual autonomy. 'Creative' responses are punished and not rewarded. On the other hand, 'liberal-democratic' teachers work from the assumption that their role is to help every child reach their inner potential, and thus encourage and reward creative behaviour in the classroom.

Ng's findings have been borne out in small studies by Martin and co-workers (Martin *et al.* 2001, 2002; Zhang *et al.* 2004), who explored pupil and teacher responses to a continuing professional development programme in China and England that offered teachers a range of support, stimulation and resources to extend pupils' critical and creative thinking. Among the findings was the suggestion that Chinese teachers were far more likely to conform to their perceptions of the cultural norm – even if it were an external one for the purposes of the project – than the English teachers (Martin *et al.* 2002; Zhang *et al.* 2004). As far as pupils were concerned, the pre-tests indicated a much greater degree of passive learning in the Chinese classrooms prior to the intervention than in the English classrooms; however, following opportunities for pupils to become more 'constructivist' in their approaches to problem finding and problem solving, there were actually very few differences in pupil responses (Martin *et al.* 2001; Zhang *et al.* 2004). This is rather an important finding, as it implies that the universalised model of creativity in education does have the potential to alter cultural perspectives and actions in terms of creativity and so lays a heavy responsibility on educators. This is particularly significant when we consider the evidence discussed earlier, for current differences in value base.

Current East–West differences are explained by Nisbett (2003), who explores the differences in values between what he calls 'Asians and Westerners'. He argues that East Asian thought can be characterised as 'holistic', focusing on the 'whole picture' (quite literally in the case of looking at, say, a painting). He suggests that Asian reasoning processes can be described as 'dialectic', seeking to find a 'middle way' between opposing thoughts. On the other hand, 'Western' thought is characterised by focusing on salient people or objects, categorising these and then applying formal logic to explaining and understanding these. Nisbett offers a social and economic account of the differences in cognition arising in these two groups, arguing that the foundations were laid in contrasting forms of social and economic organisation in ancient China and Greece. In ancient Greece individual freedom, individuality and objective thought were valued. Forms of engagement included opportunities to respond to contradictions and dissonance. The development of trading through its maritime location meant the emergence of a wealthy merchant class which valued and could afford education as a belief in knowledge for its own sake (rather than as a route to wealth and power). By contrast, in ancient China, ethnic homogeneity and centralised political control meant little opportunity to deal with difference, and, as Nisbett (2003: 32) puts it, 'the face-to-face village life of China would have pressed in the direction of harmony and agreed-upon norms for behaviour'. Given the absence of both the opportunities to explore differences and also the sanctioning of these from above or from peers, emphasis would have been put on finding means to resolve disagreement rather than ways of evaluating which proposition might be 'true'. Thus, the ancient China approach would have been focused on finding the 'Middle Way' (Nisbett 2003: 32). Underpinning the economic, social and political arrangements in the two ancient cradles of today's thought habits and patterns, of course, is the underlying ecology of the regions, as Nisbett recognises. China, whose ecology lent itself to agriculture, required a form of social organisation which was more co-operative than in Greece, the ecology of which lent itself to hunting, herding, fishing, trade and piracy – none of which, he argues, required and Indian conceptualisations of creativity (sexuality being given a role, for example, in traditional Indian readings on creativity), but suggests that what they hold in common is a focus on 'themes of development and progress towards the realisation of the universe' (Raina 2004: 30). She invokes the traditional Indian metaphor of the garland as representing creativity, to convey the sense of many diverse approaches to creativity co-existing – an inclusive world view that recognises and celebrates difference rather than expecting uniformity, universality and, ultimately, she suggests, the destruction of all that was initially diverse and unique to 'homogenous dead matter' (Raina 2004: 31).

These perspectives are also found in the work of Sen and Sharma (2004), who explored the perspectives on creativity of school teachers in India. They also acknowledge the wider values context; creativity being seen as involving spiritual expression, and personal connection to inner worlds and an outer universe, or 'beingness', rather than being seen as purely innovative problem solving (Sen and Sharma 2004; Chu 1970; Mathur 1982; Aron and Aron 1982; Sherr 1982; Kuo 1996). They cite Wonder and Blake (1992), who identify artistic, poetic and everyday life domains as being core to Eastern conceptions of creativity; and researchers who report the Indian perspective on creativity being collectivist (Hofstede 1980; Roland 1988). They also, however, discuss the perspective advanced by Bharati (1985), that there is evidence of the Indian population being both collectivist and individualist at the same time, acknowledging the dangers of oversimplifying cultural differences in a society which is itself plural, and made up of many sub-cultural groups (Sen and Sharma 2004).

To return to the social elements of the two models, both Nisbett and Ng acknowledge the finer differentiations which may be invisible in a simple categorisation that describes Asian/Western or liberal individualist/collectivist as polar opposites. For of course nationality, in a multicultural world, does not necessarily represent cultural membership. And equally, in a globalised world, where acculturation occurs across national and cultural boundaries, it is not straightforward to make comparisons because the groups being compared are not 'pure'. In addition, we may find a mix of cultures within one setting.

For example, within today's China we can find evidence of more closed, conformist traditions, where creativity may be more likely to be stifled, alongside a growing value placed on capitalism, with its demands for innovation, creativity and change. Cheung et al. (2004) report that we also may not always find what we expect as regards values, as two fairly recent large-scale Eastern studies of attitudes to creativity demonstrate. The studies, by Berndt et al. (1993) and Cheung et al. (1992), conducted in Taiwan, mainland China and Hong Kong, revealed differences in adult attitudes toward creativity such that the least positive attitude was in fact demonstrated in Hong Kong.

This, and the work of Nisbett and Ng, does bring into question any notion that it may be appropriate to foster creativity or to call for it in a way that is culture blind, for they provide evidence that the notion of creativity as discussed so far in this book and in the policy, lay and research literature, may, indeed, be quite culturally specific in its strong emphasis on individuality and the value it places on being able to think independently of social norms. And, as their work demonstrates, this may reflect values in cultures where the individual and the marketplace are held in high esteem.

When we put this together with the power held by the teacher and the system of education over young people, in terms of defining what and how it is appropriate to learn, we recognise the immense responsibility we carry with respect to fostering pupils' creativity. The small China–England study discussed briefly above (Martin *et al.* 2001; Zhang *et al.* 2004) offers disturbing findings in this respect, in that after a relatively short period of support to teachers and implementation by them, pupil behaviours and approaches were noticeably different, demonstrating acculturation to the universalised (i.e. Western) model of creativity. This is further supported on a cross-cultural study of gender and creativity by Kaufman *et al.* (2004), which found that no differences in response are detected when a universalised model of creativity within a domain is adopted with a range of distinct cultural groups. This suggests that there may be a very powerful tendency to the norm, and thus a potential for the (perhaps unwitting) domination of a universalised model of creativity.

Aside from East–West differences, there may be other cultural differences. It has been suggested (Craft 2003a) that creativity might be perceived to be less relevant and desirable in a more repressive or conformist culture. It could also be argued that cultural context may also affect a person's experiences of creativity and their ability to manifest it. However, this may not be a totally predictable relationship. Thus, in a social context where choices and personal autonomy are severely restricted, the drive to find alternatives may be quite strong. On the other hand, it may be that avoidance of social or political sanctions and socialisation into submission, would, under such conditions, suffocate creativity.

Psychologists researching creativity include those who recognise wider culture. Although this is often described in terms of the interacting parts of a system, i.e. person, the domain and the field of judges (Csikszentmihalyi, 1990), which is effectively a domain-situated perspective, the reach of creativity research to take account of wider culture has been acknowledged by Magyari-Beck (1976), cited by Csikszentmihalyi (1990). He suggests that there are four levels on which creativity could be studied: the person, the working group, the institution and the culture. He also suggests that there are three forms of creativity: the process, the product and the trait. His analysis generates the matrix shown in Figure 1. He suggests that studies may take one of four methodological approaches: quantitative/qualititive, empirical/normative. We see that there is a vast number of possible ways

	Person	Working group	Institution	Culture
Product				
Process				
Trait				

Figure 1 Matrix generated after Mayari-Beck (1976), as cited in Csikszentmihalyi (1990).

of exploring and interpreting creativity. Whether or not this particular formulation is the most relevant 30 years after it was proposed, what is useful about Magyari-Beck's approach is that it reminds us that there are several levels on which we can approach our interrogation of creativity in the wider cultural context.

Cultural capital and creativity: the 'creative and cultural agenda'

The question of culture in a slightly different, perhaps narrower, sense is particularly live for educators and others concerned with fostering creativity in learners in England, when we consider that the policy document which stimulated so much attention on creativity in education was itself concerned with both cultural and creative education. Indeed, the committee whose deliberations led to the report 'All Our Futures' was called the National Advisory Committee for Creative *and Cultural* Education (NACCCE, 1999 my emphasis). The recommendations of the committee were inclusive, and placed the connecting of wider culture – what could be described as *cultural capital* – as well as *artistic cultural achievement and development*, at the heart of promoting pupil creativity, arguing that cultural and creative development occur hand in hand. It is the narrower, artistic meaning of culture which provides additional culture for creativity in schools in England – though this too is not straightforward, since artistic creativity is interpreted increasingly widely to incorporate the 'creative industries', such as Web design and advertising.

The perspectives discussed already in this chapter that document cultural distinctions were not addressed in the NACCCE report, and it could be argued that this is problematic, in all the ways that have already been discussed. Additionally, the context of currently dominant approaches to learning, which underpin the practices of many teachers, provides a further challenge. For child development is proposed in the influential socio-cultural approaches to learning as being specific to culture, bound to context and as an inherently social process (Vass 2004a, 2004b). Vass points out how closely connected this perspective is to the constructivist

Vygotskian idea of cultural and social mediation (Crook 1994). Thus, if we adopt a constructivist approach to learning, which in Chapter 5 it was argued is both necessary to and demanded by promoting pupils' creativity, then we cannot ignore the situating of learning within wider culture in both the narrower and the wider senses discussed earlier. By the same token we must also take note of the situating of 'culture', including what counts as culture and what does not, and also windows of access to culture.

Some of the issues around the situatedness of culture itself are raised in a recent research report which explored a development project undertaken by eight secondary schools in England, aiming to develop strategies to encourage student participation in local cultural contexts (Craft *et al.* 2004b). Significant challenges to fostering participation included preconceived ideas by students and teachers, ways in which schools described events and opportunities and, perhaps by implication, what counted as 'culture' in the first place. On the other hand, success strategies included those where students took on the role of 'cultural mentor'. The cultural mentor role was characterised by Harland *et al.* (2000) as involving any or all of the following:

- apprenticeship (work-related skills shown/modelled by mentor);
- competence (mentor takes on trainer or coach role, involving observation and feedback on predefined competencies);
- reflection (mentor encourages non-judgemental and non-hierarchical exploration of own practice in a 'mutual friend' role).

In the Craft *et al.* (2004b) study, however, what was underlined was the importance of learners being able to make the transition across cultural contexts and different perspectives. Other models of student engagement included generative roles such as the 'impresario' (i.e. conceptualising and operationalising events) and the 'artist' (being a participant in the making process). The study highlighted the fact that if the fostering of creativity and culture are linked then the multiple perspectives which learners bring to this process are highly significant in terms of engagement, and this can pose practical and philosophical challenges, due to the collision of potentially different values.

Cultural differences in values around creativity, then, raise issues for us as educators. But what about other social contexts that inform values which may vary rather than being universal? We turn next, albeit briefly, to social class.

Creativity and socio-economic context

It has been argued (Craft 2003a) that creativity may be imbued with social class-based assumptions, such as resilience, self-reliance, persistence and control over one's environment – also, future-orientation and greater individualism (Craft 2002; Kluckhohn and Strodtbeck 1961). These, it is argued, form another way in which the universalisation of the notion is clearly questionable, since the assumptions (such as resilience, self-reliance, and so on) would not necessarily be shared by all people, depending on socio-economic background.

Clearly this raises issues around what it may or may not be appropriate for educators to put forward in the classroom as being of worth, since there may be an implication of one set of values being more appropriate than others. The hegemonic dimension of this is problematic, for when the so-called 'universalised' concept of creativity is concerned with inclusion and opportunity for all, this sits uneasily with the power, authority and control implied by imposing a creativity value set in the classroom which does not connect easily with some pupils' experience and understanding of how the world works.

However, it could equally be argued that educators have a responsibility to offer access to the 'dominant' (in terms of social and economic) culture to pupils who might otherwise be unaware of or unable to gain access to this. Indeed, numerous programmes aiming to foster creativity in education appear to have this perspective. It could be argued that Creative Partnerships, the government initiative scheduled to run from 2002 to 2006, is one, with its emphasis on working in areas of high urban or rural deprivation. Another organisation whose remit is to stimulate and resource the creativity of young people, as well as adults, is NESTA. Many of its funded programmes already have social inclusion at their heart, for example the Newham Sixth-Form College project (Jeffery et al. 2005), also the community arts project Image Conscious, based at Camden Arts in London (Camden Arts 2003), and the Ignite! Programme (Craft *et al.* 2004e). Each of these projects would argue vociferously that fostering the creativity of young people who might otherwise not feel they had a place in the game is of critical importance, and that connecting this work explicitly with the home and community values of which young people are a part is critical in doing so (Davidson *et al.* 2004; Jeffery 2005; Fell and Davidson 2004).

What seems to be of critical importance here is sensitivity to values which may be brought from the home and which may be in tension with those promulgated in the classroom, whether that is a nursery environment or a sixth-form workshop. So, whether it is a case of a nursery child whose parents are concerned about their daughter performing on stage in front of others (Duffy and Stillaway 2004) or a teenager whose experiences as a refugee make it difficult for them to believe that they can achieve anything they wish to (Parkes 2004), we must as educators be alive and alert to the potential for abusing the power that we hold, at the same time of being sensitised to the life-changing potential we also hold for the very same reasons (Jeffery *et al.* 2005).

Political context

The political context provides another set of influences on the extent to which creativity is encouraged in the wider culture. Piirto (1992) reminds us, for example, that during the 1950s, and throughout the 'Cold War', nationalist concerns for global domination informed investment in creativity in the USA. These contextual 'nationalist' (as she calls them) rationales still exist in the USA, with the attention turning variously to economic competition with Europe, Japan, the Pacific Rim and to military conflict with terrorists and those perceived to resource them. In the case of the economic context, the arguments for creativity are still linked to economic productivity and competitiveness.

Clearly, the wider cultural/political context may affect a person's experiences of creativity and their ability to manifest it. As already noted, we might expect that, within more repressive societies, we would see less creativity because it might be perceived to be less relevant and desirable. But even within what appears to be 'one' culture we may find variation of potential to express individual or collective views. Accordingly, at a micro-political level, it may be easier to follow a personal and individualised path in a large city than it is in a small village; equally, it may be easier to divert from the norm if one's dominant values-identity is held in a pluralised space. Thus, if fundamentalism of any kind is a part of one's value-set, being creative may seem less relevant, less desirable and also perhaps less achievable. Indeed, in his work on changing minds, Gardner (2004) argues that a fundamentalist mind set is antithetical to creativity. He takes a broad definition of fundamentalism, i.e. 'An adherent decides that he will no longer change his mind in any significant way' (ibid.: 189). He notes that this therefore means that efforts are directed toward 'shoring up the current belief system and rejecting notions that are alien to the doctrine (ibid.: 189); also that 'the fundamentalist voluntarily suspends his imagination' (ibid.: 189), meaning that creativity cannot occur.

At a macro-political level, we might say that a region or country that embraces democratic values and freedom of speech would perhaps be more likely to support the promotion of creativity in policy and practice. Subscribing to a global marketplace has meant increasing wealth in many parts of the world, which both enables people to make creative choices about their lives and also resources them to see these through. This certainly reflects arguments discussed already in this chapter by Ng (2001) and by Nisbett (2003).

On the other hand, it could be argued that to live in a 'free' country is not truly possible with such a domination of the global marketplace, which means that although we may appear to have many choices, these are actually limited by market forces. For our choices are, it could be argued, limited in terms of innovation being valued over and above an approach which says 'make do and mend'. Our choices are determined by a marketplace that both demands and creates continual innovation.

Gender

It has been argued (Goff 2004) that it is only in recent years, with the recognition that creativity is manifest lifewide and not restricted to certain domains, nor to 'high' creative activity (Craft 2001; Maslow 1970), that the creativity of women has been adequately recognised and acknowledged. Goff's argument is that the de-contextualised nature of traditional creativity tests has disadvantaged women; certainly, the issue of how children interpret tests depending on the context in which they are presented is a significant issue (Gipps and Murphy 1994). Goff acknowledges the less prominent role played by women in the public domain as regards creative achievements; as she puts it, 'Creativity is not a gender specific ability, but its recognition, acknowledgement and development are' (Goff 2004: 107). Her views may cause the reader to beg questions about how we define and reward creativity – and to what extent we acknowledge the home-based domain, a point taken up further in Chapter 11 and in the Postscript.

But Goff also suggests that the body of evidence which suggests that many women are relational learners for whom learning is grounded in first-hand experience, and for whom learning involves feelings, negotiation, and is personal (Belenky *et al.* 1986; Gilligan 1982, 1993; Goldberger *et al.* 1986, McCracken 1997), provides a contrast with models of school-based learning which may be inadequately personalised for girls. In terms of creativity, she suggests that we perhaps underestimate what kinds of opportunities will be most appropriate in fostering girls' creativity. Her own proposed solution to this is to transform traditional curricula into formats which suit women better; her particular recommendation is Torrance's Incubation Model of Teaching (Torrance and Safter 1990), which operates through three steps. First, it involves becoming aware of a dilemma, challenge or problem, or a curiosity to find out more. Second, it involves accepting the need to learn. Third, it involves incorporating what has been learned. In other words, this is an active and engaged model, which offers space for collaborative approaches to debate rather than adversarial approaches and which does not assume the transference of expertise in some sort of mechanical way.

Whether or not one agrees with Goff's solution, it is certainly the case that the global entry into the workforce and the encouragement in so many countries now of both girls and boys to develop creative pathways through their lives does raise issues regarding gender. We know from Fryer's (1996) study of English teachers that men and women saw creativity differently, with women emphasising relational aspects and self-expression and men having a more 'impersonal' model of creativity, which in turn affects the way that they provide for and interpret creativity in the classroom.

However, this is an area that warrants further investigation, as argued by Gruber and Wallace (1999), and sensitivity in the classroom.

The educator's dilemmas

In the discussions so far in this chapter, we have been exploring some significant ways in which the Western individualistic model of existence influences the framing of creativity and the discourse around creativity in education. It has been argued that the apparent 'universalisation' of the concept of creativity implies the transcendence of this model, with implications for culture, socio-economic context, and political context – and also gender.

It could be argued that the international economic and political power structure that lies behind the global market places certain organisations and governments in superordinate positions. Some might interpret this as a position on global dominance, with the USA, together with a variety of multinational companies, taking the lead.

If we accept that, at the very least, there may be some ways in which a position of universalisation is questionable, where does that leave us as educators?

One response to this question (Craft 2003a) would be to argue that both high and ordinary creativity reflect the globalisation of significant aspects of Western culture. And thus, while there may be a strong element of 'cultural saturation' in the concept of creativity, it could *also* be said that the increasing global influence of Western culture, including its markets, means that the relevance of creativity as a universal concept may grow. Taking this perspective, we would then argue that, as educators, our role is to support the universalised approach to creativity, nurturing and nourishing a homogenised approach which gradually rubs away cultural, political and socio-economic differences, and which takes no account of gender. In practice, this probably means doing nothing more than accepting the policy requirements and scaffolding offered to us as education practitioners, and implementing these.

But how appropriate is it for us to do this without, at the very least, a plural context to our pedagogy? For we still live in a world where there are distinct cultural identities both within and between nation states, as well as different traditions, value-sets and, therefore, motivations and preferences for learning and achievement.

The issues raised by the shocking terrorist responses to some aspects of globalisation and US policies in the latter part of 2001, and the subsequent response, up to the present day, of going to war with terrorism, brought into focus some of the problems which the advocacy and spread of Western values may have. For it would appear that for some of the alleged terrorists who planned and carried out those actions on 11 September 2001, the USA both represents and is a powerful source of 'cultural imperialism', pursuing its economic and other interests in the global context, as if Western values were of obvious universal validity. Hence, for those responsible for the destruction of the World Trade Center and a part of the Pentagon, the USA posed a legitimate target for a massive terrorist response. It could be argued that Western 'creativity' formed a part of the value-set perceived to have been imposed worldwide.

Further, we could argue that the response to what has become known as 'September 11th' (or 9/11), has represented an explicit and further entrenchment on cultural imperialism, the response being the 'War on Terror' which led the USA and Britain, together with other allies such as Spain and Japan, into war in Iraq. Both sides of the War on Terror could be described as 'fundamentalist', and thus not open to creative thought or perspectives. The issues are very much live; in the course of writing this chapter, I received through the post a booklet from the UK Government of the day, entitled *Preparing for Emergencies: What You Need to Know* (HM Government 2004). It is a supposed guide to survival in the face of a terrorist attack, although it cannot by definition be terribly specific.

Where does this leave the educator? We are faced with the possibility that a universalised (and market-related) notion of creativity may in fact be perceived by some as exclusive. The fact this is the case could lead to a group or organisation harnessing their creativity to further mass destruction, as the government leaflet burning a hole on my desk suggests. It could certainly be argued that the universalisation of creativity in the current world is, perhaps, premature and inappropriate. For creativity may well be limited by its cultural and, perhaps, gender specificity. Perhaps one of the big challenges we face as educators is the lack of representation of a plural perspective on creativity in education and political policy.

Summing up: where do plural perspectives leave the educator?

The discussion in this chapter begs the following question. If creativity is culturally, socially and politically specific, how appropriate is it to encourage it within education?

Stimulating creativity involves encouraging learners to adopt a way of life that not only presents itself as universal when it is not, but also the positive associations with creativity mask some possibly questionable values which are also associated with it. On the other hand, education in any cultural context will involve the teaching of some concepts as if they were universal; but, like any other concept, creativity does not necessarily have to be taught in this way. Indeed, by its very nature, being about alternatives and possibilities, it offers the potential for evaluating the worth of any creative outcome by considering the implications of any new idea, product, service, etc. Thus, although creativity is always situated within a cultural context, by interrogating this, the assumption of cultural universalism may be challenged and the perspectives of all celebrated. Chapter 11 explores this idea a little further.

8   Creativity and the environment

This chapter discusses the implications of 'innovation' as the norm. In particular it poses questions about the possible effects of innovation on the wider environment and balance, or 'ecology'. It offers reflections on these questions from the perspectives of the physical and what might be described as the existential, or spiritual.

Creativity as anchored in the marketplace?

The case for fostering creativity in education can be seen as a response to the conditions and pace of life and the global market economy, as discussed in Chapter 1. This case is made explicitly in policy documents, as already acknowledged earlier in the book. So, in England, the 1997 White Paper *Excellence in Schools* (DfEE 1997) talked of preparing young people 'successfully for the twenty-first century' by recognising the different talents of all people. This was built on by the NACCCE (1999) report, which talked of the need to provide young people with the skills and approaches required by employers. The report acknowledged that alongside high standards of academic achievement, employers now required 'people who can adapt, see connections, innovate, communicate and work with others' (NACCCE 1999: 13).

Close by geographically, the Scottish Executive published on its website in April 2004 the following statement by Frank McAveety, MSP, Minister for Tourism, Culture and Sport, regarding creativity: 'The creativity of Scots – from the classroom to the boardroom – is the edge we need in a competitive world. Our duty as an Executive is to create the conditions that allow that creativity to flourish – whether in arts, sciences, commerce or industry. . . . Creativity is as valuable in retail, education, health, government and business as in culture. The cultural sector should become the national dynamo of the creative impulse that can serve all these areas' (Scottish Executive 2004). This was the precursor to the establishment of a commission in June 2004 comprising of representatives from various sections of the cultural sector and chaired by James Boyle, to refine the cultural and creative strategy for Scotland.

These arguments and perspectives have been in emergence since the early 1990s, as the following quotation from the 'Year 2000 Framework Learning' document from the Canadian Ministry of Education (1991: 2; quoted in Woods (2002: 79)) demonstrates:

> in view of the new social and economic realities, all students, regardless of their immediate plans following school, will need to develop a flexibility and a versatility undreamed of by previous generations [and to]...employ critical and creative thinking skills to solve problems and make decisions.

The case is made, also, in the Far East. For example, Ng and Lin (2004) point out that, in Singapore, one desired learning outcome for pupils at the end of their schooling (i.e. pre-higher education), set in the context of being able to think creatively and independently, is that they should 'have an entrepreneurial...spirit' (The Ministry of Education, Singapore 1998).

Alongside this shifting education policy context, which in different parts of the world is recognising a greater explicit role creativity in the economy and, therefore, in education, in the last 10 years in particular we have seen commentators and researchers exploring ways in which creativity and the economy interact and offering more and better strategies to increase productivity and, ultimately, sales. For some, e.g. Sternberg and Lubart (1995a, 1995b), this means using the market as a tool for analysing creativity. Sternberg and Lubart propose the investment model of creativity as involving 'buying low and selling high'; they use the metaphor of the market to explain and explore creativity. They summarise the metaphor as follows: '*Buying low* means actively pursuing ideas that are unknown or out of favour but that have growth potential, whereas *selling high* involves moving on to new products when an idea or product becomes valued and yields a different return' [their italics] (ibid.: 538). Sternberg (2003: 206) later describes investment theory as '*the decision to be creative*' Sternberg's italics, in that people make the decision to buy low and sell high.

For others, the market lurks in the background as an assumed 'good'; e.g. Nagel (2000: 15) discusses creativity and public policy, and as part of his analysis proposes that public policies that tend to foster creativity are those which, among other things, relate to 'competitive business firms' and 'increased national productivity'.

For others still, performance in the market place is itself an indicator of creativity. Florida (2002), who comments on economic development, argues that we value creativity more highly than ever and cultivate it more intensely and that in North America it is led by the growth of a 'Creative Class'. Members of this group include engineers, architects, scientists, artists, educators and entertainers. He suggests that their economic function is to create new technology, new creative content and, above all, new ideas, and his thesis is that the group is growing in size and influence, with an already profound influence on work and lifestyle, in being both self-directed and high achieving. Florida asks some profound existential questions about the purpose and goals of this group, suggesting the need for a closer focus on cohesion around what might be seen as the common good. His work, which argues that urban economic development needs to bring together diversity (for example, attracting bohemians, gays and ethnic minorities) because creative workers want to live in such places, has been influential in urban redesign and regeneration in the USA. However, it also has its critics. Among them is Malangi (2004), who suggests that Florida was too quick to conclude that what attracted creative workers to urban areas was their tolerance, openness to creativity and their diversity. Malangi suggests that some of the cities that Florida cites as successful creative-age cities are underperforming and also that some of the top creative cities do not appear to attract or retain residents. He suggests that Florida overemphasises the high-tech industries' contribution to the Creative Class, and also wonders why some cities which on other indices of economic growth have expanded very fast in recent years, such as Detroit, have been omitted from Florida's list altogether, while New York, which is one of Florida's most creative cities, seems to produce fast-growing companies at less than half the rate of all big cities.

Equally, it could be argued that it is successful economies themselves (urban or not), rather than diverse urban environments, which foster the growth of the Creative Class.

In later work, Florida and Tinagli (2004) focus on global shifts in the growth of the Creative Class. By using a tool to measure this growth, Florida and Tinagli argue that the economic power of the USA and of the 'old Europe' is being challenged by what they call a 'creative crescent' of 14 northern European countries which are performing highly in the 'knowledge economy' in which creativity is a fundamental good. They argue that economic development is based on technology, talent and tolerance, and on the expansion of the 'Creative Class'. Countries in Europe with a high proportion of what they call 'Creative Class' workers include The Netherlands, Belgium, Finland, England, Ireland and Denmark. Their analysis assumes, of course, that creative people are needed to generate and maintain the economy of the twenty-first century. It can perhaps be seen as growing out of assumptions proposed by Seltzer and Bentley (1999: 9), who argue that 'knowledge is the primary source of economic productivity', requiring the fostering of 'creative potential of all citizens . . . to boost competitiveness'.

There is a strong sense, then, in which creativity is both actually and seen to be integrally linked with a Western (or perhaps increasingly globalised) model of the market.

Culture and worldview

In Chapter 7, the cultural context to creativity was discussed, and Western and Eastern models were explored as a part of this. We might note the close fit between the emphasis in the Western model on there being a 'product' to creativity, and a high value placed on the market.

Another element, however, which Lubart (1999) identifies, is the 'worldview' that underlies the different approaches to creativity. In other words, the broad conception held in a culture of the nature of the world and also of the role of people in it (Sadowsky *et al.* 1994). Drawing on Spindler and Spindler (1983), Lubart (1999: 345) suggests that the US worldview might be characterised by its emphasis on 'individualism, a work ethic of accomplishment and achievement, and a belief in progress and a better future'. The latter part of this worldview, with its emphasis on development and change as a good thing, places 'creativity' very high in value and implies, by contrast, that cultures which place a high value adherence to tradition and conformity to the norm may, in fact, stifle creativity.

Yet, despite the evidence for the existence of both Eastern and Western models of creativity discussed in Chapter 7, it would appear that the powerful global marketplace now dominates and influences foundation cultures. And thanks to growth in information and communication technologies, it reaches far into people's lives and homes worldwide. This means that the individual, family and community are inundated with advertising of evolving products and services with decreasing shelf lives, so that the role of consumer is difficult to escape. It could be argued that persistent advertising to encourage the consumer to replace current goods and services with the latest model, toy, form of food, approach to entertainment etc. conveys a model of creativity as linked with the market, and as 'a good thing'. Thus, an implicit message appears to be that the notion of market-linked creativity is a good thing, as appropriate and as universalised – whether or not a culture actually adopts this intentionally as a core value. This is apparent from some of the discussion at policy and commentator level already explored in this chapter.

Consequences of anchoring creativity in the marketplace

It could be argued that the relationship between creativity and the market-place has been one of the drivers behind government initiatives the world over to inject greater creativity into the curriculum. Crudely put, we increase the emphasis on fostering creativity in our schools, and we achieve, or remain at, the cutting edge in terms of economic prosperity and growth. The wealthier we are as nations, the more we can achieve and the easier our lives. But what kinds of consequences flow from adopting a line that emphasises the role of creativity in selling ideas and products?

One of the effects of promoting a culture that encourages and rewards continual innovation in the context of a marketplace is that the drive to innovate further becomes an end in itself. There is a danger – and plenty of evidence – that the re-use of old artefacts and ideas becomes subservient to the shiny mantra of making profit; we find ourselves living in a world of our own creation, where new is better than make do and mend. Indeed, in order to maintain demand, and therefore profit, one might be forgiven for thinking that many products and services appear to be designed with a short shelf life, in that the item ceases to work after a short period; even more significant, it is designed to be disposed of and replaced, rather than repaired or restored.

This chapter, then, asks how desirable is the norm of innovation that the global economy demands? To what extent is it desirable to encourage and sustain the 'disposable' culture, where obsolescence is built in at the design stage of many consumer goods and where fashion dictates the need for constant change and updating?

Environmental costs

There are clear environmental costs to giving high value to the market as if it were a divine force. In a world of finite resources, an increasingly global lifestyle that encourages continual disposal and replacement of products fuels a ticking time-bomb of degradation. As participants in global society, whatever our roles, whether producers, consumers, parents, educators and so on, we contribute to the costs of creativity each time we purchase an innovation which we want but do not need. Effectively, we might argue that we contribute to upsetting an ecological balance. And how often do we stop to look behind the image or resist the pressure for the latest fad, to ask what kind of life we wish to lead at a more fundamental and global level?

These are not new concerns; indeed, in 2002, an international conference was held in England to address these and other issues as they apply to education. The conference was attended by Navaho Elders and other educators from various parts of the world. Resulting in a book (Fryer 2004), the conference sought to address issues of cultural diversity and to surface implicit aspects and effects of creativity tied to a Western marketised model of existence. At another level and elsewhere, although still in England, the social, economic and environmental impacts of innovations form the focus of a number of studies based at the Innovation Studies Centre at the Tanaka Business School, Imperial College, University of London. Further afield, research has found evidence of innovation that responds to environmental impact; a Canadian study (Hanel 1999), for example, explored reasons why firms had introduced innovations, one possible set of reasons being to do with environmental impact. The survey found that one out of four innovators was motivated out of a high or very high concern to reduce environmental damage. These firms also retained a slight competitive edge over others.

Indeed, some creative processes themselves are focused particularly on the issues of environmental impact. Jones and Harrison (2000), for example, describe how the creativity process known as TRIZ (Theory of Inventive Problem Solving) has been used to further eco-innovation (i.e. ecologically sound innovations).

However, the attempt to innovate to limit environmental impact does not do away with the fundamental high value placed on creativity as a good thing, full stop. It could be argued that the purchase of consumer and other items is, in part, a replacement for meaning in a world where the market holds such supremacy (Lane 2001). Lane (ibid.: 16) describes the ascribing of power to the market as a 'consumerist mentality', which is also charac-terised by a dependency on what he describes as 'externals'; pressures from peers or from advertising, for example.

In addition, the constant drive toward making and buying occurs at the same time as massive global population growth; it could certainly be argued that unless the most wealthy and educated parts of the world start to take less of the world's resources, there will be insufficient food and water at the most basic level for the whole of the world's population. But to start to 'take' or to consume less would mean to see 'creativity' as fulfilling a wider function in society, not an apparently value-neutral contribution to consumption. It would mean seeing creativity in perhaps a more spiritual way, in terms of fulfilment, individual and/or collective. And so it could also mean taking a different kind of existential slant on life.

Coming at these issues from the perspective of human geography, Massey (1999) argues that the positioning of space as if it were time is highly problematic, in that the very language we use to describe space (and culture) can imply an unproblematic and inevitable link between global development and time. Massey's argument that space and time are not necessarily linked in this way is an example of taking a different perspective on life, in her case one which sees spatiality as open, co-constructed. She calls for a re-examination of the spatiality of cosmologies that we hold as implicit, so as to separate the inevitable tie between space and a marketised, global model of economic development and all that goes with that. As Massey's work illustrates, taking a co-constructed, negotiative approach to meaning, consumption, production and so on, affects deeply the role we then give to creativity in our lives.

Spiritual costs

As well as environmental costs there are also spiritual costs to a 'market as God' model of existence. What kind of world do we create where the market is deified? What could this mean for individuals, families, communities and nations finding purpose, meaning and connection in their lives? What does a marketised world do for retaining contact with an ethical dimension in life?

One approach to this question has been adopted by Sheldrake *et al.* (2001). In this 'trialogue'-based text, they undertake an exploration of current views of morality, reality and the nature of life. Aspects of what they explore include the relationships between our inner and outer spaces or existences, and the role of chaos in the dynamics of human creation. They challenge us, too, to consider the potential role of the sacred.

It is a very different perspective on life to the one which Lane (2001: 41) describes as underlying high consumerism, who uses the metaphor of a dream to underline his point as follows: 'the dream of our society is wealth and its multiplication. Wealth, the dream suggests, brings not only ease and beauty but unequivocal happiness'. Perhaps most significantly of all, however, Lane (2001: 41) suggests 'It allows us to do whatever we please, whatever we want to do.' Although an aspect of this is that we can be as creative as we wish, it also points up the fact that for a good idea to be put into action does not necessarily involve any or much consideration given to its possible unintended consequences, some of which may not be particularly positive.

Lane (2001), in fact, offers a vision close to the perspectives introduced by Sheldrake *et al.* (2001). He proposes a model of what he calls 'simplicity' (in which creativity and imagination are brought to transforming homes and lifestyles not through the purchase of new and better, but through making do, finding, mending and valuing) as a more spiritually generous alternative.

Creative destruction

This chapter has been edging toward discussing the potential of creativity to act as a negative force, rather than a positive one.

To what extent do we, in the marketplace at any rate, encourage innovation for innovation's sake and without reference to genuine need? How desirable is it to encourage those values that present, via the market, 'wants' as if they were 'needs'? It could be said that a culture of 'make do and mend' might be something to be fostered, rather than looking to ways of changing what may be working perfectly well already, whether that be a system, a relationship, a service or a product. And, as Lane (2001) suggests, 'making do and mending' may often require creativity of us.

Fromm (1954) described what we might now call the marketisation of society as likely to lead to mass conformity: 'such a civilization can produce only a mass man: incapable of choice, incapable of spontaneous, self-directed activities... increasingly irresponsible as his choices become fewer and fewer: a creature governed mainly by his conditioned reflexes ... [to] the sales organizations of modern business, or by the propaganda office and the planning bureaus of totalitarian and quasi-totalitarian governments'. Fromm had, perhaps, predicted the future; a world where a great deal of emphasis is laid on the surface, on acquiring and on being entertained, rather than on much more fundamental and substantive issues. As Crichton (1999) so eloquently puts it:

> everyone must be amused, or they will switch – switch brands, switch channels, switch parties, switch loyalties. This is the intellectual reality of Western society at the end of the century. In other centuries, human beings wanted to be saved, or improved, or freed, or educated. But in our century, they want to be entertained. The great fear is not of disease or death, but of boredom. A sense of time on our hands, a sense of nothing to do. A sense that we are not amused.

Quite apart from the capacity of creativity harnessed to the market to generate such a superficial existence, there is of course the whole question of creativity's darker side. The human imagination is, without doubt, capable of immense destruction as well as of almost infinitely constructive possibilities. To what extent is it possible to generate systems which stimulate and celebrate creativity within a profoundly humane framework, and which actively examine and encourage the critical examination of the values inherent in creative ideas and action? It is argued that the role of educators is perhaps to encourage students to examine the possible wider effects of their own ideas and those of others, and to evaluate both choices and worth in the light of this.

This inevitably means the balancing of conflicting perspectives and values, which themselves may be irreconcilable. This may have been, and may still be, the case in the creative act of destruction of 11 September 2001, and what might be described as the failing attempts to achieve 'closure' on this on both sides. The balancing of conflicting perspectives is explored in Chapter 11, which aims to offer a brief exploration of a practical framework for educators attempting to resolve such tensions and dilemmas that arise from such a marketised and universalised notion of creativity.

But it may also mean making more strenuous efforts than hitherto to detach creativity from innovation – bringing the ideas to market. As discussed in Chapter 2, which explored the language of creativity, innovation, while involving creativity, is commonly thought of by commentators as distinct from creativity. And yet, we perhaps muddle our everyday conceptions of the two, so that creativity and innovation are confused, resulting in a muddle of values around what is produced through creative effort, and how that is evaluated. For while bringing ideas into the marketplace in some ways may add to the quality of the lived experience of all beings on the planet, very often this is not the case. Chapter 9 explores possible ways in which educators could position themselves in fostering learner creativity in such a way that potential damaging environmental impact of generativity – creativity – is minimised, and positive impact maximised.

Part III
Constructing creativity

Part III

Introduction

Creativity as a 'good thing'

On one level it is difficult to see how creativity could be seen as anything other than 'a good thing'. Creativity is becoming a part of a universalised discourse in the Western world. It reflects the globalization of economic activity, which has led to increased competition for markets and which has developed, therefore, an integral fear of obsolescence. As well as reflecting the wider world, creativity is a response to it, as continual innovation and resourcefulness have become necessary to economic survival. The growth of the weightless, or knowledge, economy requires creativity, relying on the intellectual and creative capabilities of workers, at least as much as on their physical energy and general intelligence (Seltzer and Bentley 1999). The economy demands creativity, and a healthy economy leads to a wealthy society, which then produces assets for general consumption, in the form of better public amenities and services – as well as assets in the form of individual wealth and opportunities.

In addition, there has been a growing assumption within the discourse on creativity, perhaps voiced first by Maslow (1970), that the creative individual is a fulfilled one, and one whose life is characterised by 'agency' – the capacity to take control and make something of it. Maslow also put forward the notion that creativity is not for the few, but an everyday phenomenon of everyday people who were not necessarily the equivalent of Einstein. He suggested that there was 'a more widespread kind of creativeness' (Maslow 1970: 159), applicable across life and not simply in the arts, but also manifest in everyday occupations such as housework, as well as specialised occupations involving extensive knowledge and experience, such as medicine. Maslow's approach to the breadth of everyday life as an arena for the expression of creativity is echoed later in the work of Goleman *et al.* (1992), who argue that much innovation and problem solving occurs in everyday life.

The application of creativity by individuals within an everyday setting is one that others have also developed, as acknowledged earlier in the book (Feldman *et al.* 1994; Amabile 1996; Runco and Richards 1997; Craft 2000, 2001a, 2001b, 2002). I have come to use the phrase 'lifewide creativity' to describe the application of creativity to the breadth of contexts in everyday life (Craft 2002). Others, too, have written about creativity as a fundamental attribute to enable adaptation and response in a fast-changing world (e.g. Ripple 1989; Barron 1988; Gruber 1989; Henry and Walker 1991). The assumption is that the ordinary person can be creative (Craft 2002; NACCCE 1999; Seltzer and Bentley 1999; Weisberg 1993). It is assumed that there is some relationship between 'big c' and 'little c' creativity. Worth (2001) has argued for a continuum of creativity, with 'localised' creativity somewhere in the middle, between high creativity and ordinary creativity; Feldman (1974, 1989, 1999, 2003) has similarly argued for the existence of a spectrum. NACCCE (1999) suggested that, by fostering creative and cultural education in schools, the growth of culture (thus of high creativity) would also be promoted.

So, the argument seems to go that creativity is good for the economy and, therefore, for society. It is good for individuals, who are more fulfilled when creative and who do not need to be Einstein to manifest creativity. Education in many parts of the world and not just in England, has had a key role to play in responding to, and providing for, this 'universalised' notion of creativity.

In England, alongside statements in the National Curriculum and Foundation Stage Curriculum, numerous government-funded projects and development programmes related to education and learning sprang up in the last 10 years of the twentieth century and first years of the twenty-first century. Many of these are enumerated in Chapter 1.

This book has already explored some dilemmas and contradictions in fostering creativity in education, noting limitations produced by lack of clarity in language/terminology, and dilemmas associated with learning, curriculum and pedagogy. It has also looked more broadly at the broader social, environmental and values context for creativity. For whilst a universalised notion of creativity may be propagated by policy makers as Part II indicated, this does not mean to say that it is unproblematic for either practitioners in the classroom or researchers making sense of teaching and learning. In the next three chapters, dilemmas and tensions are discussed and some possible responses offered.

9   Dilemmas of principle in the classroom

This chapter explores some of the issues of principle that face teachers, arguing that there are no easy ways out of any of these dilemmas, but offering some possible approaches.

Three dilemmas are proposed. First, those that arise from the perspective of creativity as culturally situated or specific. Second, those that stem from creativity as necessarily tied to innovation, novelty and, most important, the market. Third, dilemmas for the teacher that arise from the relationship between creativity and the status quo. What is the appropriate balance between creativity as a response (and, therefore, as fostering the status quo) and creativity as alternative (and, therefore, challenging the status quo)?

Dilemmas posed by cultural specificity

If creativity is culturally specific, how appropriate is it to encourage it within education?

Stimulating creativity involves encouraging learners to adopt a way of life that presents itself as universal, when we have evidence and can also argue that this is not so. Chapter 7 pointed out the promotion of a particular version of creativity as a universal is in fundamental tension with how this may relate to values connected to pupils' home and family contexts, or to their wider identity affiliations in terms of culture, or socio-economic group, or other factors such as gender.

The dilemma turns on how we define creativity. Throughout this book the notion of universalised creativity has been challenged. The concept of universalised creativity, it has been argued, is umbilically connected to the market economy. This being so, creativity is framed as having an ultimate presence in the market and being significant in innovation, change and wealth creation. It is also framed as a positive process. This, it has been argued in Chapter 8, may mask ways in which creativity can be used to destructive ends. Such ends would include not only acts of war, terrorism and violence, but also the very feeding of a market-based existence at local, global, national and international levels, which holds little respect for the natural world and which, therefore, appears to be almost blind to its limited resources.

So what does the educator do in the face of the desire (or statutory responsibility, depending on their context) to stimulate creativity in the classroom with the awareness that to do so may be to promote an approach which is both culturally saturated and hold destructive potential?

In a teaching and learning context, where perhaps fewer and fewer classrooms are homogeneous in terms of their student populations, this is a live question. And, even in classrooms which are fairly homogeneous, the question is just as relevant (in the same way that multicultural education can be seen as just as relevant in mono-cultural classrooms as it is in multi-cultural ones).

In addressing the question, though, it could be argued that education in any cultural context will involve the teaching of some concepts as if they were universal; but creativity does not necessarily have to be taught in this way. Indeed, as its very nature is about alternatives and possibilities, it offers inherent potential for evaluating the worth of any creative outcome by considering the implications of any new idea, product, service, etc. This evaluative element is one which policy makers have come to emphasise increasingly over the recent years, and, as acknowledged in Chapter 3, is named in the Qualifications and Curriculum Authority's creativity frame-work (QCA, 2005a, 2005b) as a significant part of evidence that creativity is being fostered in the classroom.

How we go about encouraging the evaluation of ideas, though, also needs careful thought and consideration, since the framework in which this occurs needs to be a wide one. So, for example, having pupils consider one another's ideas for raising money for the school fair is one possible activity which both encourages creativity and also evaluation of ideas. However, asking children also to consider what the purpose of raising the money is, and to evaluate that too, takes the evaluative framework to a more funda-mental level. As educators, then, we need to pay attention to how narrowly or widely we set the task.

In theory therefore it could be argued that although creativity is always situated within a cultural context, by interrogating this context the assumption of cultural universalism may be challenged.

There is another, related, aspect to this too, however, and that is how we choose to 'assess' or evaluate creativity. For as indicated in Chapter 7, a narrow approach to evaluating creative activity has the effect of restricting what we value as creative, with the potential of putting up, perhaps unintentionally, gender-based and other barriers. Again, if we define creativity in a plural way, then the inhibition of the creativity of some in the classroom and beyond should be avoided. Thus, if we accept the lifewide notion of creativity (Maslow 1970; Craft 2001a, 2001b, 2002), and acknowledge the significance of situating tasks which demand and assess creativity, then in the classroom we are led away from de-contextualised tasks and into viewing all learning activities as offering potential for learner creativity. We can also be sensitive to possible gender bias in our own attitudes to what 'counts' as creative, considering whether we have implicit expectations based on our own gender or that of pupils we work with. We still have a great deal more to learn and understand in terms of gender and creativity, which is even more reason to be especially reflective about our own expectations.

Dilemmas posed by the 'throw-away society'

How appropriate is the implication that creativity is seen as a good thing for the economy, for the society and, therefore, for education? As discussed in Chapter 8, implicit in this is the idea that innovation, change and novelty are, of themselves, positive: that the old, or the borrowed, the inherited and the unchanging are of lesser value compared with the new, which is, by contrast, of paramount value, simply (perhaps) by virtue of its newness.

Creativity (in the sense of the process that leads to constant change and innovation in products) contributes toward the economy, in that having a product with a short shelf life means increased sales and creates market demand. Some initiatives set up by policy makers are explicitly intended to nurture the relationship between creative ideas and the development of the economy. Creative Partnerships is one such initiative, although it also aims to provoke debate around creative classrooms, creative teachers, creative partnerships and to invoke the long-term and sustainable development of creativity in pupils, teachers and partner organisations (Creative Partnerships, Slough 2004a, 2004b).

Direct implications

But how far is it appropriate for this fostering of creativity to occur without critical reflection on the environmental, social and other consequences there may be in treating the 'market as God' in this way? With regard to the implications for the classroom, these may be both direct and indirect.

To take the direct implications first; at times, pupil creativity may be fostered in the context of business enterprise; however, this, for most pupils, is a small part of their experience of creativity in education, and for some, depending on their age and context, they may experience none. For those that do experience creativity through having or exploring ideas which are directly market related, the concern with a value-neutral approach to this could be countered by the consideration of potential impact of any idea, from a range of perspectives. So, children encouraged to develop an idea for the school fair might be encouraged to think about the potential costs and benefits of their idea, for different people and from different perspectives. A fortune-dipping stall in which children find sweets could be explored in terms of dental and general health, and also age appropriateness; having identified some of the costs involved in the stall, children might consider ways of transforming these to benefits. (How would the inclusion of different prizes address these concerns and what other issues could this raise, e.g. would the price of each turn be affected?)

Indirect implications

Exploring indirect implications helps children to be aware of some of the environmental impact of their creativity, which is connected in a much more remote way to the marketplace, both as producers and consumers. On one level, children and teachers are well used to being careful with resources: cutting out from the edge of paper, felt, etc. and thus maximising the options for how the rest of it could be used by other people. However, there are also more radical ways in which children can be engaged in considering the environmental impact of their creativity, including being aware of the resources that they use to make things. Many practitioners, particularly in the early years and primary education, reuse and recycle resources for all kinds of learning purposes, e.g. using clean yoghurt pots, packaging and old boxes to make models, using fabric offcuts to explore the properties of materials, using cardboard packaging to make simple weaving looms, using found objects or even growing matter to create drums, chimes and wind instruments. In some of these cases, a part of the learning experience is to become aware of our impact on resources, and on the potential for reusing them to creative ends. In others, the environmental impact is a side issue. But could potential environmental impact be more centrally woven into the ways in which we promote pupil creativity in education? This would include not only children evaluating their creative ideas with reference to what resources they use or would use, but would also, when appropriate, go back to whether the idea was needed.

This latter point is an important one, for it is through evaluative activity that we can bring critical scrutiny to bear in creative engagement. The role of evaluation is certainly acknowledged in the framework offered by the QCA (2005a, 2005b). But rather than seeing evaluation as occurring at the end of a creative process, in many creative processes it is appropriate for critical engagement to occur during the process too. Clearly, there is a fine balance between 'letting go' and potential 'judgement', as Claxton and Lucas (2004) discuss. Their exploration is in the context of the tool 'brainstorming' that we often use with older pupils, and also adults, to generate ideas; their critique of this process includes a number of components, the most relevant to this discussion being that brainstorming is, in part, unhelpful because it involves no judgement at all. And yet, many brainstorming sessions do lead to some ideas being taken forward—but perhaps not the most exciting, innovative or thoughtful ones that could have been developed. Had they been interrogated more thoroughly at the point of being named, as happens in the Synectics process (Nolan 2004) then we might be more likely, Claxton and Lucas (2004: 150) suggest, to come up with something 'exciting or innovative...a really good idea which goes to the heart of a tough issue'. Critical scrutiny and evaluation does not necessarily have to involve others, but it does have a central role in enabling creativity which takes account of its possible environmental consequences.

All of the discussion about environmental awareness has so far focused on children as producers. A further fundamental question to consider in relation to children producing ideas and other outcomes, as raised in Chapter 8, is how the decoupling of creativity from innovation could alter the terrain. The drive to produce new ideas which go into some sort of production and ultimately to the market, could be seen as an emphasis on innovating, rather than on being creative; an implicit assumption that one leads to the other and that this is somehow 'a good thing'. A creative response at this point in environmental degradation could be to question the notion of the two being inevitably linked. This, too, as with other ideas already discussed in this chapter, could shift fundamentally the ways that we explore creativity in the classroom, again bringing into sharp focus the *impact* of ideas.

Moving away from children as producers, the same arguments can be made for children as consumers. How far are children aware of their impact on the environment through accepting, without critical scrutiny, the constant innovation, new-is-good, throwaway context in which they live as consumers? How far should our work in the classroom encompass this, too? This is as important as exploring one's own direct impact on others. This could be as simple as discussing the issues involved in putting packaged plastic toys in breakfast cereals to make the product more interesting to small children (and to draw them into the purchasing decisions in a family), or as complex as finding out more about the invention of genetically modified foods, and their implications from different perspectives. Bringing active, critical scrutiny to the perspective of being a consumer, or to what is often 'taken as read' could, then, be seen as a significant element in promoting creativity in education. In England at any rate, there is a long history of fostering this kind of thinking in school pupils, both in policy making (NCC 1990) and in commentaries (Cathcart and Esland 1990; Craft and Pearce 1991; Greig *et al.* 1987; Hodkinson and Thomas 2001; Steiner, 1996).

Creativity as feeding or challenging the status quo?

Fostering creativity in the classroom could contribute to children participating as consumers in the market, as suggested already earlier in the book and in this chapter. But fostering children's creativity could also lead to challenges to the status quo, in part by exploring consumer perspectives, and in part through openness to new possibilities which may go beyond an overarching capitalist framework, and which could potentially lead to alternative modes of existence.

So, a further dilemma faced by the educator is how can classroom pedagogy reflect the schism between the assumption that creativity leads to increased wealth and the celebration of creativity as the 'Other', or as the potential for the 'Other'. In other words, how can we offer pupils opportunities to make sense of and develop relevant skills and experience to enable them to participate in the local and global economies, and to develop disciplinary understanding, whilst also offering them opportunities to challenge conventions, including those underpinning a market-related conception of creativity?

Eisenman (1991) reminds us that there is another sense in which creativity potentially challenges the norm, through what may be seen by others to be 'deviant' behaviour. As he puts it, 'society does not take kindly to the original person, unless his behaviour can be clearly defined as part of the ongoing social process' (Eisenman 1991: 223). This begs the question of how something is defined as creative, for unless the agent of creativity can persuade their audience that their idea is useful, then it may not be accepted.

Along with what Carnell and Lodge (2002) suggest are the other 999 interactions a teacher may engage in during any normal teaching day, a question of judgement, when faced with a pupil exhibiting creative behaviour, may be: 'Is that idea or behaviour creative, or naughty, or both, or neither?' And we may in fact encourage out-of-the-box approaches and so encourage walking the fine line that separates rule-smashing with respectful rule-shifting and bending. Children can, of course, engage in this evaluative process also, considering their own ideas and those of others with critical scrutiny. But if we are to encourage creativity, then ultimately we have to accept, as Eisenman (1991) points out, that creativity threatens the existing order.

The ways in which we respond to this dilemma are also, as with so many aspects of our decision making in pedagogy, influenced by our own core values.

One continuum of core values may be seen as the spectrum between inventions/ideas that develop the current ways of doing things and ideas that could challenge the status quo. Examples of the former might include offering Foundation Stage or Key Stage 1 children the opportunities to transform a home corner by providing a range of resources, or encouraging contributions to a wall display, a musical accompaniment to a known story or ways of representing extreme weather in scientific and artistic forms of representation, using the outdoor environment to construct a living saga. Examples of developing current ways of doing things with older pupils might include offering Key Stage 3 pupils the opportunities to research, plan and help organise a school visit, or offering Key Stage 4 pupils the opportunity to write, produce and stage a school play.

By contrast, ideas which could challenge the way things are currently done might include encouraging nursery or primary children to come up with new ideas around classroom or school organisation and the way time is used, asking children to find alternative ways of combining numbers, or inviting them to develop constructive critiques of their own and others' ideas and their outcomes. Some of these could also be appropriate with older pupils, e.g. generating their own ideas about school organisation. Other examples might include charging secondary pupils with the responsibility of weighing up the pros and cons of the traditional school visit format, and, given some parameters such as learning objectives and budget, setting them the challenge of proposing, critiquing, working on and then organising an alternative style visit, to include the evaluation of it afterward. Or, it might include encouraging pupils to innovate in their end-of-term production, by being required to, perhaps, introduce some sort of dissonance, or by considering the role of the audience, or by considering where the production could be sited, and so on.

Another continuum of core values, which cuts across the status quo/ challenge one, may be represented by a spectrum that is concerned with ideas for 'the social good' at one extreme, and ideas 'for the personal good' at the other. Examples of encouraging ideas for 'the social good' might include working with children to come up with ideas for developing the outdoor or indoor space of the school – or even of the community. Ideas 'for the personal good' might include encouraging children to work at taking the next steps, both individually and in collaboration, in a range of contexts that might, for example, include model-making, story invention, scientific investigation, or exploration with water and sand.

Clearly, teachers' own professional judgements will dictate the balance between the maintenance of and the challenge to the status quo; but if creativity is to be truly creative and to offer opportunities for 'out-of-the-box' thinking, then our classrooms and schools must indeed offer the balance, and not simply opportunities for recreating what is already known or accepted.

Summing up

This chapter has discussed several dilemmas of principle, to which there are no easy answers for teachers and other practitioners in promoting creativity in schools. However, they are questions that deserve to be asked and which require some responses: creativity is not, it is argued, a panacea. In the next chapter, we explore some pedagogical dilemmas.

10   Pedagogical challenges

This chapter discusses a number of pedagogical challenges in fostering creativity, and in doing so sets out an agenda for the development of practice in promoting creativity in schools.

Three sets of dilemmas are explored in this chapter: those arising from the relationships among knowledge, the curriculum and creativity; those arising from the notion of professional artistry in the context of a technicised model of teaching; and those dilemmas which arise from the distinctions between teaching for creativity, creative teaching and creative learning.

Dilemmas arising from relationships between knowledge, the curriculum and creativity

A number of challenges arise from the relationship between knowledge, the curriculum and creativity. One set of issues arises from teacher knowledge and expertise in the relevant domain. Perhaps most fundamental is the significance of both teacher and learner developing a sufficient understanding of the domain in order to think creatively in it. A recent study of the DTI's Electronics in Schools project, designed for pupils aged 11–16 in England, illustrated a number of difficulties encountered by pupils in being creative, due to insufficient or inadequate knowledge, or where the opportunities for them to deepen their knowledge were inadequately designed (Murphy *et al.* 2004). The research team found that the following pedagogical practices limited pupil creativity:

- Strategies that prevented pupils from taking responsibility for their own learning, from making decisions and solving problems, but which instead placed them in the role of following instructions and receiving information, through spoon-feeding, or through working through the pupils' problems and offering a solution step by step as opposed to offering insights into the process of problem solving.
- Strategies that see pupils as 'receivers of information' and which assume that teacher and pupil will always make the same sense of concepts as

one another. This often leads teachers into telling pupils about abstract ideas with little opportunity for practical exploration, or making sense through experience.

- Strategies that place pupils in the role of discovering, so that pupils work out meaning for themselves, without the benefit of structured guidance and tasks. This strategy involves the teacher's role being reduced to the provision of the learning opportunities, and means that pupils are faced with drawing on their own limited experience and knowledge. It also embodies an assumption that there is some personal authenticity in the task for the learner, an assumption that is rarely checked out for validity.

Murphy *et al.* argue that such strategies result in pupils who have reduced understanding, and cannot transfer their knowledge to new situations.

To avoid such pitfalls, teachers must have a strong personal understanding of the subject they are teaching. This means developing the capacity to introduce pupils to key ideas and processes from that subject in such a way that pupils can explore, make sense and negotiate meaning. The teacher needs to be able to recognise misconceptions or difficulties and to work to negotiate meaning, such that the learner has access to the dominant beliefs of the subject area. It is only from this access point that learners can operate creatively in the subject area. It may be reasonable to expect these findings to be replicated in other subject areas and in other age groups. Indeed, evidence of the powerful potential of knowledgeable practitioners/ teachers to nurture growth in student understanding as a foundation to creative work is found in early childhood education settings (Project Zero/ Reggio Children 2001; Duckett *et al.* 2002a, 2002b; Duffy 1998). Evidence of successful work to nurture foundation understanding in disciplines and pupil creativity within and across these is also found in primary education (Beetlestone 1998; Brice-Heath and Wolf 2004; Jeffrey and Woods 2003; Woods 1995; Woods and Jeffrey 1996), and in secondary education (Craft 2003c; Sefton-Green 1999) as well as post-compulsory education (Jeffery *et al.* 2005).

In many of these examples, partnership working is a feature, with teachers working alongside practitioners, often artists, who come with expertise from beyond the classroom. From a different, but related, perspective, the notion of the teacher–artist, where the teacher is also an artist, has been well documented by many researchers (Bancroft *et al.* 2004; Brice-Heath and Wolf 2004; Duffy 1998; Jeffery 2004; Fell and Davidson 2004; Project Zero/ Reggio Children 2001) and is further explored in Chapter 11. One challenge that faces teachers and schools is to explore further what kinds of model might best facilitate the development of teachers' own knowledge. Responses to this challenge may include the adoption of sustainable partnerships with experts, models of teacher as artist, approaches to pooling and sharing teacher expertise across a school, and staff sharing expertise with others through continuing professional development. Some of this agenda was mapped out long ago (Bentley 1998), but there is still much work to be done to evolve it.

Finding the right balance between telling and exploring, between adult and learner framework, between 'knowing that', 'knowing how' and 'wondering' about these is challenging. It requires sensitivity to many factors, including individual learners' meaning-making.

So far, we have discussed some relationships between pedagogy and knowledge. But what of curriculum organisation? How can the curriculum be organised to stimulate creativity?

There are at least two ways in which this question can be approached. One concerns the kinds of knowledge that we value and recognise in the curriculum, in other words the given curriculum, or what we may consider to be the curriculum 'menu'. The other concerns the ways that practitioners organise that curriculum.

To take the question of what is on the curriculum menu first, a curriculum that is fixed, compulsory, which involves a great deal of propositional 'knowing that' knowledge, and which takes up a great deal of learning time may pose challenges to stimulating creativity – possibly more so than a curriculum that is more flexible. Indeed, Seltzer and Bentley (1999) argued for a reduction in schools' statutory curriculum content by 50% to leave more time for creative and other thinking. It could be argued, then, that the National Curriculum, given how much time it takes up, and how much propositional knowledge it contains, perhaps gives less space to creativity than the Foundation Stage curriculum does, with its greater emphasis on processes and exploration; and its greater value placed on what might be termed 'exploring how'.

The National Curriculum approach to knowledge has been called a 'realist' one (Burwood 1992). This means that it makes a virtue of public knowledge, reducing the significance of socially constructed meanings. Woods and Jeffrey (1996) argue that the personal construction of meaning is essential to creative thinking. Nevertheless, in their ethnographic study of the art of teaching in primary schools, Woods and Jeffrey demonstrate how some primary teachers succeed in transforming knowledge which is both onerous in terms of quantity and also public in terms of who 'owns' it, into personal knowledge through a range of strategies, which include:

- *Sharing and creating knowledge.* Woods and Jeffrey describe whole-class teaching where children offer ideas and perspectives to facilitate the development of an idea or technique. They describe teachers using this strategy as sharing the process of education with the children.
- *Possibility knowledge.* This involved teachers encouraging children to speculate, to play with one another's speculations and not to close on conclusions until the ideas had been explored to everyone's satisfaction. Examples they gave of such explorations included 'Is the tooth

fairy real? How does she carry the money? Why do racists behave the way they do? Why do we need trees? Is everything you see on television true? What can you tell about the person in this portrait?' (Woods and Jeffrey 1996: 118).

- *Prior knowledge.* This means building on what the children already know – often derived from the home experience or culture. Teachers who succeeded in mediating public and personal knowledge began from children's existing perspectives. Even the naming of topics for exploration drew on personal language rather than the public subject area language.

- *Shared puzzlement.* By joining in the thinking process and demonstrating their own puzzlement about phenomena, the teachers in Woods and Jeffrey's study altered the power differential between themselves and the children. As they put it: 'They look out at the world together and surmise about the future...' (Woods and Jeffrey 1996: 119). By engaging in this way and in the other ways described above, Woods and Jeffrey (1996: 119) suggest that teachers demonstrate their concern that 'a variety of knowledges are legitimated and valued, and that the nature of knowledge in political and power terms is confronted by their pupils'.

- *Valuing pupil knowledge.* The teachers in the Woods and Jeffrey study had a holistic view of their pupils, 'one that sees them as persons, to whom school is but one situation and experience in their lives' (ibid.: 120). This is perhaps an obvious point and maybe less surprising to an early years practitioner than to a primary teacher, but one which is very significant in how children's ideas are taken on in the classroom, and what space there is for them. The teachers in their study valued children's knowledge partly as an entry route to the public knowledge, but also to enhance pupil self-esteem. This included valuing home languages and cultures as much as other knowledge and perspectives that the children brought with them.

- *Developing 'common knowledge'.* Woods and Jeffrey take this term from Edwards and Mercer (1987), who use it in the context of teachers and pupils developing a shared knowledge in the process of teachers helping pupils move from the known into the unknown – or in Vygotskian terms, into the 'zone of proximal development'. The development of common knowledge in the classroom in relation to mediating 'public knowledge' encompasses, Woods and Jeffrey suggest, many aspects of the child's identity in relation to the 'public knowledge' or the given curriculum. It is through developing common knowledge that teachers can help pupils to make sense of the given curriculum.

- *Problematising knowledge.* By encouraging pupils to share knowledge and perspectives with one another, the children in Woods and Jeffrey's study were encouraged to problematise knowledge, to see it as dynamic and shifting, and also to understand their role in both creating and making sense of it.

We have evidence, then, that where the curriculum menu on offer is a form of public knowledge, rather than being personally mediated, successful primary teachers can find ways of supporting children in making their own meanings and bringing their own personal knowledge to bear on it. Although we may be tempted to surmise that this mediation of given knowledge is less common in secondary and further education, we also have some evidence that it is indeed possible (Jeffery *et al.* 2005; Parkes 2004).

It may be that other models of the given curriculum, or the curriculum menu, may be offered or defined in the future by policy makers, so that what teachers and practitioners are working with is far more relational and much less imposed. But until that time, teachers and early years practitioners face, to a degree, dilemmas and questions around how to support the development of children's knowledge in a way that is meaningful and takes account of existing learning frameworks, so that children can think creatively and generatively.

Turning to the second set of dilemmas around the curriculum, what are the best ways of organising a curriculum for creativity? The interpretation of this question, over the years, has often been based on heartfelt beliefs about the connectedness or separateness of areas of knowledge in the learning environment. Primary and early years practitioners have often argued that it is most appropriate to organise time, resources and knowledge thematically, to enable children to explore topics through several lenses (Alexander 1995; Blenkin and Whitehead 1996; Hurst 1997; Jeffrey and Woods 2003). Although the National Curriculum's definition of the curriculum in separate subject compartments led to many primary teachers and schools organising their teaching in separate subjects in order to ensure and detect progression in learning, there are also examples of schools which did not do that (Jeffrey and Woods 2003).

As discussed in Chapter 4, recent thinking, particularly at Harvard's Project Zero, around generative (or creative) thinking and subject areas notes that new knowledge is often generated through interdisciplinary work. Working (since 2000) mainly with 'expert institutions', as well as university and pre-university programmes of study, and exploring the nature of the expert 'interdisciplinary mind', the thinking of Boix-Mansilla and Gardner (2004) reminds us that finding connections between ideas and disciplines is a significant part of learning to be a generative thinker in the twenty-first century. Their work with teachers has also helped to establish possible preliminary parameters for pedagogy to enhance what they call transdisciplinary thinking. These include focusing learning opportunities around complex and often ill-defined problems, and placing disciplinary knowledge in historical context (Project Zero Website 2004). The project is moving into a systematic exploration of pedagogy at secondary school and further education level.

The Harvard team has produced initial characterizations of 'end state performances' of the interdisciplinary mind at work. These include descriptions of both explicit and implicit strategies that are used by experts in their study in order to cross disciplinary boundaries and to negotiate epistemological differences. They also propose qualities of intellectual character exhibited by these experts, such as a disposition to tackle risky and ill-defined problems and to consider alternative perspectives.

The balance that teachers have to achieve, of course, is to ensure that pupils develop sufficient disciplinary understanding to be able to make transdisciplinary connections. What some teachers and the Project Zero team may be suggesting is that it is possible to achieve disciplinary understanding through transdisciplinary work. Clearly this is more possible in the early years, primary and, to an extent and where they exist, middle school contexts. But the departmental arrangement and timetabling issues which exist in secondary schools and post-compulsory education make this more of a challenge in those contexts.

Perhaps, then, a more appropriate way of considering how the curriculum should be organised in the classroom, in terms of fostering creativity, is to consider what we are trying to achieve. Professional judgements need to be made about ways into the curriculum that offer learners sufficient opportunities to negotiate personal knowledge against public knowledge, with sufficient depth in disciplinary areas to enable them to make meaningful connections between them.

Dilemmas in the co-existence of professional artistry and centralised control

During the 1990s, English primary and secondary education underwent a period of significant reform. During this time, teaching and learning came under increasing control by government and the agencies of government. An example of these increased controls was the National Curriculum, first introduced in 1989, alongside a series of national assessments at regular points in children's school careers, that led to league tables in performance. The Office for Standards in Education (Ofsted) introduced a national system of inspections, and these too became available for public inspection and were used by parents to select schools. Education was seen as a marketplace with parents as its consumers. Schools were given far more autonomy over their own budgets, yet were also subject to performance management and self-management systems, including target setting, appraisal systems and the analysis of outputs. Although the devolution of responsibilities (particularly financial) were, for some teachers and schools, empowering, for many the effects were to place primary teachers in particular, in tension with the 'performativity' culture, particularly in relation to inspection. Many teachers felt they were being subject to a form of surveillance, which it has been argued runs counter not only to creativity, but also to professional integrity and, perhaps even more fundamentally, humanity (Wrigley 2003). Jeffrey (2003) documents the way in which a mutual instrumentalism developed between teachers and learners as they strove to meet targets and achievement levels. And yet, from the mid 1990s, alongside these initiatives came also the burgeoning of opportunities for teachers to be creative, and to foster pupil creativity.

In addition to the effects of the culture of performativity and surveillance that supported it, the *centralising of curriculum* (and also of *pedagogy*, in literacy and numeracy in the primary school) can be seen as having posed a challenge to professional artistry – and in this sense may be seen as restricting potential teacher creativity, at least in some parts of the curriculum and in some phases. The tightening of control around both curriculum and pedagogy, as well as other aspects of the management and financing of schools in England, can be seen, then, as a further paradox facing teachers (Craft 1997; Woods *et al.* 1997). For, whilst creativity was being encouraged, the means by which this and other educational goals were being achieved were extremely constraining for teachers. In response to the tightening framework within which teachers were to work, creativity became, for some, a tool for personal and institutional survival (Craft 1997, McCarthy 2001, Safran 1991, Woods 1990, Woods and Jeffrey 1996). The conflicting demands of the 'teacher as technician' model being in tension with the model of 'teacher as creative professional' aiming to foster pupil creativity were not confined to England. Sawyer (2004: 12) discusses similar pressures in North America, where the introduction of literally word-for-word scripts for teachers to read out are increasingly favoured by schools, suggesting that 'scripted teacher-proof curricula do not rely either on the teacher's creative potential or their subject matter expertise'.

So, how does a teacher balance professional creativity and judgement against the requirements to teach in certain ways? We have evidence of early years practitioners, as well as teachers and schools, who manage particularly well in relation to being creative and fostering student creativity (Duffy 1998; Craft 2003b, 2003c, 2003e; Jeffrey 2001a, 2001c; Jeffrey and Woods 2004). We have other evidence of how secondary teachers survive as creative practitioners (Wilson 2004) and how further education practitioners can stimulate very high creative achievement, at times against the odds (Jeffery *et al.* 2005).

From a socio-cultural perspective, Sawyer (2004: 12) draws on theatre studies to propose creative teaching as an 'improvisational performance', where interaction and relational engagement are necessary to the performance. He cites evidence from classrooms where conversations are evoked and sustained in such ways as to provoke creativity in pupils whilst recognising the balance between 'structure and improvisation' (Sawyer 2004: 17).

However, this is an area we are still coming to understand, and around which practitioners often face real tensions.

Dilemmas arising from distinctions and potential tensions between teaching for creativity, creative teaching and creative learning

The distinction between teaching for creativity and creative teaching was made by the NACCCE (1999) report. As discussed in Chapter 5, the more recent notion of creative learning is being theorised at present (Craft *et al.* 2005, Creative Partnerships in preparation; Jeffrey 2002, 2004a, 2004b, 2005; Jeffrey and Craft 2004).

There may be practical differences between each of these processes, which need exploration and articulation (Craft 2003b). The NACCCE (1999) report proposed that teaching for creativity would be likely to involve teaching creatively. One of the possible and perhaps unintentional effects of separating the two terms is to polarise them in some way; and, as noted in Chapter 4, in a study of an English first school, Jeffrey and Craft (2004) have explored possible relationships between teaching creativity and teaching for creativity. The argument is that sometimes both teaching for creativity and creative teaching co-occur, although at other times teachers may emphasise one over the other according to circumstances and what they see as being most appropriate. Teaching for creativity, it is proposed, may sometimes arise in situations where it was not initially intended. There is some evidence that teaching for creativity may arise in adverse conditions (Fryer 1996); however, the argument made by Jeffrey and Craft (2004) is that teaching for creativity is most likely to arise out of creative teaching. This is in part because, through creative teaching, the teacher provides a role model for learners and also because creative teaching involves a more learner-inclusive approach to the classroom and to knowledge (Jeffrey and Craft 2004).

Woods (2002) describes how creative learning arises from creative teaching, suggesting that the creative teaching he has identified in his own research could be construed as a 'reconstructed progressivism' (Woods 2002: 74). Creative teaching, proposes Woods, and as noted in Chapter 4, has four characteristics or properties: innovation, ownership, control and relevance (Woods 1990). Creative teaching, he suggests, leads to creative learning through the enactment of these four properties, as follows.

- *Innovation.* This involves the creation of something new; a 'major change' (Woods 2002: 76) for the pupil, e.g. 'a new skill mastered, new insight gained, new understanding realized, new significant knowledge acquired, new ways round a problem found' (Woods 2002: 76). The idea is that a major shift is effected rather than a gradual one.
- *Ownership of knowledge.* Here, the point is that pupils learn for themselves and not for others. As Woods (2002: 76) puts it, 'Creative learning is internalized, and makes a difference to the pupil's self'.
- *Control of learning processes.* Here, the idea is that the learner is self-motivated and not governed purely by extrinsic goals or rewards.

- *Relevance*. Teachers do their best to offer constructions of knowledge which relate to children's knowledge and interests, so that they 'construct knowledge that is meaningful within the child's frame of reference' (Woods 2002: 77).

Although Woods argues that creative teaching leads to creative learning, there are at least two problems with his account. First, it is not clear how the one leads to the other, and whether it is always the case. For, it is conceivable that a teacher's own creativity may, if not thoughtfully applied with clear learning intentions, expand to diminish the creativity of others around them.

Second, these four features do not necessarily help us to conceptualise the notion of creative learning in totality. Where, for example, would we place the notion of enabling children's 'possibility thinking' (Craft 2002) within Woods' framework? One response would be to see Woods' framework as focusing on the processes of pedagogical engagement, and the notion of possibility thinking focusing on capturing what creative learning actually is (and a current research project involving several researchers and several teachers working collaboratively is exploring just these issues; Craft *et al.* 2004c, Craft *et al.* 2005b). Jeffrey (2004b) takes the Woods framework further in exploring creative learning, recognising, for example, ways in which pupils are offered opportunities to make relevant contributions and relevant connections, to develop relevant strategies, and also ways in which teachers offer pupils control in decision.

What should be clear is that these interrelationships between creative teaching, teaching for creativity and creative learning are still being explored and defined. Teachers and schools are, therefore, faced with the challenge of refining and elaborating the ways in which we can understand and enact these approaches to teaching and learning. And, clearly, just one aspect of the challenge is the recognition that our approaches may well be socially and culturally situated, as discussed in Chapter 7, and that our actions may have an impact on our environment, as discussed in Chapter 8.

Summing up

Teachers and schools are faced with live dilemmas in fostering learner creativity. The agenda mapped out in this chapter may well not cover the whole terrain, but it has endeavoured to name some of the major challenges which not only teachers and schools, but also policy makers and researchers will need to grapple with in order to take the creativity agenda forward effectively with young learners.

11 What is left? Creative co-construction

How do we respond to the dilemmas raised by the fostering of creativity in education? This book has explored a variety of challenges that creativity poses, stemming in particular, although not exclusively, from a universalised view. Faced with such dilemmas and difficulties, what is our response as educators? This chapter explores a possible framework that could support the development of creativity in schools. It argues the case for the fostering of creativity to form a core part of the education process and calls for greater attention to be given to the notion of LifeWork – the multiple perspectives involved in creative excellence both 'facing in' as well as 'facing out'.

Posing the question

How do we respond in the classroom, to at least some of the challenges raised by problematising creativity? It could be argued that many, if not all, of the problems posed by creativity arise from a universalised perspective, which implies that creativity is uniform across time and space, and that it is also unquestionably A Good Thing. We might, then, be led to question, as this book has done, whether creativity is indeed 'A Good Thing' to foster in the classroom. And yet, in a sense the question is an unhelpful one. For it is perhaps undeniable that generative thinking is a core human attribute. Human beings seem, too, to manifest creativity even in the most unlikely and oppressive circumstances; we only have to look at the history of war, civil disruption or famine, for example, to see many examples of creativity on the part of those who suffer, and also in many instances on the part of those responsible for suffering.

If creativity is a human attribute, then we could expect our harnessing, nurturing and exploration of it to form an appropriate part of what we do in schools. However, the book has raised many questions that may be addressed through paying attention to *how* we go about promoting creativity in the classroom.

The framework offered in this chapter explores the role of creative partners, models of artistic and creative engagement, and the role of critical scrutiny in the classroom in the context of the active ethical and social environment into which new ideas are born, and also in the context of creativity as core to being human. It is this latter notion that we begin with.

Creativity in relationship

Early studies treated creativity as if it were an individual attribute (Guilford 1950; Torrance 1987, 1988; Plucker and Renzulli 1999), although recent work has situated it in systems. Csikszentmihalyi (1988, 1994, 1999) suggests that creativity is only deemed to be so by recognition of a field of experts. Simonton's (1984, 1988, 1999) historiometric work examines creative individuals in their historical context, Sternberg and Lubart (1995b) propose an economic metaphor of creativity as investment, and there are others (e.g. Williams and Yang (1999)). Situating creativity as emerging from systems implies that it has something to do with 'being in relationship'.

But how might we understand creativity in a more holistic, connected and perhaps even constructive sense of relationship? We see such a model in the work of the inspirational physicist David Bohm (Nichol 1998, 2003), who suggested that the 'general mess' (Nichol 1998: 18) in society is a consequence of so few of us being able to grasp a holistic position on our place in the social and physical world and in individual and collective consciousness. Thus, we create partial 'order', which comes into conflict or tension with other partial 'orders'.

For Bohm, true creative acts come from recognising difference and similarity: 'one first becomes aware ... of a new set of relevant differences, and one begins to feel out or otherwise note a new set of similarities, which do not come merely from past knowledge, either in the same field or in a different field' (Nichol: 1998: 16). But this also comes from a place which involves connection with other individual and collective thought; if it does so, he suggests, 'This leads to a new order, which then gives rise to a hierarchy of new orders, that constitutes a set of new kinds of structure. The whole process tends to form harmonious and unified totalities, felt to be beautiful, as well as capable of moving those who understand them in a profoundly stirring way' (Nichol: 1998: 16).

Although here he is referring to what might be called 'big c creativity', shifts in conceptualising the world and the interrogation of similarities and differences are processes he advocates in developing any level of creative thought. His contention is that small steps that are undertaken without reference to other frameworks have the effect of stagnating our capacity to truly be creative, and destroy the harmony and totality of true creativity. The process of creative engagement, he acknowledges, is confusing and can be painful, but cannot be undertaken through formulae and techniques. He suggests 'Certain kinds of things can be achieved by techniques and formulae, but originality and creativity are not among these. The act of seeing this deeply (and not merely verbally or intellectually) is also the act in which originality and creativity can be born' (Nichol: 1998: 26).

Bohm, however, argues not only that interrogation, or 'dialogue' as he calls it, is essential to a new creative order. Bohm and Peat (1989) also propose that generativity, or the development of new ideas, at an explicit level (the 'explicate order'), is born of a latent 'implicate order', which is in turn informed by a super-implicate, or second-level implicate, order. Wider societal consciousness can be understood in these terms also according to Bohm, so that the overt activities, individuals and artefacts are the explicate order of social consciousness. At the first-level implicate order is 'the pool of knowledge it has accumulated for millenia' (Nichol 2003: 289), and beneath this, at the second-level implicate order, are 'the values and meanings that inform the pool of knowledge with specificity and order, giving rise to dispositions, intentions and actions that unfold into the explicate social order' (Nichol 2003: 289). The significance of Bohm's model is the need for collective and intersubjective thinking to really produce coherence in generative thought. As Nichol (2003: 290) puts it, '[Bohm] came to feel that the efforts of scattered individuals would have only marginal effect on the generative social order, and that any enduring impact would require a collective approach, which carries the potential for exponential change'.

It could be argued that the dilemmas and tensions outlined in this book may be seen as an illustration of Bohm's 'general mess', which results from inadequately connected thinking. Bohm's framework suggests that critical engagement with ideas is essential to developing coherence. In other words, being in relationship, in dialogue, with others about our ideas and our inventions and the ways that we live our lives is core to a more balanced approach to the development of our world.

Bohm's work is very theoretical on one level, but we find similar suggestions within classroom studies. It has been argued (Sawyer 2004), as discussed in Chapter 10, that conversation situated in a discipline is necessary to the development of creativity in the classroom. Sawyer uses the notion of 'disciplined improvisation', borrowing from theatre studies, to emphasise the balance of structure and freedom in the construction of understanding, the collaborative nature of enquiry in a classroom community and the role of peer co-participation. As Sawyer notes, a particular challenge for the teacher is how to find the balance between the planned curriculum structure and knowledge goals: 'In disciplined improvisation, teachers locally improvise within an overall global structure' (Sawyer 2004: 16). On one level, it is difficult to see what might be new in what Sawyer is proposing, for, as he himself notes, 'Teaching has always involved the creative appropriation of curricula within the situated practice of a given classroom' (Sawyer 2004: 17). But he goes beyond this to emphasise the role of improvisation in fostering creativity in particular, suggesting that recognising teaching as disciplined improvisation means recognising the teacher as a creative professional rather than as a technician, and that being able to teach through disciplined improvisation requires both content knowledge and also the capacity to facilitate group improvisation effectively.

Other implications of the perspectives proposed by Bohm and by Sawyer lead us to need a better understanding of creativity as a dialogic or collaborative process. Some recent work is taking place in this area (John-Steiner 2000; Sawyer 2004; Wegerif 2004), and our understandings of how this translates into the classroom are still imperfect. However, Sawyer suggests that we could learn more as teachers from actors, using role play, verbal spontaneity, and staying 'in the moment' by building on previous comments through the 'yes-and' rule (i.e. not trying to write the whole play but being comfortable to be able to predict just one or two plot-turns ahead). The balance of remaining in touch with the goals that one has for a group of learners and enabling real conversation is clearly challenging, but it does illustrate the creativity inherent in teaching as an art.

A different sort of approach to establishing dialogue and relationship with ideas and with others in a classroom community is described by Eckstein (2004), drawing on neuro-linguistic programming. Eckstein proposes that through using the tool of 'reframing' it is possible to encourage learners (and indeed for peers to encourage one another) to see a problem or a situation from a fresh perspective in order to generate possible strategies for engaging with it. As he puts it, 'Reframing changes the original meaning of an event or situation, placing it in a new context in which an equally plausible explanation is possible' (Eckstein 2004: 39). It involves, quite literally, bringing a new set of assumptions to an existing situation, to facilitate generative thinking.

One aspect of seeing creativity as emerging through dialogue is the notion of 'being in relationship'. In one study (Craft 1997) of educators in the south-east of England, this was a theme seen as essential to genuinely fostering pupil engagement and generativity. 'Relationship' was seen as dynamic interaction, including that between learner and teacher, learner and learner, and also between teacher or pupil and themselves. It also included the relationship between the learner and the discipline itself. Creativity was construed as dialogic and not as unitary. It was seen as emerging from a constructivist framework of learning and teaching.

Disciplinary dialogue or conversation encompasses the domain in which understanding and creativity are being developed, as research by Bae (2004) illustrates. Her study of the teaching of art in early childhood education in North America suggested that children's creativity in art is mediated and enhanced through peer and adult mediation. She found that the length and depth of children's engagement was much greater when children engaged in conversations related to their art work, particularly with adults. This finding is also borne out by the work of Brice-Heath and

Wolf (2004), who explored children's creativity through art mediated by a professional artist working in partnership with a school in South East England. In each case the adult helps to guide children to new understandings, new connections and new possibilities, but in such a way that the learner constructs their own ideas drawn from and inspired by the discipline in question. And it is the learner's active engagement in making sense and making connections which is so important. This is demonstrated in a study of the 'pretend play' of children aged three to six by Gmitrova and Gmitrov (2003: 242) in the Slovak Republic, where children's creativity was far greater when adult interaction was not 'frontal direction' but rather involved 'gently facilitat[ing] playing groups, activate[ing] passive children, and allow[ing] a free-flow in the playing process'. They note that the environment was richly resourced to both provoke and support play. It was significant that 'children were free to undertake extended exploration and problem solving, often in small groups, where cooperation and disputation mingled pleasurably' (ibid.) and that although the teacher's role was unobtrusive, it nevertheless meant playing alongside children and engaging actively with their emergent ideas.

The establishment of a community of engagement is perhaps also implicit in perspectives on nurturing creativity which seek to take account of 'how ideas land'. The work of the Project Zero team at Harvard University around the notion of understanding as performance, discussed earlier in the book, offers a model whereby the creative needs of individuals are balanced against the collective needs of a group, and whereby understandings are negotiated and further developed collectively where nourishment, stimulation and support for the individual is set in the wider context of others. Applied to creativity, this classroom strategy might involve having pupils represent their ideas using certain domains of expression (for example, visual art or algebra) in order to share them as a 'performance of understanding' (Blythe 1999). Seeing how ideas how ideas 'land' and entering into a negotiation and exploration of meaning would be integral to the performance, and so the audience would be invited to offer evaluative feedback which, too, might be in the same or different form to the original performance. Feedback would not be one-way; it would be important for the creator to be able to negotiate meaning and possible implications with evaluators. Through this *interactive feedback*, an intersubjective community of enquiry and of practice would emerge, which would aim to express and deepen disciplinary understanding and to strengthen creative engagement. This strategy for fostering ethical creativity is adapted from the Project Zero Teaching for Understanding framework, in which precise understanding goals are taught through generative topics and assessed and developed through performances of understanding (Blythe *et al.* 1998; Perkins 1999).

The suggestion is that generative, thoughtful creativity in the classroom, then, takes account of the frameworks that it challenges and emerges through conversation or interaction and the consideration of potential impacts that new ideas may have. Ritchart (2002) describes the creative disposition as involving open-mindedness and curiosity. He claims that by harnessing these and other thinking dispositions in the classroom we enable learners to apply their understandings and to generate their own ideas. Of course, the underlying model of engagement needs careful thought: How far is our aim to 'battle the ideas out', as in the Western model described in Chapter 7, or to 'achieve concensus', as in the Eastern model described in that same chapter?

Thus, although we may not necessarily generate ideas in the school classroom that are domain shifting, such interaction provides a framework which both nurtures creativity and also does so in a framework that acknowledges the possible effects of creativity.

Perspectives on partnership

A further and significant dimension to developing interaction between pupils and staff is influenced and informed by partnership activity, where staff located beyond schools and classrooms seek to connect with those situated in schools to provide culturally authentic opportunities and contexts in which pupils can explore their own creativity. The presence and development of partnerships is a strong theme in current creativity work in early years settings, as well as in schools and colleges throughout England, due in part to the funding provided by the national project Creative Partnerships discussed earlier in the book. Partnership is often developed between artists and teachers, but there is also a long tradition of partnership, activity being developed between schools, local industrial and other workplaces, and the wider community in general. Much of this partnership work aims at, and succeeds in, fostering pupils' creativity.

In a case-study based approach to investigating creative partnerships, Jeffery *et al.* (2005) argue for the establishment of clear principles on which to base the partnership between teacher and (often external) artist/ collaborator. Their work is particularly focused around the creative and performing arts in a post-compulsory environment; nevertheless, the discussions raise issues common across all education contexts where institutions form relationships with groups and individuals beyond them as part of the educative process. The argument advanced by Jeffery *et al.* (2005) reflects the findings of a study undertaken by Animarts (2001), and centres on the catalytic role which artists can have when working in partnership with teachers. Both emphasise the significance of the basis of the relationship between the partners, suggesting that this should be undertaken on a mutually reflective and equal basis, where the learning process is designed collaboratively and responsibility for learning is shared, so that 'in a dialogic frame, teacher creativity and artistic creativity open up new possibilities for learners'.

Table 2 Comparing locus of control: a spectrum.

One partner has control	Shared control
Non-negotiated approaches	Approaches negotiated
Lack of shared vision	Vision shared
Resource residing with one partner	Resource seen as shared
Meaning determined by one partner	Meaning constructed

Reproduced with kind permission of Jeffery (2004).

Clearly, there are many approaches to, and models of, partnership. As Jeffery (2004) discusses, these can be seen as residing on a spectrum of control (see Table 2). At one end of the spectrum is either the external partner as the expert agreeing to provide their expertise to the insider group and determining the content, processes and outcomes, or the educational institution 'controlling' the external partner's contribution. In contrast, at the other end of the spectrum there is a shared vision of what learning opportunities will be offered, developed and possibly even delivered collaboratively.

Whichever end of that spectrum one operates in, it is certainly the case that developing relationships with external colleagues can bring valuable non-monetary connections and resources into the classroom and into the lives of learners. Jeffery (2004) notes this can lead to access for learners to extended networks that can offer opportunities for mobility and progression beyond the school classroom.

However, he also points out that there are potential power and control issues in partnerships, in that systems and procedures may in fact result in the opposite of fostering agency (or creativity). The construction of dialogic, facilitative relationships with external partners in which asking questions, listening and responding, in a quest for evolving shared goals and values, can model the engagement which such partnerships seek to offer learners. Implicit in such a collaborative model of partnership work, then, is a set of principles which values and encourages multiple perspectives and engagement with the ideas and outcomes produced by other people, in a constructive atmosphere of mutual enquiry, exploration and creativity.

The establishment of successful partnerships of this kind, though, he argues, involves careful attention to the detail of the systems that support and nourish them. This can involve forms of leadership that offer creative decision making to teachers and to artists in partnership: a democratic approach where resources follow decision making and which Jeffery calls 'redistributive leadership'.

The findings of Jeffery and co-workers (Jeffery 2004; Jeffery *et al.* 2005) and Fell and Davidson (2004) reflect those discussed by Seidel *et al.* (2001), who explored many aspects of sustaining arts partnerships in the USA. The study investigated 21 arts education partnerships in a wide mix of settings across the USA, drawing on a range of student populations, including those excluded from mainstream education as well as those firmly within the system – and including a mix of cultural perspectives, both relatively mono-cultural and richly multicultural contexts. The study concluded that:

1 *Sustaining quality was to be found in partnerships that placed the needs of pupils and schools at the heart of their intentions.* Given the perhaps inevitably competing and various priorities, needs and interests of many arts partnerships, the research team found that those which survived had, at their heart, the benefits for teachers and learners, so that this drove their organisation and implementation.

2 *Surviving arts partnerships reflect deeply held personal commitment to the educational potential of such work.* As Seidel *et al.* (2001: 3) put it: 'Arts education partnerships are created and sustained by people for whom the goal of bringing children in direct contact with art, artists, and art-making is a driving, often life-long, commitment'. Such people often hold very strong views about the positive and transformative role of arts partnerships in the community, as well as in their own personal lives and in the lives of learners.

3 *The need to listen, to learn and to change are all embraced by arts education partnerships which survive.* The research team found that those partnerships which survived were characterised by those people in key positions being talented at listening, learning and growing (though not necessarily in size); dynamic change was a given, based on heard need.

4 *A broad base of investment and ownership is essential.* Seidel *et al.* (2001) report that those arts education partnerships which were successful, encouraged ownership and investment by those beyond the initiators and primary leaders. In particular, this involved offering real control and involvement to parents and administrators, as well as to artists and teachers. The work of Jeffery and co-workers (Jeffery 2004; Jeffery *et al.* 2005) and Fell and Davidson (2004) also emphasises the need for learners to be offered control and ownership.

5 *Multiple elements of the work receive regular attention.* The research team acknowledges the complexity of arts partnerships, recognising that those that survive and thrive 'pay constant and careful attention to relationships, goals/values, leadership, funding, advocacy, educational quality and documentation/evaluation/assessment' (Seidel *et al.* 2001: 4).

The context of partnership, then, adds a further dimension to the fundamental challenges inherent in fostering creativity, and offers us, in many ways, a viable and productive forward path, in demanding and producing dialogue, and in encouraging the exchange of perspectives.

Exchanging perspectives through apprenticeship

Certainly, the establishment of genuine, authentic dialogue across perspectives in which creativity is situated seems likely to support and nurture the engagement of young people in bringing to fruition, representing and responding to their own ideas and those of others, with reference to the knowledge base that they grow out of, as Griffiths *et al.* (2004) acknowledge. They discuss the notion of 'guided participation' proposed by Rogoff (1990), often used in the context of literacy, arguing that it has strong currency for fostering creative engagement. Through their work with teachers, artists and pupils in one region of England, Griffiths and Woolf (2004) identify a cycle of learning in apprenticeship, as shown in Figure 2.

This cycle of engagement recognises the cyclical and ongoing nature of learning alongside an expert practitioner, through watching and listening, to engagement, to beginning to create, to independent creative work, and back again to watching and listening at a new level. The cycle emerged from a complex 'level-based' matrix, proposed by Nottingham Creative Partnerships, which also attempted to map out this cycle from the perspectives of artists, teachers and learners.

Thus, within Level 1, the 'Observer' level, the artist demonstrates, performs and exhibits; the teacher draws learners' attention to aspects of each of these, and takes a lead in helping learners to interpret and explore finished work, through discussion often; and learners watch an artist at work, see or experience the finished work, and pose questions about it. Examples might include pupils going on a visit to the artist's workplace, visiting an exhibition or watching a performance, or having

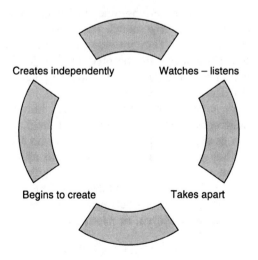

Figure 2 The cycle of learning in apprenticeship (reproduced with kind permission of Griffiths and Woolf (2004)).

an artist visit them in school to demonstrate how they do their making or performing.

At Level 2, the 'Participant' level, the artist shares techniques and skills, encouraging pupils and teachers to have a go too. The teacher learns alongside pupils, and supports and encourages learners as they try out new approaches, skills or techniques. The learners get to try out new ways of making, and collaborate with the artist on the tasks that are directed by the artist. They also have the opportunity to discuss what they are doing. Examples might include workshops linked to an exhibition or performance, participating in a Theatre in Education performance, learning to use a potter's wheel, or how to operate Adobe Photoshop® on a computer.

At Level 3, the 'Novice Practitioner' stage, the artist collaborates with individuals, small groups or the whole class, breaking down the work into manageable tasks/steps, conveying values and approaches from the 'community of practice' in which they work as a professional. The teacher helps both artist and learner to frame the activity, negotiating and sorting out practical issues, and supports both artist and learners during the activity itself. Learners work alongside the artist on a task that has been jointly agreed. They begin to work independently, discussing their work with both artist and teacher, being encouraged to self-correct and respond to advice. The learner begins to get a stronger sense of the professional world the artist inhabits. Examples might include children making their own individual ceramic tiles for a wall display overseen by the artist, pupils devising and performing a play with the advice of a professional dramatist, or pupils devising a CD-rom, in a template provided by a digital artist.

Finally, Level 4 is when pupils become 'Independent Practitioners'. In this version of the apprenticeship model, the artist acts as a fellow expert and offers critical evaluation. They provide support and advice, but when consulted and not necessarily unprompted by the learner. The teacher supervises activities, providing support and advice when necessary. Pupils are encouraged to decide on their own activity, or to identify their own problem requiring a creative solution. They work independently or with peers to find creative solutions, seeking expert help and advice when necessary. They act as expert practitioners to those who are less experienced than themselves. They are encouraged to adopt an appropriate language to critical evaluation and have a growing set of skills and knowledge in the arts area they are working in. Examples might be children composing music, or writing a stage show, to perform for others, writing and illustrating a book for younger children, or passing on skills and approaches to other children.

Key elements of apprenticeship models are expertise, guided participation and authenticity of task for the artist and, therefore, for the pupil, a finding which has emerged from other studies also (Jeffery 2003a, 2004, Jeffery *et al.* 2005; Craft and Joubert 2004; Craft *et al.* 2004d, 2004e; Murphy *et al.* 2004).

The teacher–artist

Integral to the evolving notions of partnership and what constitutes a partnership of high quality for fostering creativity, are the roles of teacher and artist. A feature of development work, policy making and research in the early twenty-first century has been an engagement (some might argue a re-engagement) with emergent models of artistry and teaching. To a degree this involves an unearthing of reflective practice approaches stemming from the work of writers such as Schon (1983, 1989) and Stenhouse (1975, 1979). Schon and Stenhouse both assumed and contributed to the develop-ment of a notion of teaching and learning as involving artistry, creativity, craft and skill. Reflection on and in this process was seen as part and parcel of professional practices; this perspective is sometimes evoked by those who challenge the technocratic conception of the pedagogic process which also exists in the current policy context, certainly in England and perhaps elsewhere too (Nias 1993; Woods 1993; Woods and Jeffrey 1996).

But approaches to the teacher–artist have moved well beyond the notion of teaching as artistry in and of itself, to approaches which encompass and welcome additional expertise, often in an arts area, in addition to the expertise of teaching. Thus, the model of the teacher–artist eloquently described by Parkes (2005), where the teacher is also a professional artist in their own right, is one that is evolving fast. In the same volume, Jeffery (2005) argues that the model proposed by Parkes emerges from a commitment to developing dialogical frameworks for learning which places interactions between learners, teachers and artists at the heart of learning, and which offers each participant ownership in the learning process, which itself is conceived of as a creative one. He acknowledges two fundamental issues that need to be addressed in the development of the teacher–artist model:

1   *In whose interest is the teacher's artistry?* Where the teacher is also an artist in their own right, and enters into a co-creative space, where does the artist end and the teacher begin, and vice versa? Whose interests are at the heart of the learning processes? Jeffery asks whether there may be a need at this point in the twenty-first century for the development of an ethical code for teacher–artist practices, one that frames the teacher–artist firmly within an overall code of teacher-professionalism rather than artist-professionalism.

2   *On what basis should arts-educating partnerships between artists and teachers be forged?* This is an extension of the first question; Jeffery argues that the fine distinctions in role need to be made explicit in the multiplicity of possible roles that may exist, where teachers may also be artists in their own right and employed for this reason. Thus, roles that need to be surfaced would include those of the overall educating institution, the artist who visits, and the teacher who is also an artist in their own right.

1 The teacher as artist	**2 The artist as educator**
The creative practice of the teacher has a personal and an institutional dimension: an inner conflict in the formation of teacher identity that, skilfully channelled, can be highly creative. Such inner conflict and dialogue can be characterised as play, deviance, bending the rules, engaging in dialogue with learners.	The artist's role is on the boundary between institutional learning and less formal, perhaps more 'real' and situated learning. The artist brings a portfolio of knowledge, ideas, technical skills and abilities that are complementary to those of the teacher.
3 The artistry of teaching	**4 Artistic work (process and product) as a model and educator.**
Pedagogy is fuelled by the cycle of research-planning-action-reflection theorised in the notion of reflective practice. The teacher is seen as making 'artistic', fine judgements about learning.	The skilled facilitation of participation in creative process. It involves attention to the work of making art, gives value to creative products (works of art) as exemplars, models, resources, and tools for exploration and questions.

Figure 3 Models of teacher–artist–teacher (Reproduced with kind permission of Jeffery 2005).

What Jeffery brings into focus is the potential inadequacy of the single-teacher, single-artist model and the need for us to recognise the multiplicity of conceptualisations of teacher–artist–teacher formulations, formulations that facilitate dialogue and which recognise the distinct but overlapping institutional roles and responsibilities of teachers as professional educators and of artists as makers who may become involved in the educative process as such. It is certainly a contested and developing area of theory and action; Jeffery offers a framework for both capture and analysis at this point in time. This is summarised in Figure 3.

Jeffery suggests that a genuinely effective creative partnership which succeeds in enabling learner creativity needs to operate across all of these four perspectives, but in such ways that enable the contexts of each kind of role to be debated and explored explicitly with learners, so as to engage with issues within the social, cultural and economic surroundings. He proposes that this should be done through investigative, interactive learning in spaces and places outside of the school or learning institution and also beyond the ordinary and everyday. This reflects, as he acknowledges, a community arts perspective where creative engagement is taken into a public and shared realm, facilitating relationships between learners (or apprentices) and professionals, in the case of the arts. Jeffery argues that further development of the notion of the teacher–artist could facilitate greater dialogic modes of learning, where creative engagement is related to cultural production and occurs within a mental, social, physical space that is negotiated rather than prescribed.

He proposes dialogic engagement at multiple, simultaneous, levels:

- internal (a teacher reflecting on their practice);
- between colleagues (building collaborations);
- between teacher and students;
- between teacher and visiting artist(s).

At the time of writing, Jeffery's (2004) models of teacher–artist roles and his discussion of space and place serve to remind us of how much further we could and perhaps need to take our conceptualisations of creative partnership and engagement if we were to place artistry right at the heart of educational engagement to the extent that we could entertain a transformation of pedagogic skills and practices in our classrooms.

It is remarkable how the issues addressed by Jeffery (who writes from the perspective of work done with young people beyond compulsory schooling age) are so similar to those highlighted in an international study for Arts Council England (Churchill Dower 2004). Through three in-depth case studies of arts–education partnership work in the early years of education, drawn from France, Italy and Belgium, and England, Churchill Dower documents, among other points:

- The significance of developing a shared language between teachers/ nursery workers and artists, in part through pre-service education and ongoing professional development. Modes of support included peer-to-peer mentoring, both within and across skill sets.
- The significance of developing long-term relationships between artists and educators, where the artist's role is one of cultural mediation, both learning about the setting, staff and children, but also working to find ways of engaging and inspiring each child with their art form, often challenging conventions and routines, and opening up perspectives on what children are capable of making and expressing. The development of long-term engagement between artist and setting not only facilitates the children's learning, but also allows for the involvement of parents and guardians in the creative process, so that discontinuities between home and setting are minimised.

Where Churchill Dower diverges from Jeffery's analysis, however, is in making the case for avoiding duplication of effort. She argues that improved networking and communication between regions and countries is needed, so that learning in the area of creative partnerships in the early years and development work are adequately supported by an infrastructure of continuing research, exploration and evaluation. It means, she suggests, moving beyond a local and organic growth of creative partnerships, to an approach which is more consistent. She suggests, referring back to an earlier study (Clarke *et al.* 2002), calling for improved co-ordination between early years infrastructures and the Arts Council's regional structure in England, proposing that a more coherent approach might include the development of a knowledge bank or network to facilitate learning and to encourage deeper communication and knowledge across both education and arts sectors.

Summing up so far

This chapter posed the question: If there are such fundamental tensions and dilemmas facing the process of fostering creativity, how do we respond to the challenge? Responses to this have included exploration of the notions of dialogic engagement and 'being in relationship' with ideas and creative impetus, both implicitly and explicitly; the roles of apprenticeship and artistry in creative teaching and learning. Emerging pedagogic models have been discussed in each area. What the discussion perhaps serves to highlight is the potential for greater coherence between the cutting-edge practices and thinking in these overlapping domains of seeing how ideas land, working across perspectives and developing creative partnerships. Through a greater coherence across emerging ideas and practices in these areas, we perhaps increase the possibility for more deeply addressing ethical and social engagement as we foster creativity in schools. It is to this set of issues that we turn next.

Ethical and social engagement

What kind of ethical and social environment are ideas born out of, and into? What is the impact of the ideas? And what role does ethical scrutiny play in the acceptance, or otherwise, of them?

Chapters 7 and 8 explored the social/cultural and wider ecological/spiritual environment in which creativity is fostered, and in which new ideas are born. Both chapters raised some ethical questions about the appropriateness of some of our apparent assumptions in promoting creativity in the classroom. They each suggested that, as educators, we have numerous dilemmas to resolve if we are to foster creativity in a way that has regard to the social, cultural, environmental and spiritual context which it arises from and affects.

So how might we bring an ethical and social dimension to our engagement with creativity in the classroom? One of the challenges, as Gardner (2004) notes in his work on changing minds, is to avoid adopting a 'fundamentalist' perspective. He describes fundamentalist positions as those where one refuses to alter one's perspective. He does not necessarily tie this to religion, although he recognises that some fundamentalist positions are related to faith. The fundamentalist perspective, he proposes, cannot, by definition, be creative, since it does not allow for change or development. And yet, in a pluralist and multicultural classroom some aspects of some pupils' and possibly teachers' beliefs may be fundamentalist. We have a responsibility to ensure that pupils each have the right to their beliefs. But, in a pluralist classroom and society, a part of the value set is to react to and encourage ideas that may not necessarily fit exactly with existing ones. Indeed, in a creative classroom we may not know where some of the interactions and ideas may lead. This is described by Durham (2001), who proposes fostering creativity through what she calls 'mysteries'. Durham (2001: 159) explores strategies for creating mysteries, puzzles, stories, adventures and explorations in thinking by bringing dilemmas into the classroom, recognising that they are 'intriguing, difficult, uncertain and problematic... we can never entirely solve the mystery'. For Durham, what is important is enjoying ideas, recognising that the chase is what is important, but all this in the framework of high expectations on the part of the teacher. Earlier in the chapter, the notion of Performing Understanding was explored in the context of creativity in the classroom, and it was suggested that the establishment of a community of enquiry around creativity could provide an appropriate evaluative framework which also offered significant intellectual, ethical and other challenges to all engaged in them, both initiators and audience.

But what is the wider context for any enquiry or process of creativity? Is it really possible to enable children to develop and express any ideas, even those that might offend, hurt or damage others or the world around them? For another aspect of our work in the classroom is that of shepherding pupils into the wider society, or helping them come to terms with their responsibilities and their rights as citizens. We cannot avoid the ethical dimension in our work as teachers, and we cannot avoid the ethical dimension in generative, or creative, thought either. To return to the ways in which we are evolving models of arts–education partnership for a moment, we need to recognise that the social, environmental and ethical challenges posed by fostering creativity are, in partnership work, the business and responsibility of not simply the teacher, but also their collaborators. At this point, we perhaps do not have an adequate model of creative partnership that encompasses these wider questions.

Looking wider still, and beyond the classroom itself, Gardner and his colleagues explore the notion of excellence and ethics, particularly in the workplace, in their large-scale GoodWork project. Gardner (2004: 207) argues that 'a society needs GoodWorkers, and especially so at a time when things are changing rapidly, our sense of time and space is being radically altered by technology, and market forces are tremendously influential, with few counter-forces of equal power'. For, as Gardner (2004: 212) so eloquently puts it, we can choose whether we use our creativity 'in ways that are selfish and destructive or in ways that are generous and life-enhancing'.

The GoodWork project grew, in part, out of a set of concerns close to those voiced in Chapter 8 of this book. In particular, the research team wished to question the pervasive nature of the market model, such that 'any human sphere threatens to be overwhelmed by the search for profit – when the bottom line becomes the only line that matters' (Gardner *et al.* 2001: 14). Thus, their long-term study of the professions emerged, looking first at veterans or senior figures in their professions (Gardner *et al.* 2001) and then at the dilemmas faced by younger people (Fischmann *et al.* 2004). Interestingly, the first book from the project was published just after the 11 September World Trade Center terrorist attack which shook the world, and the authors note an immediate and initial shift in the career choices of many young Americans, away from making money and toward those which we might see as socially oriented, e.g. teaching, intelligence, counter-intelligence, public services, the armed forces (Gardner *et al.* 2001).

The study is so far mainly confined to the USA; however, it does help us to understand the pervasive forces of the market and its influence on how successful veterans, and those eager to become so, go about leading their professions. It demonstrates many ways in which ethics and excellence struggle, and it reminds us that, in part due to the marketization of society, none of us is free from moral and ethical dilemmas. As educators, we have a responsibility to encourage learners to evaluate creative acts which occur both outside and inside the classroom and to bring a critical scrutiny to their acceptance or otherwise.

Establishing means for doing so is a part of the challenge that lies ahead for those passionate about fostering creativity in the classroom. Dialogic, intersubjective approaches to developing and scrutinising ideas would seem to be a powerful way forward. There are many examples of this, as discussed earlier in the chapter; another is provided by Siu and Kwok (2004), who describe young people participating in a collective, democratic and creative process to design a community resource in Hong Kong. Perspectives on their current living, learning and social spaces were documented by the young people and they then shared their needs self-identified through this process. Collective ideas for developing the community space then grew from conversations which enabled each person to share their own views and have these interrogated in a learning group; a similar notion was proposed earlier in the chapter as an application of the Project Zero Teaching for Understanding. Such strategies perhaps should form a focus for educators, researchers and policy makers to investigate the role of exchange and debate in enabling and promoting creativity with reference to its impact.

Sustainability

How can the development of creativity be sustained in an ethically responsible economic context? The United Nations Educational, Scientific and Cultural Organisation (UNESCO) argues that creativity is needed in order to find ways of sustaining economic development in such a way that cultural diversity is not suppressed in the ways that were discussed in Chapter 7. In other words, to avoid 'universalisation' of creativity, cultural diversity needs to be maintained. UNESCO (2002) favours a dynamic notion of cultural diversity, suggesting that it 'presupposes the existence of a process of exchanges, open to renewal and innovation but also committed to tradition, and does not aim at the preservation of a static set of behaviours, values and expressions'. By the same token, however, UNESCO acknowledges the importance of having long memories of our heritage, putting it as follows: 'If creativity is essential in the search for sustainability, then memory is in turn vital to creativity. That holds true for individuals and for peoples, who find in their heritage – natural and cultural, tangible and intangible – the key to their identity and the source of their inspiration' (UNESCO 2002).

The adoption of plural perspectives in our classrooms, which also afford opportunities for engagement with our cultural heritages and, through partnerships, those responsible for these, is critical to ensuring dynamic engagement between young learners and their cultural context.

Looking a little wider and at a more fundamental level, how is the development of creativity in a social and ethical context sustained? For there is no doubt that it is necessary to do so. One of the findings of the GoodWork project's work with younger people was that 'too many of the young workers... Espous[ed] a dubious brand of moral freedom – asserting that they were the ultimate judges of the ethics of their work'... (Fischmann *et al.* 2004: 182). This may reflect a 'consumer as always right' mirror to the 'market as God' model of living in so many parts of the world; and yet we socialise young people into believing that they alone are the judge of the appropriateness of their or anyone else's actions and ideas, to our peril. As Fischmann *et al.* (2004: 182) put it, 'the entire world could use many more individuals who unite their considerable personal capacities with a commitment to act responsibly, ethically, morally'. The project also explores the role of spirituality, and Solomon and Hunter (2002) suggest that bringing one's spirituality (which they see as 'a sense of profound connection to things beyond and/or within one's self' (Solomon and Hunter 2002: 39)) into one's working or public identity might be one step; this, too, could have implications for teachers and teaching.

Promoting children's creativity in the context of wider ethical dimensions of our existence is not an optional extra. As Fischmann *et al.* (2004: 182) put it: 'At a time when the world is inexorably interconnected and the potential for destruction has never been greater, a perennial concern with the implications and applications of work seems an imperative, not an option.' Seen from this perspective, finding ways of encouraging pupils to see how ideas land, to form communities of creativity, to engage in critical scrutiny of their own and others' ideas, and to expect this in any creative work must be a core part of the educator's role.

The GoodWork project is concerned with the notion of humane creativity, then, which faces out into the world of the workplace, where ideas are put in to practice in the name of, or in the context of, interconnected and intermeshed – although sometimes fractured – roles that people play in the world beyond the home. The team is concerned with supporting the evolution of thoughtful, responsible creativity among aspiring young people. Their focus is on excellence. But the argument for fostering creativity in its ethical context applies just as readily to young people who do not necessarily aspire to, or achieve, excellence.

LifeWork?

But perhaps our biggest challenge as educators is to work out how we do this, and how to do it in such a way that takes account of GoodWork that not only faces out to the world of work, but 'faces in', as it were, to our home and personal lives, too. What does creative GoodWork look like in the context of our personal (as opposed to work) identities? How does our creativity engage with needs and rights both inwardly (home and personal) and outwardly (work and public life)? This balance, or LifeWork, as I have come to think of it, may be the biggest challenge of all that creativity poses us. And as educators we are faced with a responsibility for finding the balance both in our own lives and in enabling those we teach to find it in theirs.

Postscript: Onward research and development

Four challenges

This book has posed some fundamental questions about the fostering of creativity in schools, has explored some of the implications for curriculum, learning and assessment, and has proposed a number of ways of addressing these. There remain a variety of areas which, it is argued, need to be explored empirically and conceptually, to take forward the fostering of creativity in schools in ways which adequately address these.

The challenges can be grouped into at least four areas: those issues concerned with learning and pedagogic practices, those focused on the methodology of investigating creativity in schools, framing and extending partnerships and, finally, those which are concerned with young people's aspirations to roles beyond their schooling.

Learning and pedagogic practices

Although learning and pedagogic practices in relation to creativity have been documented and explored in many contexts in recent years, as discussed in Chapters 4 and 5, there remain numerous areas that are under-researched. Four in particular seem significant in terms of the challenges and dilemmas facing practitioners, researchers and policy makers keen to develop creativity in education.

One of these is the question of *progression in learning*. What kinds of models of progression might be appropriate to creativity? What might an educator or creative partner expect of a learner at the ages of, for example, 3, 9, 13 and 18? How might these expectations relate to disciplinary (subject) content? How can we separate out our expectations for learner (and teacher) creativity within the disciplinary area from expectations of learner and teacher creativity which crosses disciplinary boundaries in some of the ways explored by Boix-Mansilla, Gardner and others, and discussed in Chapter 3 (Boix-Mansilla *et al.* 2003; Nikitina and Boix-Mansilla 2003)? We might consider how transdisciplinary work might provide a fruitful 'middle ground' in notions of exploring progression; in Plucker's (2004) terms, an approach which sees creativity as both content free and also domain specific. At the time of writing, a pilot study is under way (Craft *et al.* 2005a) looking to characterize creativity in three parts of the curriculum (English, music, and information and communications technology) through the learning of five cohorts of children, from pre-school through to post-compulsory education. It is hoped that this study might, therefore, begin to understand and explore some of these issues, including the depth and nature of disciplinary engagement where creative partners (e.g. artists) from beyond the classroom are involved, building on the work of Bae (2004) and Brice-Heath and Wolf (2004), as well as dialogic engagement within disciplinary areas (Sawyer 2004), all discussed in Chapter 11. However, many questions remain, not least around other disciplinary areas than the three studied this time, as well as those around interdisciplinary work. Underlying all of this, of course, is the question of culture and social context. How might models and experiences of progression in creative learning differ between social context and culture? To what extent is it possible to propose any sort of 'universalised' notion of progression in creative learning?

Related to the issue of progression is, the question of *assessing creativity*. Fryer (2000) suggests that an assessment strategy for creativity needs to:

- encompass teaching for creativity and also creative teaching;
- take affective and cognitive factors into account;
- use a variety of methods, collect information from a variety of sources;
- recognise that performance at one stage is not necessarily predictive for another;
- recognise that it is easier to assess creative achievements than creative behaviour;
- determine what criteria are to be used according to age of learner and context;
- consider the extent to which children should be encouraged to assess their own work for creativity;
- offer children the opportunity to become more creative;
- connect directly to teaching;
- be limited so as not to inhibit teaching and learning.

To this we might also add the need to be clear about how to take account of disciplinary content when we assess for creativity. If we are exploring progression in creative learning then we inevitably need to adopt strategies for assessing creativity. These will need to take account of social and cultural context and, therefore, are likely to be very different from the early approaches to assessing creativity which divorced the assessment from any wider context (Torrance 1966, 1974, 1988).

Another set of questions exists around *the balance between individual and collective creativity*, an area that Amabile (1983, 1988, 1996, 1997) highlighted and which others have continued to research (Craft 1997; John-Steiner 2000; Miell and Littleton 2004; Sawyer 2004; Sonnenburg 2004; Wegerif 2004). How do the two interrelate? How can we best harness and develop the creativity of both the individual and the collective? What can we learn from strategies such as the Performance of Understanding framework (Gardner 1999, 2000; Blythe *et al*. 1998; Perkins 1999) explored in Chapters 3, 5 and 11, about how the understanding and ideas of an individual can be enhanced by engagement with the ideas and understandings of other people? How does Eckstein's (2004) 'reframing' tool, taken from neuro-linguistic programming, and discussed in Chapter 11, foster creative engagement from multiple perspectives? How might Bohm's notion of creativity being born of collective and intersubjective engagement at explicate and implicate levels of order (also explored in Chapter 11) broaden our conceptions of what it means to engage individual and collective creativity? How might individual and collective questions be related to social and cultural context? The entire area of collective and individual engagement warrants further development and research, to better inform classroom practices.

A fourth set of questions remain live around *the nature of adult/expert engagement in nurturing creativity*, as explored in Chapter 11. How do we best frame partnership, apprenticeship, the notion of the artist and the teacher? What can we learn about models of engagement that hold critical scrutiny at their heart? And how widely applicable are some of the models proposed recently regarding creative partnership in particular? For example, how widely applicable are the levels of engagement documented by Griffiths and Woolf (2004) explored in Chapter 11? How can we further characterize and understand notions of expertise, guided participation and authenticity of task for artist and pupil, as documented by Jeffrey and his colleagues (CLASP 2002) and Murphy *et al*. (2004), also discussed in Chapter 11?

How do we further conceptualise and develop the notion of the teacher–artist as proposed by Jeffery *et al*. (2005) and explored in Chapter 11 also? How might the framework of the teacher as artist and the artist as educator be further characterized through documentation of practice, in all phases of school education? How do we further document and nurture the development of shared language as discussed in Chapter 11 and as highlighted by Jeffery *et al*. (2005), and also by Churchill Dower (2004), at interestingly different ends of the school education spectrum? All of these questions and the possible responses to them are, of course, situated in social and cultural context, which itself may be affected by the findings of studies that address these questions. For example, how might we need to reconceptualise the role of the classroom teacher in nurturing creativity, in light of emerging notions of artistry and partnership? And how do we explore the questions of ethical, social and environmental responsibility in fostering creative engagement when these are shared in a creative partnership between teachers and artists?

All of these, then, are areas for further development and research in terms of learning and pedagogy. What of methodology?

Methodologies for investigating creativity in schools

Methodology for exploring creativity in schools has expanded in recent years, perhaps reflecting generalized changes in educational research cultures, certainly in Europe and perhaps, increasingly, globally too. The major shift has been toward an emphasis on trying to capture the complexity and minutiae of social and other interactions which form the lived experiences of those in the research site. As Denzin (1994: 83) put it, this approach goes 'beyond mere fact and surface appearances... [presenting] details, context, emotion, and the webs of social relationships that join persons to one another'. This generalized move to qualitative (characterizing) methodologies, either in place of, or often alongside, quantitative approaches, has led to the expansion of methods adopted by researchers, as well as an extension in perspectives.

Methods include an increasing focus on the anthropological method of ethnography (used in a number of landmark studies in English research since the late 1960s; e.g. Ball 1981, 2003; Filer and Pollard 2000; Gewirtz *et al.* 1995; Hargreaves 1967; Jeffrey and Woods 2003; Lacey 1970; Pollard 1985; Reay 1998; Willis 1977; Woods 1990, 1993, 1995; Woods and Jeffrey 1996), in which long-term immersion in the research site is seen as essential to the documenting of experiences in it. Aside from the ongoing debate regarding credibility between champions of the quantitative and qualitative approaches, numerous challenges face those adopting qualitative approaches. As Jeffrey and Troman (2004) argue, ethnographic approaches can be seen as distinct from other qualitative approaches in their depth and in terms of the amount of time that has, classically, been involved in this approach.

The qualitative approach in part reflected an increased concern to represent and attempt to understand perspectives on any given situation, leading to expansion of perspectives addressed in terms of whose viewpoints are explored. In common with other educational research, children's voices have been more commonly documented (Burgess-Macey 2004; Burnard 2004; Craft and Joubert 2004; Cullingford 2004; McAuliffe 2004; Vass 2004a, 2004b; Jeffery *et al.* 2005; Jeffrey and Woods 2003). Other adult perspectives, such as that of the creative partner, or artist (Best and Craft 2004; Griffiths and Woolf 2004), the teacher (Grainger 2004; Haydn *et al.* 2004; Jeffery 2004) and that of the student teacher (Taylor and Clark 2004) have also been a focus of documentation in recent times.

The continued exploration of methodologies appropriate to documenting creative learning is ongoing and, among other initiatives, was the focus of an international symposium held at Cambridge University in April 2005 (Burgess-Macey and Loewenthal 2005; Chappell 2005; Cheng and Lau 2005;

Churchill-Dower 2005; Craft *et al.* 2005b; Gabel-Dunk 2005; Hope *et al.* 2005; Martin 2005; Ng 2005; Raggl 2005; Smythe 2005; Spendlove and Wyse 2005; Vong 2005; Wai-Yum 2005). The international grouping of scholars and teachers seeks to explore answers to the 'what', 'how' and 'why' of documenting creative learning. One hope for this group is that it may surface some of the social, cultural and ethical issues with which this book has been concerned, in order to compare perspectives on them. The documentation of creative learning, and the ways that it is situated, certainly warrants greater attention in the coming years.

Creativity and aspirations beyond school

A knowledge-based economy, and an increasingly global emphasis on creativity, encourages young people to aspire to creative engagement with opportunities to shape ideas and develop personal pathways and journeys beyond their schooling. This may involve young people in choosing paths that diverge from conventions, or from what their peers select, or both. What do we know about the issues experienced by young people in this process of choice and in becoming visible?

Some exceptional young people are offered tailored opportunities to develop their talents, e.g. Ignite!, a state-funded programme for exceptional young people aged 10 to 21, in England. This particular programme, funded by NESTA, offered a combination of residential Creativity Labs (for 10- to 15-year-olds) and Creativity Fellowships with mentors and creative advisers built in (for 16- to 21-year-olds) was researched, in its first (and pilot) year by an Open University research team. Among the findings was the issue of choice and visibility for young people choosing to be different (Craft *et al.* 2004e).

The accounts of the 10- to 15-year-olds highlighted the need to overcome fear of failure and feeling self-conscious; leaders of this group experienced challenge in fostering feelings of pride and self-confidence. The theme of needing to overcome a fear of exposure, of feeling isolated, lonely and frightened (of not succeeding, of their outcomes not being liked, of being judged) was present within the 16- to 21-year-old group also, although less prominent. In addition, there was a significant minority of young people who were selected for participation in the programme who ultimately chose not to participate. Initial explorations revealed that, for this older group too, visibility may have been a factor, not only for the young people themselves but sometimes also for their families (who sometimes perceived that participation in this scheme could have implications in other ways, perhaps particularly economic where being involved in a government-sponsored scheme might affect a hitherto invisible informal economy).

The theme of visibility for the young people themselves is also present in another, current, study of inner city teenagers being offered opportunities to work through a contemporary art venue with a variety of artists

(Craft *et al.* 2004d). Initial evaluation data revealed that in this programme, Image Conscious, also funded by NESTA, many young people experienced anxiety about being in the public eye. Some, but not all, of this seemed to be related to the public exhibition/dissemination that each was encouraged to create as part of the experience and process. For some, local peer pressures were also significant, particularly where participation in the programme at all was affected by rivalry between friendship groups – both geographically and socially anchored.

These kinds of issues could be probed further, not only for those young people considered to be exceptional, but also for the majority. What kinds of challenges and dilemmas do young people, particularly those in their teens, face when selecting creative courses of action? How does peer pressure and identity impact on creative choice? How might choices and actions be affected by how young people view themselves in relation to their peers, and what other sorts of influences might there be on which choices and options are taken up and which are not?

Related to this are the questions of ethics and excellence. For young people who aspire to excel creatively in a chosen area, what sorts of moral and ethical dilemmas do they face?

There are various potential lines of enquiry here. These might include documenting the kinds of 'creative courses of action' that young people choose, and the extent to which these courses and choices are imbued with dilemmas relating to, for example, peer group values, individual identity and wider ethical issues.

We know, from the work of Fischmann *et al.* (2004), about the kinds of issues faced by young people aspiring to do work which is both ethical and excellent in journalism, genetics and acting. This work forms part of a wider study exploring these issues in a wider group of professions, including medicine, law and philanthropy (Gardner *et al.* 2001). The work of Fischmann *et al.* does highlight the significance of peer influence over ethical decision making and the decreasing influence on young people of influential, 'heroic' public figures. It appears that for the young people in their study the radar circle of influences on their decision making is altering to include those physically close (teachers, family members). Interestingly, in this study, some young people cited no hero influences beyond these at all, and others gave examples from sport or entertainment (where, as Fischmann *et al.* (2004: 170) point out, 'moral caliber may be low').

Further lines of enquiry might include probing the *sort of moral/ethical model* that may lie behind such choices. For we can debate the so-called 'stages' of moral development posited by Kohlberg (1981, 1984), through which young people pass without fail (a model based on the Piagetian model of logical – mathematical cognitive development (Piaget 1932; Piaget and Inhelder 1969). The Kohlbergian approach stands in contrast to that proposed by Gilligan (1982), who claimed that this is a masculine model – indeed, it is based solely on studies of male subjects. She suggests it is not applicable to girls and women, for whom an ethic of care is dominant, and offers her own stage theory of moral development for women. It has, like Kohlberg's, three major stages: pre-conventional, conventional and post-conventional. However, according to Gilligan it is changes in the sense of self, or in personal identity, that fuel the transition between stages, rather than, as Kohlberg had argued, changes in cognitive capability. Gilligan's approach is based not on a 'developmental' approach, but rather on one which modifies Freud's approach to the development of the ego – the personal identity. One of the contributions that Gilligan's work has made is in helping us to realize that there may be more than one way of looking at the development of moral or ethical decision making. Although Gilligan's critique is not accepted universally (Crain, 1985), it has certainly reminded us of the influence of the explanatory models that we may be using even unconsciously to explain behaviour.

And bringing that back to the question of the sorts of dilemmas that young people may face in making creative choices, clearly the model that we use for how moral or ethical behaviour is conceived of *and* how it develops will affect the way that we make sense of how young people make 'creative' choices and what influences these.

There are also other issues that we understand little about. These include gender roles and parenting. It could be argued that the expansion of equality of opportunity in the world beyond the home for both women and men leads to a further set of dilemmas as creativity is poured into contexts that could be described as 'facing out' rather than 'facing in'. Although we are beginning to have a good sense of what might be involved in doing excellent creative work that 'faces out' – and in particular some of the moral and ethical dimensions to this (Gardner *et al.* 2001) – we have yet to document and understand the issues involved for children's creativity when their parents are both 'facing out'.

Kubo (2004) explores the fostering of creativity in Japan and Singapore. He argues that a major threat to creativity is in the subcontracting of parenting of very small children (under threes). It is an issue, he notes, that young people do not consider home-making as a viable option. He argues that, traditionally, the home was seen as the crucible of a successful economy where 'Japanese women played an important role in the family and were respected by Japanese men for their dedication and devotion to taking care of children of the next generation . . . [there was] harmonious co-operation between male and female . . . housework was regarded as equally important as working for a company . . . [it was] one of Confucious' core teachings for a healthy country' (Kubo 2004: 78–9). However, nowadays, Kubo (2004: 79) suggests, 'it is unlikely that the younger generation will consider work at home, such as home management and raising children, as the foundation of human development and education, even in Japan'. In this way, Kubo documents the transference of focus for creative engagement to the external context, to include (and possibly further than merely including, actually to emphasize) for both genders the world beyond the family itself as a context for creativity.

The extent to which this pattern is found in other cultural contexts has yet to be determined. Kubo's thesis is that the transference of focus to outside of the home and family has a deleterious effect on creative engagement in the home. This appears to rest on the assumption that paid childcare workers are less able to nurture children's creativity than their own parents are. That assumption needs further testing, through careful documentation and analysis.

From the perspective of adults, how does the shift of focus affect their own creativity? For those adults who 'face out' in order to work creatively or otherwise, and thus have the dual role of worker and carer, it could be argued that this double act in itself brings demands for creativity – for survival. Equally, there is some evidence that those who aspire to creativity and excellence at work rely on strong support from those close to the creator, including those in the home (Gardner 1993). But how this shifting balance in the role of carers (traditionally, but not exclusively, women) in the twenty-first century society engages not only with gender roles and expectations, but also the creativity of all involved, has yet to be explored. Although there is increasing awareness of and concern with the general issues involved in the intersection between the economy and particularly early childhood care and education (HM Treasury *et al.* 2004), there is still little research attention focused on the interrelationships between creativity in particular that faces in and creativity that faces out.

In terms of creativity that faces out, the stories of women such as Judith Richards Hope, the first female associate director of the White House Domestic Council and in the first class of women admitted to study Law at Harvard, and others like her (Richards Hope 2003), are testimony to the creative challenges and opportunities that the dual roles bring. How might we explore this issue in relation to other extraordinary achievers like Richards Hope?

And what of those whose creativity faces in, and whose lives may be more ordinary but just as demanding? Some are beginning to ask questions about what Gardner (1993), in his study of high creators, called 'The Creator's Faustian Bargain'. These include asking what role creativity plays in the home for both children and their parents (Schwager 2005). Again, this could perhaps form a focus in the onward development and research agenda.

Framing, brokering and extending partnership

The potential of creative partnerships, between schools and creative practitioners of a variety of kinds, has been explored in various places in this book. Although the nature of relationships between artists and schools is increasingly well documented, as are the models for exploring aspects of teachers as artists and artists as teachers in development

(Jeffery *et al.* 2005), as discussed in Chapter 11, what is perhaps less well documented is what kinds of infrastructure work well in brokering, maintaining and sustaining those relationships. Some recent work begins to characterise these (Best and Craft 2004), but there is plenty more that needs to be done. Best and Craft (2004) identified a number of approaches adopted by 'Creative Friends' who were appointed from 2002 until 2003 by a region of Creative Partnerships in England, to take on a brokering role between schools and imaginative opportunities for fostering pupil creativity through the creative and cultural sectors. One particularly significant contextual theme that emerged in the data was the notion of 'framed distance'; in other words, the process of determining relational distance. The concept, taken from Dorothy Heathcote's drama-in-education work (Wagner 1979), relates to the framing of experiences and events using steps of ever-increasing distance in order to obtain a better view, or understanding, while still remaining connected.

Applying this to the role of the Creative Friend, there were complex layers of relationship and communication that impinged upon or supported the outcomes of their creative role. The notion of 'framed distance' also acted as a reminder that any one interaction or experience is framed for each person by the experiences around them; and this being the case, it may not be possible for any one person involved to see all of the potential frames at any one time. Thus, as the study explored how the different roles involved (creative friends, school co-ordinators and artists) perceived one another, so the levels of engagement emerged as a dominant theme.

Two continua of engagement were identified. The first defined the relational processes according to proximity (near to far), i.e. the Creative Friend being close, in the middle, or distant. This was the most prevalent in the way that both Creative Friends and School Co-ordinators saw the relationships formed. Descriptors for close engagement included the terms 'supportive', 'the glue that makes coherence'. In-between engagement was described as 'the conduit', the 'translator', emphasising perceptions of the 'go-between' element of the role. Descriptors for more distant engagement included such terms as *active spectator* and *strategic*.

The other continuum defined the levels of engagement vertically, with the location of the Creative Friend being either on the ground, or above the activities, i.e. in the sky with some sort of overview, or moving between the ground and sky. Examples of descriptors included *hands on* for being on the ground, *bridge* for permitting movement between sky and ground, and *hovering* for being above. The descriptors for both continua are combined within Figure 4.

The framing and development of partnership is discussed by others (Griffiths and Woolf 2004); but, as partnership work continues to evolve, to include the early years (Churchill Dower 2004) through to post-compulsory and higher education (Jeffery *et al.* 2005), scrutiny about how these relationships are set up, nurtured and sustained, how they relate to notions

CLOSE	⟺	IN THE MIDDLE	⟺	DISTANT
'holding her hand'	*'participatory'*	*'translator'*	*'lighter touch'*	*'visionary'*
				'strategic'
'getting hands dirty'	*'supportive'*	*'listening'*	*'careful distance'*	
		'enabling'		*'advisor'*
'buddy'	*'provoking'*		*'active spectator'*	
'glue that makes coherence'		*'conduit'*		*'hovering'*
		'bridge'		*'overviewer'*
'hands on'	⟺		⟺	

Figure 4 Levels of engagement proximity and verticality (reproduced with permission from Best and Craft (2004)).

of 'teacher' and 'artist' as discussed in Chapter 11, and their contribution to nurturing the creativity of all involved will continue to be important lines of enquiry, as will exploring these issues in differing social and cultural contexts.

Concluding thoughts: what is it all for?

Running through all three themes discussed so far in this postscript is the theme of what ends creativity is put to. So, in addition to further work being needed in all of these three areas, this book as a whole has been arguing that we need a closer interrogation of the purposes to which we put creativity. As educators we need to explore possible links between the means and the ends.

Possible ends for creativity, all discussed within this book, may include those focused on:

- economic development, as proposed by Robinson (2001) and Seltzer and Bentley (1999);
- alternative views of space, place and existence which argue against the globalisation which seems to be implicit in notions of 'economic development' (Amin *et al.* 2000; Massey 1999, 2005);
- community development, particularly at a local level, as exemplified by Jeffery *et al.* (2005);
- social justice, as developed by Griffiths *et al.* (2004).

There is also the question of disciplinary-focused ends. Educators need to consider the balance between disciplinary and interdisciplinary approaches;

e.g. to what extent might we use creativity for:

- the development of individual disciplinary areas, such as the use of creativity to develop learning in English, as documented by Jackson (2001); or, by contrast,
- the combining of disciplinary areas (one example being Soundproof (NESTA 2005), focusing on science and music).

This book as a whole has drawn attention to the social, cultural, ecological and spiritual dimensions of creative engagement, as a backdrop to our identification and evaluation of the ends we put creativity to, both our own and that of pupils, in our schools.

Creativity then, characteristically, poses educators with both opportunities and challenges. The maps of creativity that we can share and compare are partially drawn. Many questions remain, both about how the territory can be charted and how we make our way through it, on what informs the turnings that we take, the boundaries that we perceive and the ways that we deal with what may seem like dead-ends, highways, blind corners, vantage points and the square metre of a field for wide-awake contemplation that Tim Smit describes in his Foreword. There is much still to be learned. This book has argued for inclusive approaches to and perspectives on our map-making.

Perhaps most significantly, we must remember the potential that the creative imagination offers us, to question the parameters and to ask why we are making the creative journey at all, and, as suggested in Chapter 11, to pay serious attention, therefore, to what ends our creative potential may be serving. In doing so we might consider how we nurture each learner's own LifeWork – creative engagement that *both* faces 'in' (to home, family and self) *and* faces 'out' (to work, public life and the wider environmental, physical, social and spiritual contexts).

Perhaps this is the big challenge for teachers and schools who want to foster creativity in the twenty-first century.

Glossary

ACE	Arts Council (England)
AST	Advanced Skills Teacher
CP	Creative Partnerships (a large national creativity project in England funded over 3 years by the DCMS, Arts Council and DfES)
CPD	Continuing professional development
DfEE	Department for Education and Employment (a UK Government department, replaced by the DfES)
DfES	Department for Education and Skills (a UK Government department)
DCMS	Department of Culture, Media and Sport (a UK Government department)
DTI	Department of Trade and Industry (a UK Government department)
FS	Foundation Stage (for children of 3–5 years old) of education in England
GCSE	General Certificate of Secondary Education
ICT	Information and communications technology
KS1	Key Stage 1 (for children aged 5–7) of education in England
KS2	Key Stage 2 (for children aged 7–11) of education in England
KS3	Key Stage 3 (for children aged 11–14) of education in England
KS4	Key Stage 4 (for children aged 14–16) of education in England
NACCCE	National Advisory Committee on Creative and Cultural Education (a UK Government-appointed task force which deliberated over 2 years, and was charged with setting out the agenda for creative and cultural education in England; it reported in 1999)
NESTA	National Endowment for Science, Technology and the Arts (a forward-looking funding partially government-related body for creativity in England established through an endowment in 1998 from the National Lottery)
Ofsted	Office for Standards in Education
QCA	Qualifications and Curriculum Authority
SST	Specialist Schools Trust

References

Alexander, R. (1995). *Versions of Primary Education*. London and New York: Routledge/The Open University.

Alexander, R. (2004). Still no pedagogy? *Cambridge Journal of Education* 34(1), 7–33.

Alexander, R., Rose, J. and Woodhead, C. (1992). *Curriculum Organisation and Classroom Practice in Primary Schools: A Discussion Paper*. London: HMSO.

Amabile, T.M. (1983). *The Social Psychology of Creativity*. New York: Springer-Verlag.

Amabile, T.M. (1988). A model of creativity and innovation in organizations. In: Staw, B.M. and Cunnings, L.L. (Eds), *Research in Organizational Behavior*. Greenwich, CT: JAI.

Amabile, T.M. (1989). *Growing up Creative: Nurturing a Lifetime of Creativity*. Buffalo, NY: CEF Press.

Amabile, T.M. (1990). Within you, without you: the social psychology of creativity and beyond. In: Runco, M.M. and Albert, R.S. (Eds), *Theories of Creativity*. London: Sage.

Amabile, T.M. (1996). *Creativity in Context (Update to the Social Psychology of Creativity)*. USA: Westview Press.

Amabile, T.M. (1997). Motivating creativity in organisations: on doing what you love and loving what you do. *California Management Review* 40(1).

Amin, A., Massey, D. and Thrift, N. (2000) *Cities for the Many not the Few*. Bristol: Policy Press.

Animarts (2001). Report available at www.animarts.org.uk.

Aron, E.N. and Aron, A. (1982). An introduction to Maharishi's theory of creativity: its empirical base and description of the creative process. *Journal of Creative Behavior* 16(1), 29049.

Athey, C. (1990). *Extending Thought in Young Children*. London: PCP Ltd.

Bae, J.-H. (2004). Learning to teach visual arts in an early childhood classroom: the teacher's role as a guide. *Early Childhood Education Journal* 31(4).

Balke, E. (1997). Play and the arts: the importance of the 'unimportant'. *Childhood Education* 73(6), 353–60.

Ball, S.J. (1981). *Beachside Comprehensive*. Cambridge: Cambridge University Press.

Ball, S.J. (2003). *Class Strategies and the Education Market: The Middle Classes and Social Advantage*. London: RoutledgeFalmer.

Bancroft, S., Fawcett, M., and Hay, P. (2004). $5 \times 5 \times 5 =$ Creativity in the Early Years 2003–2004. Bath: Arts Development, Bath, and North East Somerset Council.

Barron, F. (1988). Putting creativity to work. In: Sternberg, R.J. (Ed.), *The Nature of Creativity*. Cambridge: Cambridge University Press.

Beetlestone, F. (1998). *Creative Children, Imaginative Teaching.* Buckingham: Open University Press.

Belenky, M.F., Clinchy, B.M., Goldberger, N.R. and Tarule, J.M. (1986). *Women's Ways of Knowing.* New York: Basic Books.

Bellah, R.N., Madsen, R., Sullivan, W.M. Swidler, A. and Tipton, S.M. (1985). *Habits of the Heart: Individualism and Commitment in American Life.* New York: Harper & Row.

Bentley, T. (1998). *Learning Beyond the Classroom: Education for a Changing World.* London and New York: Routledge.

Berger, S. and Dore, R. (Eds) (1996). *National Diversity and Global Capitalism.* Ithaca, NY: Cornell University Press.

Berndt, T.J., Cheung, P.C., Lau, S., Nau, K.-T. and Lew, W.J.F. (1993). Perceptions of parenting in China, Taiwan and Hong Kong: sex differences and societal differences. *Developmental Psychology* 29, 156–64.

Bernstein, B. (1990). *The Structuring of Pedagogical Discourse. Class, Codes and Control,* Vol. 4. London: Routledge.

Best, P. and Craft, A. (2004). Brokering creative opportunities: the creative friend model. Presented at *BERA National Conference,* September 2004, UMIST, in a symposium of the Special Interest Group, Creativity in Education.

Bharati, A. (1985). The self in Hindu thought and action. In: Marsella, A.J., Devos, G. and Hsu F.L.K. (Eds), *Culture and Self: Asian and Western Perspectives.* New York: Tavistock; pp. 185–230.

Blenkin, G.M. and Whitehead, M. (1996). Creating a context for development. In: Blenkin, G.M. and Kelly, A.V. (Eds), *Early Childhood Education: A Developmental Curriculum* (2nd edition). London: Paul Chapman Publishing.

Blythe, T. (1999). Approaching poetry: entry points to understanding. In: Hetland, L. and Veenema, S. (Eds), *The Project Zero Classroom: Views on Understanding.* Cambridge, MA: Project Zero, Harvard University Graduate School of Education.

Blythe, T. and the teachers and researchers of the Teaching for Understanding Project (1998). *The Teaching for Understanding Guide.* San Francisco: Jossey-Bass.

Boey, K.W. (1976). Rigidity and cognitive complexity: an empirical investigation in the interpersonal, physical and numeric domains under task-oriented and ego-oriented conditions. Unpublished doctoral dissertation, University of Hong Kong.

Bohm, D. and Peat, P.D. (1989). *Science, Order and Creativity.* London: Routledge.

Boix-Mansilla, V. and Gardner, H. (2004). GoodWork Paper 26: Assessing interdisciplinary work at the frontier: an empirical exploration of "symptoms of quality". Part of series edited by Jeff Solomon. Cambridge, MA: Harvard University Project Zero.

Boix-Mansilla, V., Dillon, D. and Middlebrooks, K. (2003). Building bridges across disciplines: organizational and individual qualities of exemplary interdisciplinary work. Cambridge, MA; Harvard Project Zero Working Paper.

Brice-Heath, S. and Wolf, S. (2004). *Visual Learning in the Community School.* London: Creative Partnerships.

Brown, S. and McIntyre, D. (1993). *Making Sense of Teaching.* Buckingham: Open University Press.

Burgess-Macey, C. (2004). Diasporic creativities: children reflecting on their learning in schools carnivals in UK and Trinidad and Tobago. Paper presented at *British Educational Research Association Conference,* UMIST, September 2004.

Burgess-Macey, C. and Loewenthal, A. (2005). Documenting creative learning in children aged 3–11: carnival. Paper presented at *Documenting Creative Learning Symposium: What, How and Why?* University of Cambridge, April 2005.

Burnard, P. (2004). Creativity and pupil–teacher voices in education. Paper given at *British Educational Research Association Conference*, Manchester, England, September 2004.

Burwood, L.R.V. (1992). Can the National Curriculum help reduce working class under-achievement? *Educational Studies* 18(3), 311–21.

Carnell, E. and Lodge, C. (2002). *Supporting Effective Learning*. London: Paul Chapman Publishing.

Camden Arts (2003). *Box*. London: Camden Arts Centre.

Carter, S., Mason, C. and Tagg, S. (2004). *Lifting the Barriers to Growth in UK Small Businesses: The FSB Biennial Membership Survey, Report to the Federation of Small Businesses*. London: Federation of Small Businesses.

Cathcart, H. and Esland, G. (1990). The compliant-creative worker: the ideological reconstruction of the school leaver. In Esland, G. (Ed.), *Education, Training and Employment, Volume 2: The Educational Response*. Wokingham, UK: Addison-Wesley Publishing/The Open University.

Central Advisory Committee for Education (1967a). *Children and Their Primary Schools (The Plowden Report), Volume 1*. London: HMSO.

Central Advisory Committee for Education (1967b). *Children and Their Primary Schools (The Plowden Report), Volume 2: Research and Surveys*. London: HMSO.

Chao, R.K. (1993). East and West: concepts of the self as reflected in mothers' reports of their child rearing. Unpublished manuscript, University of California, Los Angeles.

Chappell, K. (2005). Conceptions of and approaches to creativity in dance education. Paper presented at *Documenting Creative Learning Symposium: What, How and Why?* University of Cambridge, April 2005.

Chen, E.K.Y. and Kwang, C.H. (Eds) (1997). *Asia's Borderless Economy: The Emergence of Subregional Economic Zones*. Sydney: Allen and Unwin.

Cheng, V.M. and Lau, S. (2005). Consensual assessment of creativity in teaching ideas. Paper presented at *Documenting Creative Learning Symposium: What, How and Why?* University of Cambridge, April 2005.

Cheung, P.C., Conger, A.J., Hau, K.-T., Lew, W.J.F. and Lau, S. (1992). Development of the multi-trait personality inventory (MTPI): comparison among four Chinese populations. *Journal of Personality Assessment* 59, 528–51.

Cheung, P.C., Lau, S., Chan, D.W. and Wu, W.Y.H. (2004). Creative potential of school children in Hong Kong: norms of the Wallach–Kogan creativity tests and their implications. *Creativity Research Journal* 16(1), 69–78.

Chu, Y.K. (1970). Oriental views on creativity. In: Angott, A., and Shapiro B. (Eds), *Psi Factors in Creativity*. New York: Parapsychology Foundation; pp. 35–50.

Churchill Dower, R. (2004). *International Creative Practice in Early Years Settings – Research Report Full Report*. London: Arts Council of England.

Churchill-Dower, R. (2005). Key strategies for fostering creative learning from the earliest years – three international case studies. Paper presented at *Documenting Creative Learning Symposium: What, How and Why?* University of Cambridge, April 2005.

Clark, G., Day, M., and Greer, D. (1987). Discipline-based art education: becoming students of art. *The Journal of Aesthetic Education* 21(2).

Clarke, A., Heptinstall, E., Simon, A. and Moss, P. (2002). *The Arts in the Early Years – a National Study of Policy and Practice*. London: Arts Council England.

CLASP (2002). *Creative learning and student perspectives*. A European Commission, Economic and Science Research Council and Open University research project. Milton Keynes, The Open University.

Claxton, G. and Lucas, B. (2004). *Be Creative: Essential Steps to Revitalize Your Work and Life*. London: BBC Books.

Copland, A. (1980). *Music and Imagination*. Cambridge, MA: Harvard University Press.

Craft, A. (1997). Identity and creativity: education for post-modernism? *Teacher Development: An International Journal of Teachers' Professional Development* 1(1), 83–96.

Craft, A. (1999). Creative development in the early years: implications of policy for practice. *The Curriculum Journal* 10(1), 135–50.

Craft, A. (2000). *Creativity Across the Primary Curriculum*. London: Routledge-Falmer.

Craft, A. (2001a). Little c creativity. In: Craft, A., Jeffrey, B., Leibling, M. (Eds), *Creativity in Education*. London: Continuum.

Craft, A. (2001b). Creativity across the primary curriculum. *Teaching Thinking*. Autumn 2001 (magazine now called *Imaginative Minds*).

Craft, A. (2002). *Creativity in the Early Years: a Lifewide Foundation*. London: Continuum.

Craft, A. (2003a). The limits to creativity in education. *British Journal of Educational Studies* 51(2), 113–27.

Craft, A. (2003b). A language for creativity? Paper presented as part of *BERA Creativity SIG Creativity in Education*, Heriot-Watt University, Edinburgh, Scotland, September 2003.

Craft, A. (2003c). Creativity in education: pedagogical and conceptual frameworks. A report commissioned for Qualifications and Curriculum Authority, July 2003, Department for Education and Employment, Qualifications and Curriculum Authority.

Craft, A. (2003d). *Creativity and Learning, Study Unit 7*. Open University Course E123: Working with Children in the Early Years, Milton Keynes: The Open University.

Craft, A. (2003e). Early years education in England and little c creativity: the third wave? *Korean Journal of Thinking and Problem Solving* 13(1), 49–59.

Craft, A. (2004). Creativity in education: challenges. Keynote address at *Creative Partnerships Conference*, Plymouth, February 2004.

Craft, A. and Pearce, I. (1991). The establishment of economic and industrial understanding as a cross-curricular theme within the National Curriculum in England. In: Whitehead, D. and Dyer, D. (Eds), *New Developments in Economics and Business Education: A Handbook for Teachers*. London: Kogan Page/Institute of Education, University of London; pp. 32–42.

Craft, A. and Joubert, M. (2004). Creative learning by partnership. Paper presented at *British Educational Research Association Conference*, UMIST, September 2004.

Craft, A. and Martin, D.S. (2004). Proposal for international symposium on creative learning, unpublished working paper, April 2004.

Craft, A., Burnard, P. and Grainger, T. (2004a). Research proposal for possibility thinking in Year 1 music-making and literacy – pilot project. Unpublished working paper, April 2004.

Craft, A., Jeffrey, B. and Joubert, M. (2004b). *Let's Get Going! Evaluation of the Schools and Cultural Venues Project*. London: Calouste Gulbenkian Foundation and Arts Council England.

Craft, A., Burnard, P., Grainger, T. and Woods, P.E. (2004c). Documenting possibility thinking. Unpublished working paper, November 2004.

Craft, A., Chappell, K. and Best, P. (2004d). Evaluation of Image Conscious. Internal interim report to Image Conscious, Camden Arts Centre, North London, November 2004.

Craft, A., Miell, D., Joubert, M., Littleton, K., Murphy, P., Vass, E. and Whitelock, D. (2004e). Final report for the NESTA's Fellowship Young People project, Ignite, September 2004.

Craft, A., Burnard, P. and Grainger, T. (2005a). Research design for Progression in Creative Learning project (PICL). Funded by Creative Partnerships – internal working paper, January 2005.

Craft, A., Burnard, T., Grainger, T., Woods, P., Burns, D., Duffy, B., Leese, M., Keene, J., Haynes, L. (2005b). Documenting possibility thinking. Paper presented at *Documenting Creative Learning Symposium: What, Why and How?* University of Cambridge, April 2005.

Craft, A., Grainger, T., Burnard, P. (2005) Documenting Creative Learning: Reflections After the Symposium. April, 2005: unpublished working paper.

Crain, W.C. (1985). *Theories of Development*. Prentice-Hall; pp. 118–36.

Creative Partnerships (2004a). Creative learning. Internal working paper.

Creative Partnerships (2004b). Catalyst: This is how education should be, isn't it? Summer 2004. London, Creative Partherships.

Creative Partnerships (2004c) Creative Partnerships Website: http://www.creative-partnerships.com/aboutcp/ (last access July 2004).

Creative Partnerships (2005). http://www.creative-partnerships.com/ (last access 26 January 2005).

Creative Partnerships, Slough (2004a). Young People TOTAL Working Paper, June 2004 (unpublished).

Creative Partnerships, Slough (2004b). Youth Think Tank, Minutes, February 2004, internal working paper (unpublished).

Crichton, M. (1999). *Timeline*. Alfred A. Knopf.

Crook, C. (1994). *Computers and the Collaborative Experience of Learning*. London: Routledge.

Cropley, A. (2001). *Creativity in Education and Training: A Guide for Teachers and Educators*. London: Kogan Page.

Csikszentmihalyi, M. (1988). Society, culture and person: a systems view of creativity. In: Sternberg, R.J. (Ed.), *The Nature of Creativity*. Cambridge: Cambridge University Press; pp. 325–39.

Csikszentmihalyi, M. (1990). The domain of creativity. In: Runco, M.A. and Albert, R.S. (Eds), *Theories of Creativity*. Newbury Park, CA: Sage.

Csikszentmihalyi, M. (1994). Creativity. In: Sternberg, R.J. (Ed.), *The Encyclopedia of Human Intelligence*. New York: Macmillan; pp. 298–306.

Csikszentmihalyi, M. (1999). Implications of a systems perspective for the study of creativity. In: Sternberg, R.J. (Ed.), *Handbook of Creativity*. Cambridge: Cambridge University Press.

Cullingford, C. (2004). Learners' perspectives on creativity. Paper presented at *British Educational Research Association Conference*, UMIST, September 2004.

Cunliffe, L. (1998). Art and art education as a cognitive process and the National Curriculum. In: Burden, R. and Williams, M. (Eds), *Thinking Through the Curriculum*. London: Routledge.

Davidson, K., Fell, R. and Jeffery, G. (2004). Building pathways into creativity: what do students and teachers need? Paper presented at *ESRC Seminar: Creativity, the Arts and Achievement*, Canterbury Christ Church College, 5 July 2004.

Denzin, N. (1994). The art and politics of interpretation. In: Denzin, N.K. and Lincoln, Y.S. (Eds), *Handbook of Qualitative Research*. London: Sage.

Dewett, T. (2003). Understanding the relationship between information technology and creativity in organizations. *Creativity Research Journal* 15(2–3), 167–82.

DfEE (1997). *Excellence in Schools*. London: HMSO.

DfEE/QCA (2000). *Curriculum Guidance for the Foundation Stage*. London: Qualifications and Curriculum Authority.

DfES (2003). *Excellence and Enjoyment*, London: HMSO.

DfES (2004a). Personalised learning for every child, personalised contact for every teacher. Press Notice 2004/0050.

DfES (2004b). Personalised learning around each child. DfES Website http://www.standards.dfes.gov.uk/personalisedlearning/about/ (last access December 2004).

DfES (2004c). *A National Conversation about Personalised Learning*. Nottingham: DfES Publications.

DfES (2005a). http://www.standards.dfee.gov.uk/excellence (last access 24 January 2005).

DfES (2005b). http://www.teachernet.gov.uk/professionaldevelopment/resourcesand research/bprs/search/ (last access 24 January 2005).

DfEE and QCA (1999a). *The National Curriculum Handbook for Teachers in Key Stages 1 and 2*. London: Qualifications and Curriculum Authority.

DfEE and QCA (1999b). *The National Curriculum Handbook for Teachers in Key Stages 3 and 4*. London: Qualifications and Curriculum Authority.

DTI (2005). http://www.dti.gov.uk/bestpractice/innovation/innovation-creativity.htm (last access 26 January 2005).

Duckett, R., Holmes, C. and Lines, L. (Eds) (2002a). *The Mouse House: Woodland Children*. Newcastle-upon-Tyne: Sightlines Initiative.

Duckett, R., Mason, E. and Lines, L. (Eds) (2002b). *Feathers: Woodland Children*. Newcastle-upon-Tyne: Sightlines Initiative.

Duffy, B. (1998). *Creative Children, Imaginative Teaching*. Buckingham: Open University Press.

Duffy, B., Stillaway, J. (2004). Creativity: working in partnership with parents. In: Miller, L. and Devereux, J. (Eds), *Supporting Children's Learning in the Early Years*. London: David Fulton Publishers.

Dunn, J., Zhang, X. and Ripple, R. (1988). A study of Chinese and American performance on divergent thinking tasks. *New Horizons* 29, 7–20.

Durham, C. (2001). *Chasing Ideas*. Sydney: Finch Publishing.

Eckstein, D. (2004). 'Reframing' as an innovative educational technique: turning a perceived inability into an asset. *The Korean Journal of Thinking and Problem Solving* 14(1), 37–47.

Edwards, C.P. and Springate, K.W. (1995). ERIC clearing house on elementary and early childhood education. http://ceep.crc.uiuc.edu/eecearchive/digests/1995/edward95.html (last access 7 April 2005).

Edwards, D. and Mercer, N. (1987). *Common Knowledge: The Development of Understanding in the Classroom*. London: Methuen.

Eisenman, R. (1991). Creativity: is it disruptive? Society does not take kindly to the original person. *The Creative Child and Adult Quarterly* XVI(4).

Ekvall, G. (1991). The organizational culture of idea management: a creative climate for the management of ideas. In: Henry, J. and Walker, D. (Eds), *Managing Innovation*. London: Sage.

Ekvall, G. (1996). Organizational climate for creativity and innovation. *European Work and Organizational Psychology* 5, 105–23.

Elliott, R.K. (1971). Versions of creativity. *Proceedings of the Philosophy of Education Society of Great Britain* 5(2), 139–52.

Emilia (1996). *The Hundred Languages of Children*. Reggio Emilia: Reggio Children.

Feldman, D.H. (1974). Universal to unique. In: Rosner, S. and Abt L. (Eds), *Essays in Creativity*. Croton-on-Hudson, New York: North River; pp. 45–85.

Feldman, D.H. (1989). Creativity: proof that development occurs. In: Damon W. (Ed.), *Child Development Today and Tomorrow*. San Francisco: Jossey-Bass; pp. 271–79.

Feldman, D.H. (1999). The development of creativity. In: Sternberg R.J. (Ed.), *Handbook of Creativity*. Cambridge, UK: Cambridge University Press; pp. 169–88.

Feldman, D.H. (2003). The creation of multiple intelligences theory: a study in high-level thinking. In: Sawyer, R.K., John-Steiner, V., Moran, S., Sternberg, R.J., Feldman, D.H., Nakamura, J. and Csikszentmihalyi, M. (Eds), *Creativity and Development*. Oxford: Oxford University Press.

Feldman, D.H., Csikszentmihalyi, M. and Gardner, H. (1994). *Changing the World*. Westport, CT: Praeger Publishers.

Fell, R. and Davidson, K. (2004). Successful vocational learning for intermediate performing arts students: key findings from the *Pathways into Creativity* research project. Paper presented at *British Educational Research Association Creativity in Education Symposium: Learners' Perspectives on Creativity*, UMIST, September 2004.

Filer, A. and Pollard, A. (2000). *The Social World of Pupil Assessment*. London: Continuum Books.

Fischmann, W., Solomon, B. Greenspan, D. and Gardner, H. (2004). *Making Good: How Young People Cope with Moral Dilemmas at Work*. Cambridge, MA: Harvard University Press.

Florida, R. (2002). *The Rise of The Creative Class: And How it Is Transforming Work, Leisure, Community and Everyday Life*. Perseus Books Group.

Florida, R. and Tinagli, I. (2004). *Europe in the Creative Age*. London: DEMOS.

Froebel, F. (1887). *Education of Man*. Appleton Press.

Froebel, F. (1895). *Pedagogies of the Kindergarten*. Appleton Press.

Fromm, E. (1956). *The Sane Society*. London: Routledge/Kegan Paul.

Fryer, M. (1996). *Creative Teaching and Learning*. London: PCP.

Fryer, M. (2000). Assessing creativity in schools. In: Nolan, V. (Ed.), *Creative Education*. Synectics Education Initiative.

Fryer, M. (Ed.) (2004). *Creativity and Cultural Diversity*. Leeds: The Creativity Centre Educational Trust.

Gabel-Dunk, G. (2005). The tunnel, the dragon car, the escaping butterfly house, Ben's future car – Where did they come from? Where are they going? An examination and reflection on how the creative process can be encouraged, supported and documented. Paper presented at *Documenting Creative Learning Symposium: What, How and Why?* University of Cambridge, April 2005.

Gabel-Dunk, G. and Craft, A. (2002). Baselining creative thinking with children aged 5 and 6. Paper presented at *Changing Minds International Conference on Thinking*, Harrogate, England, June 2002.

Gage, N. (1978). *The Scientific Basis of the Art of Teaching*. New York: Teachers College Press.

Galton, M., Hargreaves, L., Comber, C., Wall, D. and Pell, A. (1999). *Inside the Primary Classroom: 20 Years On*. London: Routledge.

Gardner, H. (1993). *Creating Minds*. New York: BasicBooks.

Gardner, H. (1999). *Intelligence Reframed*. New York: BasicBooks.

Gardner, H. (2000). *The Disciplined Mind: Beyond Facts and Standardized Tests, the K-12 Education That Every Child Deserves* (2nd edition). Harmondsworth, Middlesex: Penguin Books .

Gardner, H. (2004). *Changing Minds: The Art and Science of Changing Our Own and Other People's Minds*. Cambridge, MA: Harvard Business School Press.

Gardner, H., Csikszentmihalyi, M. and Damon, W. (2001). *Good Work: When Excellence and Ethics Meet*. New York: BasicBooks.

Gewirtz, S., Ball, S.J. and Bowe, R. (1995). *The Managerial School: Post-Welfarism and Social Justice in Education*. London: RoutledgeFalmer.

Gilligan, C. (1982). *In a Different Voice*. Cambridge, MA: Harvard University Press.

Gilligan, C. (1993). *In a Different Voice*, second edition. Cambridge, MA: Harvard University Press.

Gipps, C. and Murphy, P. (1994). *A Fair Test? Assessment, Achievement and Equity*. Buckingham: Open University Press.

Gmitrova, V. and Gmitrov, J. (2003). The impact of teacher-directed and child-directed pretend play on cognitive competence in kindergarten children. *Early Childhood Education Journal* 30(4).

Goff, K. (2004). Women's creative development. In: Fryer, M. (Ed.), *Creativity and Cultural Diversity*. Leeds: The Creativity Centre Educational Trust.

Goldberger, N., Tarule, J., Clinchy, B. and Bellenky, M. (1986). *Knowledge, Difference and Power*. New York: Basic Books.

Goleman, D., Kaufman, P. and Ray, M. (1992). *The Creative Spirit*. New York: Dutton.

Grainger, T. (2004). Teachers as writers: travelling *British Educational Research Association Conference* creatively forwards. Paper given at *Learners' Perspectives Symposium* as part of Special Interest Group Creativity in Education strand, UMIST, September 2004.

Greig, S., Pike, G. and Selby, D. (1987). *Earthrights: Education as if the Planet Really Mattered*. London: Kogan Page/World Wildlife Fund.

Griffiths, M. and Woolf, F. (2004). Report on Creative Partnerships Nottingham Action Research. Nottingham, Nottingham Trent University.

Griffiths, M., Berry, J., Holt, A., Naylor, J. and Weekes, P. (2004). Learning to be in public spaces: Using a new model for working with artists in schools. Presented to 'Creating Learning Communities: Learners' Perspectives', in the ESRC Seminar Series, *Creativity in Education* and *Knowledge and Skills for Learning to Learn*, November 2004, Newcastle University.

Gruber, H.E. (1980). Afterword. In: Feldman, D.H. (Ed.), *Beyond Universals in Cognitive Development*. Norwood, NJ: Ablex.

Gruber, H.E. (1989). The evolving systems approach to creative work. In: Wallace, D.B. and Gruber, H.E. (Eds), *Creative People at Work: Twelve Cognitive Case Studies*. Oxford: Oxford University Press.

Gruber, H.E. and Davis, S.N. (1988). Inching our way up Mount Olympus: the evolving-systems approach to creative thinking. In: Sternberg, R.J. (Ed.), *The Nature of Creativity*. New York: Cambridge University Press; pp. 243–70.

Gruber, H.E. and Wallace, D.B. (1999). The case study method and evolving systems approach for understanding unique creative people at work. In: Sternberg, R.J. (Ed.), *Handbook of Creativity*. New York: Cambridge University Press; pp. 93–115.

Guilford, J.P. (1950). Structure of intellect. *Psychological Bulletin* 53, 267–93.

Halliwell, S. (1993). Teacher creativity and teacher education. In Bridges, D. and Kerry, T. (Eds.), *Developing Teachers Professionally*. London: Routledge.

Handy, C. (2001). *The Elephant and the Flea: New Thinking for a New World*. London: Hutchinson.

Hanel, P. (1999). Note de Recherche: Impact of innovation motivated by environmental concerns and government regulations on firm performance: a study of survey data. Quebec, Montreal, Centre Intrauniversitaire de Recherche sur la Science et la Technologie. http://www.cirst.uqam.ca/PDF/note_rech/ 2003_08.pdf (last access 28 July 2004).

Hargreaves, D.H. (1967). *Social Relations in the Secondary School*. London: Routledge & Kegan Paul.

Harland, J., Kinder, K., Lord, P., Stott, A., Schagen, I., Haynes, J., Cusworth, L., White, R. and Paola, R. (2000). *Arts Education in Secondary Schools: Effects and Effectiveness*. Slough: NFER.

Haydn, T., Oliver, A. and Barton, R. (2004). Providing time for the development of creative approaches to subject pedagogy: three case studies. Paper given at *British Educational Research Association Conference*, Manchester, September 2004.

Hefner, R.W. (Ed.) (1998). *Market Cultures: Societies and Values in the New Asian Capitalisms*. Singapore: Institute of Southeast Asian Studies.

Henry, J. and Walker, D. (Eds) (1991). *Managing Innovation*. London: Sage.

HM Government (2004). *Preparing for Emergencies: What You Need to Know*. London: HMSO.

HM Treasury, DfES, Department of Work and Pensions and DTI (2004). *Choice for Parents, the Best Start for Children: A Ten Year Strategy for Childcare*. Norwich: HMSO.

Ho, D.Y.F. (1994). Filial piety, authoritarian moralism and cognitive conservatism in Chinese societies. *Genetic, Social and General Psychology Monographs* 120, 349–65.

Hodkinson, S. and Thomas, L. (2001). Economics education for all. In: Whitehead, D. and Dyer, D. (Eds), (2001). *New Developments in Economics and Business Education: A Handbook for Teachers*, London: Kogan Page/Institute of Education, University of London; pp. 43–51.

Hofstede, G. (1980). *Cultures' Consequences: International Differences in Work-Related Values*. Beverley Hills, CA: Sage.

Hope, G., Barnes, J. and Scoffham, S. (2005). Creativity in context. Paper presented at *Documenting Creative Learning Symposium: What, How and Why?* University of Cambridge, April 2005.

Horsman, M. and Marshall, A. (1994). *After the Nation State: Citizens, Tribalism and the New World Disorder*. London: HarperCollins.

Hubbard, R.S. (1996). *A Workshop of the Possible: Nurturing Children's Creative Development*. York, ME: Stenhouse Publishers.

Hirst, P. (1979). Professional studies in initial teacher education: some conceptual issues. In: Alexander, R.J. and Wormald E. (Eds), *Professional Studies for Teaching*. Guildford: SRHE; pp. 15–29.

Hurst, V. (1997). *Planning for Early Learning: Educating Young Children*, 2nd edition. London: Paul Chapman Publishing.

Imison, T. (2001). Creative leadership: innovative practices in a secondary school. In: Craft, A., Jeffrey, B. and Leibling, M. (Eds), *Creativity in Education*. London; Continuum.

Innovations Unit (2004). Personalised learning page. http://www.standards.dfes. gov.uk/innovation-unit/personalisation/personalisedlearning/ (last access December 2004).

Isaksen, S.G. (1995). Some recent developments on assessing the climate for creativity and change. Paper presented at the *International Conference on Climate for Creativity and Change*, Centre for Studies in Creativity, Buffalo.

Jackson, A. (2001). Creative family literacy. In: *Literacy Today*, June Issue. National Literacy Trust. http://www.literacytrust.org.uk/Pubs/jackson.html (last access 25 January 2005).

Jeffery, G. (2004). Teacher as social or cultural entrepreneur? Exploring the boundaries of teachers' professional identities through partnership working.

Paper presented at *British Educational Research Association Creativity in Education Symposium: Learners' Perspectives on Creativity*, UMIST, September 2004.

Jeffery, G. *et al.* (2005). *The Creative College: Building a Successful Learning Culture in the Arts*. London: Trentham Books.

Jeffrey, B. (2001a). Challenging prescription in ideology and practice: the case of Sunny first school. In: Collins, J., Insley, K. and Soler, J. (Eds), *Developing Pedagogy: Researching Practice*. London. Paul Chapman.

Jeffrey, B. (2001b). Primary pupil's perspectives and creative learning. *Encyclopaideia* 9(Spring).

Jeffrey, B. (2001c). Maintaining primary school students' engagement in a post-reform context (unpublished working paper).

Jeffrey, B. (2003). Countering student instrumentalism: a creative response. *British Educational Research Journal* 29(4), 489–503.

Jeffrey, B. (2004a). End of Award Report: Creative Learning and Student Perspectives (CLASP) project, submitted to ESRC November 2004.

Jeffrey, B. (2004b). Meaningful creative learning. Paper presented at ECER, Crete, September 2004. http://opencreativity.open.ac.uk/current-projects.cfm?sm=pro-projects&pg=current-projects (last access 7 April 2005).

Jeffrey, B. (2005). Final Report of the Creative Learning and Student Perspectives Research Project (CLASP), a European Commission funded project through the Socrates Programme, Action 6.1, Number 2002–4682/002–001.SO2–61OBGE, Milton Keynes. http://clasp.open.ac.uk.

Jeffrey, B. and Woods, P. (1997). The relevance of creative teaching: pupils' views. In Pollard, A., Thiessen, D. and Filer, A. (Eds), *Children and their Curriculum: The Perspectives of Primary and Elementary Children*. London: Falmer; pp. 15–33.

Jeffrey, B. and Craft, A. (2001). The universalization of creativity in education. In: Craft, A., Jeffrey, B. and Leibling, M. (Eds), *Creativity in Education*. London: Continuum.

Jeffrey, B. and Craft, A. (2003). Creative teaching and teaching for creativity: distinctions and relationships. Paper given at the *British Educational Research Association Special Interest Group in Creativity in Education Conference*, 3rd February, The Open University, Walton Hall, Milton Keynes.

Jeffrey, B. and Woods, P. (2003). *The Creative School: A Framework for Success, Quality and Effectiveness*. London: RoutledgeFalmer.

Jeffrey, B. and Craft, A. (2004a). Teaching creatively and teaching for creativity: distinctions and relationships. *Educational Studies* 30(1).

Jeffrey, B. and Craft, A. (2004b). Creative practice and practice which fosters creativity. In: Miller, L. and Devereux, J. (Eds), *Supporting Children's Learning in the Early Years*. London: David Fulton Press.

Jeffrey, B. and Troman, G. (2004). Time for ethnography, in *British Journal of Educational Studies* 30(4).

Johnson, C.M. (1971). Freedom in junior schools. In: Cox, C.B. and Dyson A.E. (Eds), *The Black Papers on Education*. London: Davis-Poynter Ltd.

John-Steiner, V. (2000). *Creative Collaboration*. New York: Oxford University Press.

Jones, E. and Harrison, D. (2000). Investigating the use of TRIZ in Eco-Innovation. In *TRIZCON2000 Conference Proceedings*, the Altshuller Institute, May 2000.

Kaufman, J.C., Baer, J. and Gentile, C.A. (2004). Differences in gender and ethnicity as measured by ratings of three writing tasks. *Journal of Creative Behavior* 38(1).

Kessler, R. (2000). The soul of education: helping students find connection, compassion and character at school. USA: Association of Supervision and Curriculum.

Klein, J.T. (1996). *Crossing Boundaries: Knowledge, Disciplinarities And Interdisciplinarities*. Charlottesville and London: University Press of Virginia.

Kluckhohn, F.R. and Strodtbeck, F.L. (1961). *Variations in Value Orientation*. Westport, CT: Greenwood Publishers.

Kohlberg, L. (1981). *Essays on Moral Development*, Vol. I. San Francisco: Harper & Row.

Kohlberg, L. (1984). *Essays on Moral Development*, Vol. II. San Francisco: Harper & Row.

Kubo, Y. (2004). Challenges for creativity in Singapore and Japan: Confucious' influence and professionalism. In Fryer, M. (Ed.), *Creativity and Cultural Diversity*. Leeds: The Creativity Centre Educational Trust.

Kuo, Y.Y. (1996). Taoistic psychology of creativity. *Journal of Creative Behavior* 30(3), 197–212.

Lacey, C. (1970). *Hightown Grammar*. Manchester: Manchester University Press.

Lane, J. (2001). *Timeless Simplicity: Creative Living in a Consumer Society*. Totnes, Devon: Green Books Ltd.

Leach, J. (2001). A hundred possibilities: creativity, community and ICT. In: Craft, A., Jeffrey, B. and Leibling, M. (Eds), *Creativity in Education*. London: Continuum.

Leadbeater, C. (2004). *Personalisation for Participation: A New Script for Public Services*. London: DEMOS. Also available through http://www.demos.co.uk.

Levine, R., Locke, C., Searls, D. and Weinberger, D. (2000). *The Cluetrain Manifesto: The End of Business as Usual*. Harlow: Pearson Education Limited.

Lim, H.A. (2004). Creativity, culture, and entrepreneurialship. *Symbiosis* (February), 4–10.

Lindqvist, G. (2003). Vygotsky's theory of creativity. *Creativity Research Journal* 15(2–3), 245–51.

Loveless, A. (2003). Creating spaces in the primary classroom: ICT in creative subjects. *The Curriculum Journal* 14(1), 5–21.

Lubart, T.I. (1999). Creativity across cultures. In: Sternberg, R.J. (Ed.), *Handbook of Creativity*. Cambridge: Cambridge University Press.

Lucas, B. (2001). Creative teaching, teaching creativity and creative learning. In: Craft, A., Jeffrey, B. and Liebling, M. (Eds). *Creativity in Education*, London: Continuum; pp. 35–44.

Lucas, B., Greany, T. and Rodd, J. (2002). *Teaching Pupils How to Learn: Research, Practice and INSET Resources (Campaign for Learning)*. London: Network Educational Press Ltd.

Lunn, S., Davidson, M. and Murphy, P.F. (2003). Towards a model of collaborative exchange in creative problem-solving. Paper presented at *Symposium of Special Interest Group Creativity in Education at British Educational Research Association Conference*, University of Edinburgh, September 2003.

McAuliffe, D. (2004). Pedagogising art – an enquiry into the particulars and universals of art making and learning in primary, secondary and tertiary education in England. Paper presented at *British Educational Research Association Creativity in Education Symposium: Learners' Perspectives on Creativity*, UMIST, September 2004.

McCarthy, K. (2001). Poised at the edge: spirituality and creativity in Religious Education. In: Craft, A., Jeffrey, B. and Leibling, M. (Eds), *Creativity in Education*. London: Continuum; pp. 126–43.

McCracken, J.L. (1997). Women who invent: examining the impact of formal and informal education on their creativity. Doctoral dissertation, Oklahoma State University.

McNiff, S. (2003). *Creating with Others: The Practice of Imagination in Life, Art and the Workplace*. Boston, MA: Shambhala Publications.

Maduro, R. (1976). *Artistic Creativity in a Brahmin Painter Community*, Research Monograph 14. Berkely: Center for South and Southeast Asia Studies, University of California.

Magaluzzi, L. (1996). *The Hundred Languages of Children, Catalogue of the Exhibition*. Reggio Emilia, Italy: Reggio Children.

Magyari-Beck I. (1976). *Kiseriet a Tudomanyos Alkotas Produktumanak Interdiszciplinaris Maghatarozasara*. Budapest: Akadamiai Kiado [cited in Cszikszentmihalyi, 1990].

Malangi, S. (2004). The curse of the creative class. In: *The Wall Street Journal*, 19 January 2004. http://www.opinionjournal.com/extra/?id=110004573 (last access 27 July 2004).

Markus, H.R. and Kitayama, S. (1991). Culture and the self: implications for cognition, emotion and motivation. *Psychological Review* 98, 224–53.

Markus, H.R. and Kitayama, S. (1994). A collective fear of the collective: implications for selves and theories of selves. *Personality and Social Psychology Bulletin* 20(5), 568–79.

Martin, D.S. (2005). Outcomes of teaching higher-level thinking to deaf learners in two cultures: an international study. Paper presented at *Documenting Creative Learning Symposium: What, How and Why?* University of Cambridge, April 2005.

Martin, D.S., Craft, A. and Zhang, N.S (2001). The impact of cognitive strategy instruction on deaf learners: an international comparative study. *American Annals of the Deaf* 146(4), 366–78.

Martin, D.S., Craft, A. and Tillema, H. (2002). Developing critical and creative thinking strategies in primary school pupils: an inter-cultural study of teachers' learning. *British Journal of In-Service Education* 28(1), 115–34.

Maslow, A.H. (1970). *Motivation and Personality*, third edition. London: Harper Collins.

Massey, D. (1999). Imagining globalization: power-geometries of time–space. In: Brah, A. *et al.* (Eds), *Global Futures: Migration, Environment and Globalization*. Basingstoke, Macmillan; pp. 27–44.

Massey, D. (2005). *For Space*. London: Sage.

Mathur, S.G. (1982). Cross-cultural implications of creativity. *Indian Psychological Review* 22(1), 12–19.

Miell, D. and Littleton, K. (2004). *Collaborative Creativity*. London: Free Association Books.

Mills, C.W. (1959). *The Sociological Imagination*. New York and Oxford: Oxford University Press.

Ministry of Education, Singapore, The. (1998). The desired outcomes of education in Singapore. http://www1.moe.edu.sg/desired.htm (last access 7 April 2005).

Montessori, M. (1914). *Dr Montessori's Own Handbook*. London: William Heinemann.

Murphy, P., McCormick, B., Lunn, S., Davidson, M. and Jones, H. (2004). *Electronics in Schools, Final Evaluation Report, Executive Summary*. London/ Milton Keynes: The Department of Trade and Industry/The Open University.

NACCCE (1999). *All Our Futures: Creativity, Culture and Education*. London: Department for Education and Employment.

Nagel, S. (2000). Creativity and policy studies. *The Innovation Journal* 5(3).

NCSL (2005). http://www.ncsl.org.uk/index.cfm?pageid=randd-activities-creativity (last access 26 January 2005).

NCC (1990). *Curriculum Guidance 4: Economic and Industrial Understanding.* York: National Curriculum Council.

NESTA (2003). *Issue: Creativity* 3(June). (NESTA journal.)

NESTA (2005). http://www.nesta.org.uk/ourawardees/profiles/4196/index.html (last access 25 January 2005).

Ng, A.K. (2001). *Why Asians are Less Creative than Westerners.* Singapore: Prentice-Hall.

Ng, A. K. (2002). The development of a new scale to measure teachers' attitudes toward students (TATS). *Educational Research Journal* 17(1), 63–78.

Ng, A.K. (2003). A cultural model of creative and conforming behaviour. *Creativity Research Journal* 15(2–3), 223–33.

Ng, A.K. (2005). The cultivation of moral creativity in the Asian classroom. Paper presented at *Documenting Creative Learning Symposium: What, How and Why?* University of Cambridge, April 2005.

Ng, A.K. and Lin, K.H.K. (2004). Teaching attitudes, emotional intelligence and creativity of school teachers in Singapore. Submitted to *Educational Research Journal based in Chinese University of Hong Kong.*

Nias, J. (1993). Changing times, changing identities: grieving for a lost self. In: Burgess R. (Ed.), *Educational Research and Evaluation: For Policy and Practice?* London: Falmer Press.

Ng, A. K. and Smith, I. (2004). Why is there a paradox in promoting creativity in the Asian classroom? In: Sing, L., Hui A. and Ng, G (Eds), *Creativity: When East Meets West.* Singapore: World Scientific Publishing; pp. 87–112.

Ng, A. K. and Smith, I. (in press). The paradox of promoting creativity in the Asian classroom: an empirical investigation. *Genetic, Social and General Psychology Monographs.*

Nichol, L. (Ed.) (1998). *On Creativity: David Bohm.* London and New York: Routledge.

Nichol, L. (Ed.). (2003). *The Essential David Bohm.* London and New York: Routledge.

Nikitina, S. and Boix-Mansilla, V. (2003). Three strategies for interdisciplinary math and science teaching: a case of the Illinois Mathematics and Science Academy. Cambridge, MA, Harvard Project Zero Working Paper.

Nisbett, R. E. (2003). *The Geography of Thought.* New York: The Free Press.

Nolan, V. (2004). Creativity: the antidote to the argument culture. In: Fryer, M. (Ed.), *Creativity and Cultural Diversity.* Leeds: The Creativity Centre Educational Trust.

OFSTED (2003a). Expecting the unexpected: developing creativity in primary and secondary schools. HMI Report 1612, E-publication, August 2003.

OFSTED (2003b). Improving city schools: how the arts can help. HMI Report 1709, E-publication, August 2003.

O'Brien, R. (1992). *Global Financial Integration: The End of Geography.* New York: Council on Foreign Relations Press.

Ohmae, K. (1990). *The Borderless World: Power and Strategy in the Interlinked Economy.* London: Collins.

Ohmae, K. (1995). *The End of the Nation State: The Rise of Regional Economies.* London: HarperCollins.

Parkes, J. (2005). Home case study. In: Jeffery, G. *et al., The Creative College: Building a Successful Learning Culture in the Arts.* London: Trentham Books.

Parkes, J. and Califano, A. (2004). Home: an educational resource pack. London: NewVIc New Media. Available from www.newvic-creative.org.uk.

Passmore, J. (1980). *The Philosophy of Teaching*. London: Duckworth.

Perkins, D. (1999). From idea to action. In: Hetland, L. and Veenema, S. (Eds), *The Project Zero Classroom: Views on Understanding*. Cambridge, MA: Project Zero, Harvard University Graduate School of Education.

Perkins, D.N. (1981). *The Mind's Best Work*. Cambridge, MA: Cambridge University Press.

Piaget, J. (1932). *The Moral Judgment of the Child*. London: Routledge & Kegan Paul.

Piaget, J. and Inhelder, B. (1969). *The Psychology of the Child*. London: Routledge & Kegan Paul.

Piirto, J. (1992). *Understanding Those Who Create*. Dayton: Ohio University Press.

Pinn, D.M. (1969). What kind of primary school? in: Cox, C.B. and Dyson, A.E. (Eds), *Black Paper Two: The Crisis in Education*. London: Critical Quarterly Society.

Plucker, J.A. (2004). Generalization of creativity across domains: examination of the method effect hypothesis. *The Journal of Creative Behavior* 38(1).

Plucker, J.A. and Renzulli, J.A. (1999). Psychometric approaches to the study of human creativity. In: Sternberg, R.J. (Ed.), *The Handbook of Creativity*, first edition. Cambridge: Cambridge University Press.

Pollard, A. (1985). *The Social World of the Primary School*. London: Holt, Rinehart & Winston.

Pollard, A., Triggs, P., Broadfoot, P., McNess, E. and Osborn, M. (2000). *What Pupils Say: Changing Policy and Practice in Primary Education*. London: Continuum.

Project Zero/Reggio Children (2001). *Making Learning Visible: Children as Individual and Group Learners*. Reggio Emilia: Reggio Children srl.

Project Zero Website (2004). http://www.pz.harvard.edu/Research/GoodWork.htm (last access 7 April 2005).

QCA (2005a). *Creativity: Find it, Promote – Promoting Pupils' Creative Thinking and Behaviour across the Curriculum at Key Stages 1, 2 Video Pack*. London: Qualifications and Curriculum Authority.

QCA (2005b). *Creativity: Find it, Promote it*. http://www.ncaction.org.uk/creativity/about.htm (last access 7 April 2005).

QCA and DfEE (1999a). *The National Curriculum Handbook for Primary Teachers in England*. London: Department for Education and Employment/Qualifications and Curriculum Authority.

QCA and DfEE (1999b). *The National Curriculum Handbook for Secondary Teachers in England*. London: Department for Education and Employment/Qualifications and Curriculum Authority.

Raggl, A. (2005). The attempt to build bridges. Paper presented at *Documenting Creative Learning Symposium: What, How and Why?* University of Cambridge, April 2005.

Raina, M.K. (2004). I shall be many: the garland-making perspective on creativity and cultural diversity. In: Fryer, M. (Ed.), *Creativity and Cultural Diversity*. Leeds: The Creativity Centre Educational Trust.

Reay, D. (1998). Setting the agenda: the growing impact of market forces on pupil grouping in British secondary schooling. *Journal of Curriculum Studies* 30(5), 545–58.

Rhyammar, L. and Brolin, C. (1999). Creativity research: historical considerations and main lines of development. *Scandinavian Journal of Educational Research* 43(3), 259–73.

Richards Hope, J. (2003). *Pinstripes and Pearls: The Women of the Harvard Law Class of '64 who Forged an Old-Girl Network and Paved the Way for Future Generations*. New York, NY: A Lisa Drew Book/Scribner.

Ripple, R.E. (1989). Ordinary creativity. *Contemporary Educational Psychology* 14, 189–202.

Ritchart, R. (2002). *Intellectual Character: What It Is, Why It Matters and How To Get It*. San Francisco, CA: Jossey-Bass.

Robinson, K. (2001). *Out of our Minds: Learning to Be Creative*. Oxford: Capstone.

Rogers, E.M. (2003). *Diffusion of Innovations*, fifth edition. New York: Free Press.

Rogoff, B. (1990). *Apprenticeship in Thinking: Cognitive Development in a Social Context*. Cambridge: Cambridge University Press.

Rogoff, B., Mosier, C., Mistry, J. and Goncu, A. (1998). Toddlers' guided participation with their caregivers in cultural activity. In: Woodhead, M., Faulkner, D. and Littleton, K. (Eds), *Cultural Worlds of Early Childhood*. London: Routledge.

Roland, A. (1988) *In Search of Self in India and Japan: Towards a Cross-Cultural Psychology*. New Jersey: Princeton University Press.

Rowe, S. and Humphries, S. (2001). Creating a climate for learning at Coombes Nursery and Infant School. In: Craft, A., Jeffrey, B. and Leibling, M. (Eds), *Creativity in Education*, London: Continuum.

Roy, R. (2003). *Open University Course T211 Design and Designing, Block 3: Creativity and Concept Design*. Milton Keynes: The Open University.

Runco, M.A. and Richards, R. (Eds) (1997). *Eminent Creativity, Everyday Creativity and Health*. Connecticut: Ablex Publishing Company.

Ryle, G. (1949). *The Concept of Mind*. London: Hutchinson.

Sadowsky, G.R., Maguire, K., Johnson, P., Ngumba, W. and Kohles, R. (1994). World views of white American, mainland Chinese, Taiwanese and African students. *Journal of Cross-Cultural Psychology* 25(3), 309–24.

Safran, L. (2001). Creativity as mindful learning: a case from learner-led home-based education. In: Craft, A., Jeffrey, B. and Leibling, M. (Eds), *Creativity in Education*. London: Continuum.

Sawyer, R.K. (2004). Creative teaching: collaborative discussion as disciplined improvisation, *Educational Researcher* 33(1), 12–20.

Schon, D. (1983). *The Reflective Practitioner*. London: Temple Smith.

Schon, D. (1989). Professional knowledge and reflective practice. In: Sergiovanni, T. and Moore J.H. (Eds), *Schooling for Tomorrow*. Boston: Allyn and Bacon.

Schwager, I. (2005). Parenting challenges for the new millennium. http://www.creativeparents.com/ar020200.html (last access 25 January 2005).

Scottish Executive (2004). Cultural Policy Statement. http://www.scotland.gov.uk/library5/education/ncs04-00.asp (last access 7 April 2005).

Scruton, R. (1974). *Art and Imagination*. London: Methuen.

Sefton-Green, J. (Ed.) (1999). *Young People, Creativity and New Technologies: The Challenge of Digital Arts*. London and New York: Routledge.

Seidel, S., Eppel, M. and Martiniello, M. (2001). *Arts Survive! A Study of Sustainability in Arts Education Partnerships*. Cambridge, MA: Project Zero at the Harvard Graduate School of Education.

Seltzer, K. and Bentley, T. (1999). *The Creative Age: Knowledge and Skills for the New Economy*. London: Demos.

Sen, R.S. and Sharma, N. (2004). Teachers' conceptions of creativity and its nurture in children: an Indian perspective. In: Fryer, M. (Ed.), *Creativity and Cultural Diversity*. Leeds: The Creativity Centre Educational Trust.

Shallcross, D.J. (1981). *Teaching Creative Behaviour: How to Teach Creativity to Children of All Ages*. Englewood Cliffs, NJ: Prentice Hall.

Sheldrake, R., McKenna, T., Abraham, R. and Houston, J. (2001). *Chaos, Creativity and Cosmic Consciousness*. Park Street Press.

Sherr, J. (1982). The universal structures and dynamics of creativity: Maharishi, Plato, Jung and various other creative geniuses on the creative process. *Journal of Creative Behavior* 16(3), 155–75.

Simonton, D.K. (1984). Artistic creativity and interpersonal relationships across and within generations. *Journal of Personality and Social Psychology* 46 (6), 1273–86.

Simonton, D.K. (1988). Quality and purpose, quantity and chance. *Creativity Research Journal* 1, 68–74.

Simonton, D.K. (1999). Creativity from a historiometric perspective. In: Sternberg, R.J. (Ed.), *The Handbook of Creativity*. Cambridge: Cambridge University Press.

Simonton, D.K. (2003). Scientific creativity as constrained stochastic behavior: the integration of product, person and process perspectives. *Psychology Bulletin* 129(4), 475–94.

Siu, K.W.M. and Kwok, J.Y.C. (2004). Collective and democratic creativity: participatory research and design. *The Korean Journal of Thinking and Problem Solving* 14(1).

Skinner, B.F. (1960). *The Behavior of Organisms: An Experimental Analysis*. New York: Appleton-Century-Crofts.

Skinner, B.F. (1974). *About Behaviourism*. New York: Random House.

Smith, P.B. and Bond, M.J. (1993). *Social Psychology Across Cultures: Analysis and Perspectives*. Hertfordshire, UK: Harvester, Wheatsheaf.

Smythe, P. (2005). Documenting creativity: insights into imaginative thinking from children's drawings. Paper presented at *Documenting Creative Learning Symposium: What, How and Why?* University of Cambridge, April 2005.

Soler, J., Craft, A. and Burgess, H. (2000). *Teacher Development: Exploring Our Own Practice*. London: PCP/The Open University.

Solomon, J. and Hunter, J. (2002). A psychological view of spirituality and leadership. *The School Administrator* (September).

Sonnenburg, S. (2004). Creativity in communication: a theoretical framework for collaborative product creation. *Creativity and Innovation Management* 13(4), 254–62.

Spendlove, D. and Wyse, D. (2005). Definitions and barriers: teachers' perceptions of creative learning. Paper presented at *Documenting Creative Learning Symposium: What, How and Why?* University of Cambridge, April 2005.

Spindler, G.D. and Spindler, L. (1983). Anthropologists view American culture. *Annual Review of Anthropology* 12, 49–78.

SST (2004). *Creative Learning and Specialist Schools (CLASS) project*. http://www.schoolsnetwork.org.uk/item.asp?page=12&item=3366 (last access December 2004).

Starko, A.J. (2001). *Creativity in the Classroom: Schools of Curious Delight*, 2nd edition. Mahwah, NJ: Lawrence Erlbaum Associates, Publishers.

Steiner, M. (Ed.) (1996). *Developing the Global Teacher: Theory and Practice in Initial Teacher Education*. Stoke-on-Trent, Staffordshire: Trentham/World Studies Trust.

Stein, M. (1974). *Stimulating Creativity*, Vol 1. New York: Academic.

Steiner, R. (1922). *Theosophy: An Introduction to the Supersensible History of the World and the Destination of Man*. London/New York: Rudolph Steiner Publishing Co./Anthroposophic Press.

Stenhouse, L. (1975). *An Introduction to Curriculum Research and Development*, London: Heinemann.

Stenhouse, L. (1979). *Case Study and Case Records: Towards a Contemporary History of Education*. Norwich: CARE, UEA.

Sternberg, R. (2003). *Wisdom, Intelligence and Creaivity Synthesized*. Cambridge: Cambridge University Press.

Sternberg, R.J. and Lubart, T.I. (1995a). An investment perspective on creative insight. In: Sternberg, R.J. and Davidson, J.E. (Eds), *The Nature of Insight*. Cambridge, MA: MIT Press.

Sternberg, R.J. and Lubart, T. (1995b). *Defying the Crowd: Cultivating Creativity in a Culture of Conformity*. New York: Free Press.

Sternberg, R.J. and Lubart, T.I. (1999). The concept of creativity: prospects and paradigms. In: Sternberg, R.J. (Ed.), *Handbook of Creativity*. New York: Cambridge University Press; pp. 3–15.

Synectics Education Initiative, Esmee Fairbairn Foundation, DfES and The Open University (2004). *Excite! Excellence, Creativity and Innovation in Teacher Education*. London: SEI.

Taylor, H. and Clark, J. (2004). Creativity in ITT "I couldn't be any other sort of teacher". Paper given at *British Educational Research Association Conference*, Manchester, September 2004.

Torrance, E.P. (1962). *Guiding Creative Talent*. Englewood Cliffs, NJ: Prentice-Hall.

Torrance, E.P. (1965). *Rewarding Creative Behaviour*. Englewood Cliffs, NJ: Prentice-Hall.

Torrance, E. P. (1966). *Torrance Tests of Creativity*. Princeton, NJ: Personnel Press.

Torrance, E.P. (1969). *Creativity. What Research Says to the Teacher*. Series No. 28. Washington, DC: National Education Association.

Torrance, E.P. (1974). *Torrance Tests of Creative Thinking*. Lexington, MA: Ginn & Company (Xerox Corporation).

Torrance, E.P. (1984). *Mentor Relationships: How they Aid Creative Achievement, Endure, Change and Die*. Buffalo, NY: Bearly.

Torrance E.P. (1987). *The Blazing Drive: Creative Potential*. Buffalo, NY: Bearly.

Torrance, E.P. (1988). Creativity as manifest in testing. In: Sternberg, R.J. (Ed.), *The Nature of Creativity*. Cambridge: Cambridge University Press; pp. 43–75.

Torrance, E.P. and Safter, H.T. (1990). *The Incubation Model of Teaching*. Buffalo, NY: Bearly Limited.

UNESCO (2002). Ensuring sustainable development through cultural diversity. http://portal.unesco.org/en/ev.php-URL_ID=1219&URL_DO=DO_TOPIC &URL_SECTION=201.html, last updated 2002 (last access July 2004).

Vass, E. (2004a). Developing creative writing through peer collaboration. Paper given at *British Educational Research Association Conference*, UMIST, September 2004.

Vass, E. (2004b). Understanding collaborative creativity. An observational study of young children's classroom-based joint creative writing. In Miell D. and Littleton K. (Eds), *Collaborative creativity*. London: Free Association Press.

Vong, K.I. (2005). Towards a creative early childhood program in Macau-SAR and Zhuhai-SER, the People's Republic of China. Paper presented at *Documenting Creative Learning Symposium: What, How and Why?* University of Cambridge, April 2005.

Vygotsky, L.S. (1965). *Thought and Language*. Cambridge, MA: MIT Press.

Vygotsky, L.S. (1978). *Mind in Society: the Development of Higher Psychological Processes*. Cambridge, MA: Harvard University Press.

Vygotsky, L.S. (1995). *Fantasi och kreativitet I barndomen* [*Imagination and Creativity in Childhood*]. Gothenburg: Diadlos.

Wagner, B.J. (1979). *Dorothy Heathcote: Drama as a Learning Medium*. London: Hutchinson.

Wai-Yum, V. (2005). The Yin Yang approach on enhancing creativity: a case study on a transforming early childhood principal. Paper presented at *Documenting*

Creative Learning Symposium: What, How and Why? University of Cambridge, April 2005.

Wegerif, R. (2004). Reason and creativity in classroom dialogues. Unpublished paper based on seminar given at The Open Creativity Centre Seminar Series, Milton Keynes, UK, March 2003.

Weisberg, R.W. (1986). *Creativity, Genius and Other Myths*. New York: Freeman.

Weisberg, R.W. (1988). Problem Solving and Creativity. In: Sternberg, R.J. (Ed.), *The Nature of Creativity: Contemporary Psychological Perspectives*, Cambridge, MA: MIT Press; pp. 148–76.

Weisberg, R.W. (1993). *Creativity: Beyond the Myth of Genius*. New York: Freeman.

Weisberg, R.W. (1995) Case studies of creative thinking: reproduction versus restructuring in the real world. In: Smith, S.M. Ward, T.B. and Finke R.A. (Eds), *The Creative Cognition Approach*. Cambridge, MA: MIT Press; pp. 158–96.

Weisberg, R.W. (1999). Creativity and knowledge: a challenge to theories. In: Sternberg, R.J. (Ed.), *Handbook of Creativity*. Cambridge: Cambridge University Press.

Williams, W.M. and Yang, L.T. (1999). Organizational creativity. In: Sternberg, R.J. (Ed.), *The Handbook of Creativity*. Cambridge: Cambridge University Press.

Willis, P. (1977). *Learning to Labour*. Farnborough: Saxon House.

Wilson, D.F. (2004). *Supporting Teachers Supporting Pupils*. London: Routledge-Falmer.

Wonder, J. and Blake, J. (1992). Creativity East and West: intuition versus logic. *Journal of Creative Behavior* 26(3), 172–85.

Woods, P. (1990). Teacher Skills and Strategies. London: Falmer Press.

Woods, P. (1993). Critical events in teaching and learning, Lewes: Falmer Press.

Woods, P. (1995). Creative teachers in primary schools. Buckingham: Open University Press.

Woods, P. (2002). Teaching and learning in the new millennium. In: Sugrue, C. and Day, D. (Eds), *Developing Teachers and Teaching Practice: International Research Perspectives*. London and New York: RoutledgeFalmer.

Woods, P. and Jeffrey, B. (1996). *Teachable Moments: The Art of Creative Teaching in Primary Schools*. Buckingham: Open University Press.

Woods, P., Jeffrey, B., Troman, G. and Boyle, M. (1997). *Restructuring Schools, Reconstructing Teachers: Responding to Change in the Primary School*. Buckingham: Open University Press.

Worth, P.J. (2000). Localised creativity. Unpublished PhD thesis, Milton Keynes, The Open University Institute of Educational Technology.

Wrigley, T. (2003). *Schools of Hope: A New Agenda for School Improvement*. Stoke on Trent: Trentham Books Limited.

Yeung, H.W. (1999). Under siege? Economic globalization and Chinese business in Southeast Asia. *Economy and Society* 28(1), 1–29.

Zhang N.S., Huang L.-J., Martin, D.S., Craft, A. and Lin GU. (2004). The impact of cognitive strategy instruction on deaf learners: an international comparative study. *Psychological Science* 27(1), 193–7.

Author Index

Subject Index